Praise for *Help*

"Marianne Power had me at hello. I'd o[...] blog-turned-memoir, *Help Me!*, and I [...] cheeky . . . reads like a novel, with full-color recurring characters, including love interests, an increasingly exasperated roommate and Power's pragmatic, farm-raised mom always ready with a one-liner. 'You're not going to go all American, are you?' she asks Power at the start of her experiment. 'You know . . . happy.' . . . Bridget Jones does self-help."   —Rachel Rosenblit, *Washington Post*

"Equal parts touching and hilarious, Power's account of the year she spent following the tenets of self-help books will make you feel better about your own flawed life."   —*People*

"A meta book about the [self-help] genre."   —*Forbes*

"Bold, earnest, and utterly hilarious . . . You'll laugh. You'll cry. You might even achieve the level of self-acceptance Power reaches by the end."   —*Refinery29*, "Best Books of January"

"Self-help is a huge industry—but does it actually work? Journalist Marianne Power decided to find out. . . . With the rollicking, easy-to-read voice of a Sophie Kinsella or Bridget Jones novel, this book showcases how complicated the notion of changing your life actually is—and questions some of the inherent problems with self-help in the first place, while recognizing its very real ability to transform one's life. It also acts as a sampler platter of self-help books that are actually worth your time. If you're looking to make changes in the new years and wondering where to begin, this is a great jump-start."

—*Mindbodygreen*, "Best Books of January"

"Harrowing, often side-splitting . . . Throughout this consistently entertaining book, [Power] writes with unflinching honesty—and bald hilarity, especially as she encountered deadpan reality checks from her mother, sisters, and skeptical friends—about the throes of facing her fears, tackling money issues, living in the present, opening herself up to rejection, and getting over her hang-ups with men . . . Bridget Jones meets Buddha in this plucky, heartwarming, comical debut memoir." —*Kirkus Reviews* (starred review)

"Couldn't put this book down—Marianne's honesty and wit shone through. There's something everyone can relate to, whether or not you like self-help—just a hugely enjoyable, fantastic read." —Poorna Bell, author of *Chase the Rainbow*

"Sparkling . . . a laugh-out-loud odyssey, with embarrassing incidents and downright disasters aplenty. But the real triumph of the book is the way it transcends its 'Bridget Jones gazes at her navel' premise to ask searching questions both about the purported effectiveness of self-help in the light of a multi-million dollar personal development industry; and about how we can really best find contentment. If you've ever worried that self-help might be a euphemism for self-obsession, then this is a book for you." —*Bookseller*

"Power is such an engaging writer, it's hard not to empathise with what she's saying . . . Plus, she's very funny . . . Marianne Power is a delightful companion and one who (putting all natural misanthropy aside) acts a powerful reminder that the traditional ways of denigrating or demanding too much of ourselves ain't going to get us anywhere . . . Excellent." —*Emerald Street*

"Funny and fearless, I loved *Help Me!* almost as much as I loved Marianne's mum who was always on hand with some no-nonsense advice and really needs to write her own self-help book." —*Red* magazine

"A sweet sharp read, and the last chapter made me cry. As someone a bit dubious of self-help books, it's perfect: Power spends a year trying to live a month per book. It's quite a fun journey through the ups and downs of negotiating ourselves through life, but underneath that is a serious, generous message, and it really does feel like you've learned something by the end of it." —Jessie Burton, author of *The Miniaturist*

"A laugh-out-loud funny book that also manages to be thought-provoking, perceptive, and devastatingly honest. I loved it." —Lucy Diamond, author of *Summer at Shell Cottage*

"Sublime and ridiculous, in equal measure. I tore through it hungrily. One minute I was having an existential epiphany, the next I was honking with laughter. Britain's answer to Sarah Knight, with Amy Schumer's naked hilarity and Matt Haig's soul-deep profundity chucked in."
—Catherine Gray, author of *The Unexpected Joy of Being Sober*

"Marianne's writing makes me smile and has moved me to tears more than once. She combines a journalist's no-nonsense investigative skills with a tenderness and honesty that sets her apart. In her blog she wrote frankly and movingly about issues that so many women are dealing with but can find it hard to talk about because we've all got caught up in trying to present our best faces to the world. Her writing has been a starting point for so many conversations that brought me closer to friends I thought I knew intimately, and from the comments on every post I know that hundreds of others felt the same. In helping herself, it turned out that Marianne was helping all of us."
—Erin Kelly, author of *He Said/She Said* and *The Poison Tree*

MARIANNE POWER

Help Me!

One Woman's Quest to Find Out
If Self-Help Really Can Change Your Life

Grove Press
New York

First published in Great Britain in 2018 by Macmillan
an imprint of Pan Macmillan

Printed in the United States of America

First Grove Atlantic hardcover edition: January 2019
First Grove Atlantic paperback edition: January 2020

ISBN 978-0-8021-4828-5
eISBN 978-0-8021-4688-5

Library of Congress Cataloging-in-Publication data is available for this title.

Grove Press
an imprint of Grove Atlantic
154 West 14th Street
New York, NY 10011

Distributed by Publishers Group West

groveatlantic.com

20 21 22 23   10 9 8 7 6 5 4 3 2 1

To G – my person

Mum: About this book . . .

Me: Yes.

Mum: Please tell me you don't use the word 'journey' in it.

Me: I don't.

Mum: Good.

Me: I prefer the term 'spiritual path'.

Mum: Oh, Marianne . . .

Contents

Help Me!

The stained office chair is covered with grey, scratchy material. I try not to think about the origin of the dark splodge as I let my fluffy dressing gown drop to the floor and sit down. Naked.

The cool air of the draughty hall hits my skin. My heart pounds.

I am naked. In front of people. Naked. Under a spotlight. Naked.

My thoughts race. What if someone I know walks in? Someone I work with? Or an old teacher?

'Just find a position you are comfortable in and relax,' says the teacher from the back of the room. 'I promise you nobody will be thinking of your nudity – they'll be too focused on their art.'

Patronizing sod, easy for you to say in your jeans and jacket. You are one hundred per cent more dressed than me right now.

I cross my legs and put my arms in my lap, just to cover something. I look down at my mozzarella tummy and the blonde hairs on my white legs glowing under the bright lights. The noise of pencil scratching paper is the only thing to distract me from the voice inside my head. A voice that's yelling: *What the hell are you doing here? Why aren't you at home watching telly like a normal person? And why didn't you shave your legs? Surely that's the first thing you do when you are about to get naked in public? Some basic bloody hair removal?*

Out of the corner of my eye I see movement. Someone has come in late. It's a man. He is tall. Dark curly hair. I raise my head slightly. He's wearing a navy sweater. God, I'm a sucker for a nice sweater . . . The reality dawns: a hot man has walked in while I am sitting with no clothes on in a village hall.

This is the stuff of nightmares.

I stare at a ball of fluff on the floor like my life depends on it.

I take a deep breath and worry that breathing makes me look fat. Fatter.

Stop it, Marianne. Think of something else . . . like what you will have for dinner when you get home. Maybe a chicken stir-fry? Or cheese on toast?

'OK, Marianne, why don't we try a standing pose? Perhaps with your back to the room? And your arms up?'

My legs shake as I turn.

I wonder how these budding Michelangelos are going to capture my cellulite. Is this something they get taught how to do? A bit like learning perspective and how to recreate the sky? I wonder what Mr Sweater is going to think of my bum? He'll hate it, I'm sure. I bet all his girlfriends are the perfect size and have bums like peaches . . .

I think about cheese on toast. I wonder what kind of bread we have left.

My arms burn with the effort of keeping them up. Two drops of sweat trickle down the side of my body. Then the teacher's talking again.

'Feel free to move to a better position,' he tells his students. 'Move closer to the model. Find a good angle to work from.'

Chairs scrape on the wooden floor. Mr Sweater is now sitting three feet away from me. He's so close, I can smell his aftershave. It smells clean and sea-like.

I bet he thinks you're a weirdo for being naked in public on a Sunday night. I bet he thinks your hairy thighs are huge and ugly. I bet . . . Stop it, Marianne!

I go back to the fluff. I wonder why the floors of halls are always so dusty and whether I can get away without doing any laundry when I get home. Then the teacher is telling me to get dressed.

The minute he does, I feel even more naked. He'd told me to bring a robe – conjuring up images of Parisian garrets and models in silk gowns – but all I had was a fleecy dressing gown. I put it on, take a breath and move over to Mr Sweater.

'I'm sorry, I'm a bit out of practice,' he mumbles, looking at his easel. 'I didn't get your nose right, and the forehead is a bit big . . .'

I look at the outline of my naked form in chaotic charcoal strokes. 'Sod the forehead!' I want to shout. 'You've made my arse the size of Australia!'

I go into the toilets and try to dress quickly on the icy, chipped tiles. I struggle to get my tights back on in the confines of the cubicle. I sit on the loo.

I feel more embarrassed than empowered.

Why am I doing any of this . . .?

The Life-Changing Hangover

There comes a point in every woman's life when she realizes that things cannot carry on the way they are. For me that point came on a hungover Sunday.

I don't remember what I'd done the night before – except, evidently, drink too much and pass out fully clothed, with my make-up on. When I woke my eyes were glued shut with crusty mascara and my skin was an oil slick of foundation and night sweat. My jeans were digging into my tummy. I needed the loo but was too lazy to move so I undid the zip and lay with my eyes closed.

Everything hurt.

Sometimes with a hangover, you get away with it. You awake feeling bleary but cheery, euphoric even, and you bump your way through the day until your hangover makes a soft landing around 4pm. This was not one of those hangovers. This was a full-frontal, no-ignoring-it hangover. My head felt like a bomb had gone off in it. My stomach was churning like a washing machine full of toxic waste. And my mouth, well, as the saying goes – someone, or something, had died in it.

I rolled over, reaching for the glass on my bedside table. My hands shook so much the water spilt down my front and onto the sheets.

The strip of light coming through the curtains hurt my eyes. I closed them again and waited for it to come . . . Oh yes, there it was . . .

That tidal wave of anxiety and self-loathing that washes over you after a big night. That certainty that you have done something very bad, that you are a bad person and nothing but bad things are going to happen to you for the rest of your pathetic life, because this is what you deserve.

I was suffering from what my friends call The Fear but it wasn't just a hangover making me feel this way. The feelings of dread, anxiety and failure were always there, humming in the background. The hangover just turned up the volume.

It wasn't that my life was bad. Far from it.

After spending my twenties stressing my way up the career ladder in newspapers, I was now a successful free-lance writer living in London. I got paid – actually paid – to road-test mascaras. A month before this life-defining hang-over I'd been sent to an Austrian spa, where I hung out with rich housewives paying thousands to eat nothing but broth and stale bread. I was given the trip for free, lost five pounds and came home with a fancy collection of miniature sham-poos.

Shortly before that I'd been given a masterclass in seduc-tion from Dita Von Teese in her suite in Claridge's for a newspaper article. I'd even interviewed James Bond and listened for weeks to the voicemail left by the late, great Roger Moore thanking me for the 'bloody good piece'.

Professionally, I was living the dream.

Outside of work, life looked good too. I had friends and family who cared about me. I bought over-priced jeans and drank over-priced cocktails. I went on holidays. I did a pretty good impression of someone having a good time.

But I wasn't. I was lost.

As friends re-grouted bathrooms and planned villa holidays, I spent weekends drinking, or lying in bed watching *The Real Housewives* or *The Kardashians*.

When I did go out, my social life consisted of a string of engagement drinks, weddings, housewarmings and baby christenings. I smiled and did my bit. I bought the presents. Signed the cards. Toasted their happiness. But with every celebration of somebody else's landmark I felt more left behind, alone, irrelevant. At thirty-six, my friends were ticking off the various life stages while I was stuck in the same life I'd had since my twenties.

I was always single, I didn't own a house, and I didn't have a plan.

Friends would ask me if I was OK, and I said I was. I knew I was unhappy but what reason did I have to be unhappy? I was lucky. I was obscenely lucky. And so I moaned about being single because that seemed to be something that people could relate to – but I didn't even know if that was the source of my unhappiness. Would a boyfriend solve all my life's problems? Maybe, maybe not. Did I want to get married and have kids? I didn't know. Either way, the point was academic. Men were not falling at my feet.

The truth was that men still scared the hell out of me and this was a huge source of embarrassment. Why couldn't I do this thing that everybody else could do? You know, meet someone, fall in love, get married.

I felt defective.

But I didn't say any of this to anyone. Instead, I'd nod as people assured me that I'd meet someone soon and then we'd change the subject and I'd go home alone and continue my slow descent into nothingness, if I wanted to be dramatic about it. Which, given the hangover, I did.

I looked around the squalor of my bedroom in the exorbitantly expensive basement flat I was renting. Old tights and knickers on the floor, a damp towel next to them, a bin overflowing with face wipes and empty water bottles. One, two, three half-empty coffee cups . . .

Surveying the scene, I heard a voice from deep within me:

What are you doing?

And then again, this time louder and more insistent:

What are you doing?

This is always what happens at these rock-bottom moments in books, isn't it? A voice comes from nowhere, telling the protagonist something has to change? That voice might be God, or a dead mother, or I don't know, the ghost of Christmases past – but there is always a voice.

I never believed in that kind of stuff, of course. I figured it was just a literary device cooked up by over-dramatic attention seekers – but it turns out it's true. Sometimes you really do get to the point where you hear voices.

Mine had been coming at me for months, waking me up most mornings at 3am, when I'd find myself sitting bolt upright in bed, heart pounding as this voice demanded:

What are you doing? What are you doing?

I did my best to ignore it. I went back to sleep, back to work and back to the pub. But as the months passed it was getting harder to push down the feeling that something wasn't right. The truth was I had no clue what I was doing with my life. And the cracks were beginning to show. I was finding it hard to keep my smile up, and the tears that were usually confined to my bedroom were now making public appearances – in the pub, at office dos, friends' parties – until finally, I'd become that woman at weddings, the one who lurched from drunkenly dancing to Beyoncé's 'Single Ladies' to sobbing in the bathroom.

I'd never ever wanted to be that person. But there it was. It had happened.

The phone rang when I was on my fourth hungover hour of hanging out with the Kardashians. I still hadn't showered.

It was my sister Sheila.

'What are you doing?' she asked. Her voice bright and breezy. She was walking.

'Nothing, I'm hungover. What about you?'

'Just been to the gym, and now I'm going to meet Jo for brunch.'

'Cool.'

'You sound miserable,' she said.

'I'm not miserable! I'm just hungover,' I snapped.

'Why don't you go for a walk? That always helps.'

'It's raining,' I said. It wasn't but Sheila didn't know that. She lived in New York, in her fancy apartment with her fancy job and her fancy friends who had fancy brunches. I pictured her bouncing down her Manhattan street, all clean and buzzy from exercise, her expensive highlights shining in the sun.

'What are you going to do with your day?' she asked. I hated the judgement implicit in that question.

'I don't know. The day's nearly over, it's 4pm here.'

'Are you OK?'

'Yes, I'm just tired.'

'OK, I'll leave you to it.'

I was going to hang up, to let her get on with her fabulous life, and continue my slide into self-pity but instead I found myself crying.

'What's wrong? Did something happen last night?' Sheila asked.

'No, nothing like that.'

'So what is it?'

'I don't know . . .' I said, my voice cracking. 'I don't know what's wrong with me.'

'What do you mean?'

'I'm unhappy all the time and I don't know why.'

'Oh, Marianne . . .' Her voice lost its usual abrasive edge.

'I just don't know what to do anymore. I've done all the things you're supposed to do – I work hard, I try to be nice, I pay stupid rent on this stupid apartment, but what's the point? What's the point of any of it?'

Sheila couldn't give me the answer, so at three in the morning, unable to sleep or tolerate any more of the Kardashians, I turned to someone, or rather something, that would.

I was twenty-four when I read my first self-help book. I was drinking cheap white wine in All Bar One by Oxford Circus, moaning about my crappy temping job, when my friend handed me a battered copy of *Feel the Fear and Do It Anyway* by Susan Jeffers.

I read the tagline out loud: 'How to turn your fear and indecision into confidence and action . . .'.

I rolled my eyes before turning it over and reading the back: 'What is stopping you from being the person you want to be and living your life the way you want to live it? Fear of tackling an issue with your boss? Fear of change? Fear of taking control?'

I rolled my eyes some more. 'I'm not scared, I'm just in a crap job.'

'I know it's cheesy but read it,' my friend urged me. 'I promise it'll make you want to go out and DO stuff!'

I couldn't see what it had made her do other than get drunk with me, but no matter. That night I read half of the book in a wine blur. The next night I finished it.

I might have been an English lit graduate with literary pretensions but there was something about the shouty capital letters and exclamation marks that was intoxicating. That American can-do attitude. It was the exact opposite of my English/Irish pessimism. It made me feel like anything was possible.

After reading it I quit my temping job even though I had no other work lined up. A week later I heard that a friend of a friend of a friend was working at a newspaper. I called her and when she didn't pick up, I kept calling. And kept calling. I showed a tenacity that was entirely new to me. Finally, she called me back and told me I could come in on work experience. Two weeks later I was offered a job.

That was my start in journalism. The risk paid off.

After that I was hooked on self-help. If a book was promising to change my life in my lunch hour, give me confidence/a man/money in five easy steps and had Oprah's seal of approval, I'd buy not only the book but the t-shirt and the audio course.

Books such as *The Little Book of Calm*, *The Rules of Life* and *The Power of Positive Thinking* were all read, cover to cover. Passages underlined. Notes in the margin. Each one seemed to promise a happier, saner, more fulfilled me . . . but did they work?

Did they hell!

Despite reading *I Can Make You Rich* – written by Paul McKenna, a former radio DJ turned hypnotist who had indeed made himself very rich with his new brand of self-help – I was a disaster with money. Give me a tenner and I'd have spent twenty by the time you put your wallet back in your pocket.

Even though I'd read *Men Are from Mars, Women Are from Venus* and *Why Men Love Bitches*, I was always single.

And while *Feel the Fear* had got me started in my career, any further success was not thanks to reading *The Success Principles* – it was down to an all-consuming fear of failure, which made me work obsessively.

While helping me pack for one of my many flat moves, my friend Sarah found it hysterically funny that in every room there was a stash of self-help books. Under the sofa, under my bed, stacked next to the wardrobe.

'A lot of them are for work,' I argued. Which was true, to a point. Sometimes I did write about them. But most of the time I'd bought these books for another reason: I thought they were going to change my life.

'Don't they all say the same thing?' asked Sarah. 'Be positive. Get out of your comfort zone? I don't get why they need 200 pages to say something that's summed up in a paragraph on the back.'

'Sometimes the message needs to be repeated for it to sink in,' I said.

Sarah picked up a book which was sitting on top of the fridge next to two phone chargers and a pile of takeaway curry menus.

'*How to Stop Worrying and Start Living*,' she said, reading out the title of a well-thumbed book.

'That's a good one!' I said.

She laughed.

'No, really it is, it's a classic, it was written in the Great Depression. I've read it at least three times.'

'You've read it three times?' said Sarah.

'Yes!'

'And you think it's helped you.'

'Yes!'

'You don't worry anymore . . .?'

'Well . . .'

By now she was doubled over, tears coming out of her eyes.

I wanted to get annoyed but I couldn't. I worried more than anybody I knew.

I was a poor advert for that book and indeed for any of the books on my shelf – or rather the ones hidden under my bed. I was proof of the argument that if self-help really worked you'd just need to read one and you'd be sorted. As it was I was buying at least one a month – and yet here I was, hungover, depressed, neurotic, alone . . .

So why did I read self-help if it didn't, well, help?

Like eating chocolate cake or watching old episodes of *Friends*, I read self-help for comfort. These books acknowledged the insecurities and anxieties I felt but was always to ashamed to talk about. They made my personal angst seem like a normal part of being human. Reading them made me feel less alone.

Then there was the fantasy element. Every night I'd devour their rags-to-riches promises and imagine what life would be like if I was more confident and more efficient, if

I didn't worry about anything and jumped out of bed to meditate at 5am . . . There was just one problem. Every morning I'd wake up (not at 5am) and go back to life as normal. Nothing changed because I didn't do anything the books told me to do. I didn't do the 'journaling', I didn't say any affirmations . . .

Feel the Fear changed my life the first time I read it because I took action: I felt the fear and quit my job. But since then I hadn't stepped out of my comfort zone – I'd hardly stepped out of bed.

And then with Sunday's hangover finally fading, while I re-read Feel the Fear for the fifth time, I had an idea. An idea that would stop me being a depressed, hungover mess and turn me into a happy, highly functioning person:

I wasn't just going to read self-help, I was going to DO self-help.

I would follow every single bit of advice given to me by the so-called gurus to find out what happened if I really did follow the 7 Habits of Highly Effective People. Really felt The Power of Now. Could my life be transformed? Could I get rich? Skinny? Find love?

The idea came to me fully formed: One book a month, followed to the letter, to see if self-help really could change my life. I would do it for a year – so twelve books in all. And I would systematically tackle my flaws one book at a time: money, worrying, my weight . . . Then, at the end of the year, I'd be . . . perfect!

'OK, but you've got to actually do stuff,' said Sheila when I told her my idea on the phone a few days later. 'You can't just read books that make you analyse your feelings for the whole year.' Her tone implied I'd just use this as a massive opportunity to navel-gaze and become even more self-obsessed than usual.

'I will do stuff!' I snapped. 'That's the whole point.'

'Which books are you going to follow? Have you got a plan?'

Again, a dig. Sheila knows I never have a plan.

'I'm going to start with *Feel the Fear and Do It Anyway* because that had a big effect the first time I read it and then I think I'll do a money book and then, I don't know. In self-help land they talk about the right book finding you at the right time,' I said.

I knew I sounded flaky.

'Are you going to do books you've read before or new ones?' she asked.

'A mixture,' I said.

'Are you going to do a dating book?'

'Yes.'

'Which one?'

'I don't know yet.'

'And when?'

'I don't know, Sheila! Later in the year. I want to work on myself first, then I'll think about a man.'

I hated that I used the phrase 'work on myself'.

'So what exactly do you want to get out of all this?' Sheila asked. This is why she gets paid the big bucks. To see the flaw in any plan.

'I dunno. I'd just like to be happier and more confident and get out of debt. I'd like to get healthier and drink less—'

'You don't need a book to drink less,' Sheila interrupted.

'I know you don't!' I said, taking a quiet gulp of wine.

'OK, but you have to actually DO things. Not just talk about them.'

'Yes, Sheila, I get it. I will.'

But even Sheila's realism couldn't get me down. I got off the phone, closed my eyes and imagined how perfect I would be at the end of the year.

Perfect Me would not worry or procrastinate, she'd get her work done easily. She would write for all the best newspapers and magazines and earn obscene amounts of money doing it – enough to get braces to fix her dodgy teeth. Perfect Me would be living in a gorgeous apartment with big windows. She'd have bookshelves full of highbrow literary books that she actually read. At night she'd go to swanky gatherings where she'd look gorgeous in low-key but expensive clothes. And she'd go to the gym all the time. Oh, and she'd have a handsome man in a cashmere sweater by her side. Goes without saying.

You know the kind of perfection you see in magazines: those interviews with perfect people in their perfect homes with their perfect outfits talking about their perfect lives? I was going to become one of them!

It was November now, so I'd start in January. New Year, New Me.

I felt a jolt of excitement. This was it. This was the thing that was *really* going to change my life.

I had no idea then that my neat twelve-month plan would turn into a sixteen-month roller coaster in which every bit of me was turned inside out.

Yes, self-help changed my life – but was it for the better?

1

Feel the Fear and Do It Anyway,
by Susan Jeffers

*'Take a risk a day – one small or bold stroke that
will make you feel great once you've done it.'*

Wednesday 1st January and I'm standing on a wooden deck,
looking down at the mud-brown pond. Icy air is whipping
my legs and it's starting to rain.

A blackboard propped on a chair announces the temperature of the water: five degrees Celsius. Nearly freezing.
Goosebumps stand to attention on every inch of my skin.

'Have you swum in the Ladies' Ponds before?' asks the
matriarch standing guard by the water. Her voice is as bracing as the weather and her accent suggests she may own
half of Hampshire.

'No,' I reply.

'The water can be quite dangerous at this time of year.
It's extremely cold.'

'OK,' I say.

'When you get in you should take a long breath out.'

'OK.'

'That will stop you hyperventilating.'

Oh, God.

I look around at the huddle of middle-aged women with

damp hair holding cups of steaming tea. If they can do it,
so can I. Right?

I put my first foot onto the icy-cold metal step and then
my second. Then down another step. My right foot hits
water. A shot of pain.

'Fuck!' I say.

My left foot goes in. I shriek again.

I don't want to go any further. This was a really bad idea.
I am not the kind of person who swims in the middle of
winter. I get cold standing by an open fridge.

I turn around and see a queue forming behind me. I can't
back out now, everyone is looking at me.

I keep going until I am in up to my waist. I gasp for
breath. Then it comes: the sensation of being stabbed by a
million tiny icicles.

The icicles were Sarah's idea. She might not be a fan of self-
help but she would cheer me on no matter what I did. I
could have told her I was becoming a Scientologist and
she'd say 'Cool, you'll meet Tom Cruise!'

'I was thinking about scary things you could do in January,' she said, when we met before Christmas, in a pub off
Charlotte Street.

'I was watching *Kitchen Nightmares* last night and was
thinking you could work in one of Gordon Ramsay's kit-
chens and have him swear at you,' she continued, shouting
over Slade wishing everyone a Merry Christmas on the
speakers.

'That would be scary,' I agreed, to humour her. There
was no way on earth I was going to do that.

'And Steve says you could streak at a football match . . .'

'Right . . .'

'Or shave your hair off . . .'

'I don't want to shave my hair off!' I said, unable to indulge this line of thinking any longer.

Sarah looked at her phone and read out more suggestions from a list: 'Dump a friend and tell them exactly why you hate them. Not me, obviously . . . Oh, and this is the best one! You could write an erotic story and send it to your mother!'

'Oh my God. Why the hell would I want to do that?'

'It's scary, isn't it?'

'No. It's just gross.'

'It's scary gross.'

'Where are you getting this stuff from?' I asked.

'I don't know, I was lying in bed last night and they just kept coming to me!' said Sarah.

'The point is to face fears I have in my everyday life – not do a load of random stuff which is going to get me arrested. And anyway, how exactly am I going to get into a Gordon Ramsay kitchen?' I asked.

'You'll figure it out – you're a journalist, aren't you?' said Sarah.

'I write about mascaras.'

'So what are you going to do, then?'

'I don't know – things like open my bank statements and answer the phone, do my tax return . . . the real things I'm scared of.'

'You're going to spend January picking up the phone?' said Sarah in a tone that made it clear that I was not going to be allowed to do that.

'I think you should start by jumping into Hampstead Ponds on New Year's Day. Face your fear of the cold.'

And actually that was a good idea. I really was scared of the cold. Sarah and I once went to my best friend Gemma's house in Ireland in February. I was so freezing I went to bed wearing every item of clothing I'd packed – including my coat. I spent most of the week too scared to leave the radiator.

And so it was that on 1st January I took an outdoor swim on one of the coldest days of the year.

Sarah did not come with me. She had been out till 4am and was now lying in a darkened room sending me text messages with splashy emojis. Gemma was cheering me in spirit from Dublin, where she was looking after her newborn baby, James.

Instead my friend – and new flatmate – Rachel had agreed to come. Just before Christmas, she'd taken pity on me, offering me her spare room so that I could get out of the bankrupting basement.

She'd promised to swim with me as if it was no big deal. I didn't think she meant it. I figured that she'd wake up on New Year's Day, look at the stormy skies and suggest we do lunch instead. I'd be able to get out of it and blame her. It didn't happen that way. Rachel knocked on my door at 10am, with a towel over her shoulder.

'Ready?' she asked.

'Are we really doing this?'

'Yes, of course. It'll be fun.'

'But look, it's raining outside, it looks horrible.'

'We're going to get wet anyway.'

'We could just go and get some lunch somewhere . . .' I said.

'Don't be a wimp. This was your idea.'

And that was the problem. I was good at ideas. I was also

quite good at *talking* about ideas. Doing them, though, well, that was different.

As we walked through the dense wooded path to the ponds, the chatter of voices got louder. We arrived to find at least thirty women, dressed in woolly hats and padded anoraks, gathered around a makeshift table full of sausage rolls, mince pies and a giant vat of mulled wine.

It looked fun. If only we could skip the bit where you get into the water.

'Is it very cold?' I asked an elderly woman getting dressed in the changing hut.

'It's over very quickly,' she said, smiling with blue lips.

And it was.

At first the water felt so cold I thought I was going to die.

I panted and splashed my way through it like a frantic puppy.

Within seconds I could feel a cramp in the back of my neck and another in my right foot.

It hurt. The water hurt. Every bit of my body hurt.

I kept moving though and, slowly, I started to feel warmer. Well, maybe not so much warm as numb, but that was fine with me.

I started to calm down.

Everything went silent bar the sound of my heart pounding in my ears.

I looked at the weeping willows watching over me, as my limbs cut through the silky water.

This is what it's like to be alive, I thought.

I kept moving.

It was beautiful.

And then it was done. I grabbed the silver rails and pulled myself up the steps.

A woman in an orange swimming hat was rubbing herself down with a towel. She must have been seventy and was wearing a pair of pink Marigolds. She beamed at me.

'Can you think of a better start to the year?'

My body flushed with warmth. I was tingling and grinning from ear to ear. Every inch of me felt alive.

'No, I really can't,' I said.

And I meant it. In that freezing five-minute dip, I had crossed a major line – the line that takes you from being someone who talks about things to being someone who actually does them. The world felt full of possibility. My year had started.

Feel the Fear and Do It Anyway by Susan Jeffers was published in 1987, the era of shoulder-pads, Margaret Thatcher and *Cosmopolitan* magazine.

While other self-help books at the time were written by men, telling women how to find love and keep love, *Feel the Fear* was written by a woman telling other women to just go out and do something – do *anything*. Not for someone else but for themselves. Its tone is upbeat but no-nonsense – and as I re-read it during the no man's land between Christmas and New Year, I felt a familiar rush of motivation. The trick now was to act on it, just as I had in my twenties.

Susan's basic premise is that if we sit around waiting for the day that we feel brave enough to do the things we want to do, we'll never do anything.

The secret of happy and successful people is not that they are any less scared, she says, but that, you guessed it, they 'feel the fear and do it anyway'.

In fact, according to Susan, we should be scared every day because that's a sign that we're pushing ourselves and moving forwards. If you are not feeling any fear you are not growing.

'Basically, I have to do something scary every day,' I said to Rachel, when we were back at the flat making bolognese after our swim.

'So what is the scariest thing you can think of doing?' asked Rachel.

'Stand-up comedy. The thought of it makes me want to be sick.'

'Hang on,' she said – running off to the living room and coming back with a notepad. 'Write that down.'

'Why? I'm not going to do stand-up.'

'Yes, you are.'

'No, come on. I'll do scary stuff, I promise, but I don't need to go that far.'

But it was no good. She'd written 'STAND-UP' in capital letters.

'What else?' she said, pen in hand.

I felt panic rising.

'Um. Asking a guy out or chatting up a guy, or anything guy related.'

'You should ask a man out on the Tube in rush hour.'

'What?'

'Just to make it interesting.'

'No way. I'm not doing that.'

She raised her eyebrows.

'OK,' I answered.

By the end of the evening, we'd come up with a list of scary things for me to do in January:

1. Stand-up comedy
2. Chat up a guy on the Tube
3. Ask out a stranger
4. Sing in front of a crowd
5. Public speaking
6. Pose naked for a photographer or an artist
7. Watch a scary film (which I hadn't done since *Misery* traumatized me, aged thirteen)
8. Go to a spin class
9. Confront someone about something they've done to upset me
10. Ask for a discount in a shop or haggle (mortifying)
11. Get the four fillings I need
12. Get the mole on my back checked out
13. Eat offal (puke, I was a coward about any meat with chewy bits, mushy bits . . . or just bits in general)
14. Skydive or do something daredevil-y
15. Cycle in London
16. Find out what people think of me (the bad stuff)
17. Parallel parking
18. Drive on motorway
19. Lose my temper (I never did. Ever. I was too repressed and scared it would make people hate me)
20. Use the phone every day (I really hated the phone).

That night I couldn't sleep. My brilliant idea now felt very real and I didn't like it. I did not want to jump out of a plane and never in a million years did I think I'd do stand-up comedy. That was for other people. Wacky, thrill-seeking, masochistic people. People who were, possibly, a bit nuts.

Was I a bit nuts?

I started small on 2nd January – with a spot of parallel parking. Not exactly dramatic, but I hadn't tried it since my driving test when I was seventeen. On the rare occasions I did drive, I preferred to park three miles away than to suffer the stress and embarrassment of trying to get into a spot while cars piled up behind me. It seemed so stupid to let such a tiny thing, a thing that people do every day, become something I avoided my whole life.

Susan says there are three 'levels' to every fear. The first level is the 'surface story' – in this case the fact that I hate parking. Underneath this fear is the 'Level 2 fear' – which is the deeper 'ego' fear of looking like an idiot. Susan writes: 'Level 2 fears have to do with the inner state of mind, rather than exterior situations. They reflect your sense of self and your ability to handle this world.' But underneath this fear is the deepest fear of all, the fear which Susan says is underneath all fears – a fear that you won't be able to handle the feeling of being an idiot who can't park. Susan has one answer to this: 'YOU'LL HANDLE IT.'

I'd gone back to my mum's flat outside London to collect some stuff, so I borrowed her battered Peugeot 205 and drove to the local town, Ascot.

It is famous for the races and not a lot else; I grew up there and worked in the local cafe. My heart always went out to the poor tourists who would come in to ask, 'Where is Royal Ascot?'

I'd have to tell them, You're in Ascot. This is it. The petrol station, cafe and Martin's newsagents. This is all the glamour you're going to get.

So anyway, it's not exactly a metropolis but it was surprisingly busy for 2nd January. I circled the area three times before I saw a space. It was a bit tight and I got flustered when a white van came up behind me. I went in too steep and hit the pavement.

My heart started pounding and my sweaty palms slipped on the steering wheel.

I tried to fix it but I just seemed to get more wedged in. I worried that the white van was going to start tooting. I imagined the two men in it were laughing at me. I felt a stress totally disproportionate to the situation. In a panic I mounted the kerb. The white van went past.

The road was quiet now. I tried to drive out and get back in a couple of times but it didn't work. I kept going up on the kerb.

But strangely this didn't bother me.

A park of vague parallelity took place and according to Susan: 'You're not a failure if you don't make it, you're a success because you try.'

And I really did feel like a success, kerb or no kerb.

Susan says that avoiding small things can have a big effect. Putting off driving on motorways, opening bank statements or picking up the phone adds to the belief that the world is scary and that we can't cope. Every time we avoid doing something it makes us feel weaker, while facing a fear, even if it's a small one, makes us feel strong, em-powered and in control. And that's how I wanted to feel. Not just with driving but with everything.

At home my bold step into the world of fear-fighting was not greeted with excitement.

'I just did a parallel park!' I told Mum, swinging the car keys on my fingers like a man of the road, an easy rider. She looked up from the sink full of dishes.

'Does your book tell you to park?'

'No, it's just about doing scary things. Confronting your fears. And parking is scary.'

Mum looked bewildered. She didn't find parking scary. She could fit a truck on a postage stamp and would make no big deal about it.

When she was my age she had three children and a house to run, she wasn't 'challenging' herself by parking or jumping into icy ponds.

She didn't have time for self-discovery or, as she puts it, 'I was not brought up to contemplate my toenails.' Funnily enough, self-help wasn't big on the farm in rural Ireland, where she grew up, one of seven children.

When I had told her about my idea at Christmas, she opened her mouth to say something, then closed it again. Then she opened it. And closed it.

'Most people would say your life is already very good, Marianne.'

'I know it is, but what's wrong with wanting to be a bit happier?'

'Nobody can be happy all the time. It's just not the way life is.'

'Well, that's miserable.'

'No, it's not. It's realistic. Maybe you would feel better if, instead of always looking for more, you were grateful for what you have.'

The familiar wash of Catholic guilt poured over me.

So on 5th January when I drove to see an old school-friend – via the M25, M3 and M4 motorways – I kept my act of breathtaking bravery to myself.

———

The next afternoon I was on the Tube home, listening to Rihanna on my phone, when I remembered that I should be chatting up men.

Anyone who lives in London knows that it's not socially acceptable to look people in the eye on public transport, let alone talk to them. It's why all over the Underground there are posters advertising dating sites, which pretty much say: 'Do you fancy that guy/girl opposite you? If so log on to our site so that you can sift through tens of thousands of people in the microscopic hope that you may see him/her again.'

The option of just smiling and talking wasn't an option. Until now.

I did a mental inventory of how I looked. OK jeans on, my good coat (Whistles, £300 down to £150), scruffy Converse and unwashed hair.

No.

I couldn't chat up a stranger with greasy hair.

Definitely not.

I'd do it next time. When I had good hair.

But I knew that that was a cop-out. Susan says that we are only fooling ourselves when we put things off. She calls it the 'when/then' game – we tell ourselves we'll approach the guy we like when we're slimmer or we'll apply for the promotion when we have more experience. We think that fear will go if we just wait for the right time but when we get to the right time we find more excuses. Doing something new is always going to be scary. The only way for it to stop being scary is to do it.

I looked around for a target.

Directly in front of me was a guy with shaven hair and a baseball jacket. A heavy bass thudded out of his giant headphones and he was nodding in time with the beat. No, not him.

To my left was a man in a dark navy suit. He was holding a battered old brown leather briefcase. He looked like a barrister or something clever. I wondered if I'd be too stupid for him. I looked down at his hands. He was wearing a wedding ring.

I started a train of thought about how all the good guys are married and how, at thirty-six, I'd missed the boat . . .

Focus, Marianne. Focus.

Standing by the doors was a tall, skinny, pale guy, also in a suit. He was good looking but not too good looking. He had a knackered-and-fed-up-with-life expression on his face. I'm not sure what it says about me but I liked knackered and fed up.

Normally I couldn't even smile at a guy I liked, let alone talk to him. Instead I imagined all the reasons he would not be interested in me: too fat, too ginger, too badly dressed. It was a fun game I played.

But this was not normal me. I was now Fear-Fighting Me. So I moved over to be nearer him. I looked down at his hands. No ring.

Right. OK. You can do this.

I opened my mouth to say 'Hello' but nothing came out.

Maybe I couldn't do this.

I should say at this point that, despite the fact that the train was packed, it was strangely quiet. Almost silent, in fact. All the commuters were locked in their own post-work misery, reading books or listening to music. If I started a conversation everybody would hear it.

Pull yourself together, Marianne. Say something.

'Is the train always this crowded?' I blurted out.

Mr Knackered-but-Handsome looked up from his phone, confused – as if I'd just woken him. He had watery blue eyes.

'Er, yes,' he said before looking back down at his phone.

'I don't usually travel at this time,' I continued. My heart thud-thud-thudding in my chest.

He raised his head again with an expression that said: Why are you telling me this? Why are you talking to me? Don't you know the rules?

I kept going.

'Where do you live?' I asked. I realized as soon as I said it that it was a very stalker-y question.

I was also aware that we now had an audience. A woman standing next to us, in a pencil skirt and trainers, had taken out one of her white headphones and the man sitting on the seat nearest to us was smirking.

Mr Knackered-but-Handsome looked scared now. I could see he was torn between not wanting to be rude and worrying that he had a nutter on his hands. Politeness won out. He informed me he lived in Bermondsey.

'Is it nice?' I asked.

'Er, yeah,' he said.

I kept going: 'Have you lived there long?'

'Yes, WE'VE lived there a couple of years' – heavy emphasis on the 'we'. Message received, loud and clear. He had a girlfriend, but just to ram the message home he informed me that 'WE'VE just bought a house.'

The guy who was smirking let out a snort. He actually snorted.

I carried on smiling and chatting, just to let Mr Knack-ered know that my world had not ended because he had a girlfriend (which it hadn't) and I could see him relax. We made small talk about property prices and then he got off at Waterloo.

And that was it!

I'd done it! I couldn't believe it but I had! I had seen a handsome man on the train and I had talked to him.

It wasn't exactly a successful attempt at chatting up, but I did it! Yes, it was embarrassing but so what? Embarrassment doesn't kill you, it turns out!

I felt electricity charge around my body. Or adrenalin. Electricity, adrenalin, whatever! I was lit up.

Until I locked eyes with Mr Smirker, who was still smirking. Then I felt a hot rush of embarrassment followed by fury. Sod him, with his hipster beard and hipster jeans! He had no idea that I was facing my fears and seizing the day and being the best me I could be! I bet he wouldn't have the guts to do that!

So I made a strange decision: I would show him that I was not remotely embarrassed by what had happened by . . .

'What are you reading?' I asked, sitting down next to him.

He smirked some more, bemused that he was now the target of my attention.

'It's *The History of the World in 100 Objects*,' he said. 'It was a Radio 4 series.'

'It's very big.' I said.

'It is,' he agreed.

There was a pause. I didn't know what else to say. My nervous energy was waning now and I was beginning to wish that I hadn't got on this stupid train.

'I bought it for my brother for Christmas but I ended up keeping it,' he added.

Yay! He'd filled the silence. And he read clever books!

'It looks like a good book to read on the toilet,' I said.

'Er, yes, I suppose so.'

Why did you have to bring the loo into it, Marianne?

'So did you get your brother something else?' I asked.

'Yeah, I got him a t-shirt.'

'Cool.'

I hate how much I say 'cool'. I'm thirty-six, I should have found a better word by now.

We carried on chatting. There was no mention of the royal 'We'. I started to see his smirk as a lovely smile.

'Where are you heading to?' I asked.

'I have to pick up some stuff from a friend's house, then I'm going home.'

'Cool. What do you do?'

'I'm an artist's assistant.'

'What kind of art?'

'Conceptual stuff.'

I didn't know what 'conceptual stuff' meant but I imagined all the tasteful art work our house would have.

I wondered what it would be like to kiss someone with such a big beard and whether it mattered that it was a bit ginger . . .

I once went on a date with a fellow redhead and when he went in to kiss me, I panicked. 'People will think we're brother and sister!' I said. The email I sent the next day, offering to dye my hair brown, did not get a reply.

'Where do you work?' asked Mr Smirker.

'I work at home. I'm usually still sitting in egg-stained pyjamas at this time,' I said.

His face didn't know how to arrange itself in response to this comment.

Why do you say these things?

'This is me,' I said, as we got to Archway.

'Me too,' he said. Smiling. We walked up the escalators together and then went through the turnstiles and hovered for a second.

'Well, bye, then . . .' he said.

'Bye . . . it was nice to meet you,' I replied.

'Yeah, you too.'

'Have a nice night.'

'You too . . .'

He gave me a final smirk/smile and went on his way.

For half a second I let myself dwell on the thought that he didn't like me because he didn't ask for my number, but then another part of me thought that maybe he was too shy to ask.

And even if it was a rejection, weirdly, I didn't care. I was too delighted with my total and utter HEROISM.

The next morning, high on my triumph, I made plans for the rest of the month.

Life was already feeling different. Susan says that every time you take action you get in touch with your 'Powerful self' and she was right. I felt powerful. Like I could do anything. Then I saw the words 'stand-up comedy' on my list and I immediately felt less powerful. I made the executive decision to wait until the end of the month before I tackled that one. Instead I would warm up with a bit of public nudity.

I googled 'life modelling' and sent an email to a local class asking if I could take part. Then I researched public speaking.

Most people fear public speaking more than they fear being buried alive, according to one of those polls that crop up every year. (Other common fears are men with beards and wooden lollipop sticks, apparently.)

My only experience of public speaking was at two friends' weddings. Both induced panic so great that I decided I'd rather pay for a honeymoon than get up behind the pulpit and read another Love Is . . . poem. Even talking in meetings of two or three people brought on a hot flush.

Rachel suggested I try speaking at Speakers' Corner, but I pretended I didn't hear that. Instead I found a local Toast-masters group – an organization that meets every week to help people practise public speaking – and got hold of Nigel, the vice president.

He told me that it would go against every rule in their book to let a stranger come in and talk straight away.

'There's protocol,' he said on the phone.

'Of course there is,' I said.

I persisted and he told me that he'd talk to his president to see if an exception could be made. Many high-level phone calls were made and, four minutes later, Nigel called me back. 'You're in,' he said. 'We meet on Thursday nights, in the church hall opposite the curry house.'

I got an email telling me that my speech would need to be five to seven minutes long. There would be a traffic-light system timing me (green when I've reached my minimum time, amber to tell me I'd reached six minutes and red to warn that I had thirty seconds to wrap up or be disquali-fied). I would have an 'Evaluator' assessing me, as well as a 'Grammarian' who would count the number of 'ums' I used. I could talk about anything but was not allowed to read from any notes.

I decided I'd talk about my self-help mission.

It was now Tuesday morning, which meant I had two days to prepare. By which I mean pretend it wasn't happening. On Thursday morning I could pretend no more.

As I practised my speech in my bedroom, I worried I'd get up on the stage and forget everything. Nothing would come out of my mouth and everybody would be staring at me and I would want to die. I kept telling myself that it didn't matter – that there was absolutely nothing riding on it. It didn't matter if it was a total disaster: I wouldn't have to see these people again. Still I was terrified. Why?

I read articles online. One explained that in our cave woman days we relied on being part of the group for survival and so doing anything that sets us up for potential rejection feels terrifying because how are you going to fight off a sabre-toothed tiger if you are on your own? It was something I'd never thought about. Another article suggested I imagine that I had to either do a quick speech or face a sabre-toothed tiger. They reckoned that when we compare public speaking to vicious mutilation, the talk seems OK.

So, basically, it all came down to tigers.

I did my speech for Rachel while she timed me on her phone.

What I thought was seven minutes turned out to be just over three.

'But it did feel longer,' admitted Rachel, who was worried I had a cold.

'No, I'm OK,' I said.

'It's just that your voice sounds croaky and kind of monotone. I thought maybe you were coming down with something.'

'I think that's my voice when I'm scared.'

'Marianne, you're talking in a church hall to probably twenty people, it's not exactly the O2.'

OK. Good. Perspective is good.

As I walked through the graveyard, I thought of Jerry Seinfeld's routine about how most people are so scared of public speaking that at a funeral they'd rather be in the coffin than giving the eulogy. Too bloody right.

The brightly lit hall was full of people chatting by plastic chairs. At the front was a rickety music stand with a blue satin Toastmasters sign hanging from it.

There were three speeches before mine. First up a fabulously surreal one about a Custard Cream factory at war with the Jammy Dodger manufacturers.

Then one about why the area needed a new sex shop.

'Imagine how much happier people would be if they had access to whips and nipple tassels!' said a white-haired man who looked like Captain Birdseye.

Finally a talk on the benefits of smoking – 'It keeps people who make those oxygen canisters in work,' said a young man in a Bob Marley t-shirt. 'What else would they do? Would you really want their families to starve?'

They were as funny as anything you'd see on television.

Then it was me. I made my way to the front, bumping people's knees and apologizing. My blood fizzed with fear.

'My heart is beating so loud I think you might all be able to hear it,' I said.

The audience smiled encouragingly.

My tongue felt like it had tripled in size.

'I haven't done this before, so please be kind . . .'

They kept smiling but this time there was a hint of 'OK, love, get on with it'.

The lights felt bright. I blinked a few times.

Come on, Marianne. You can do it. It's seven minutes of your life. Go, go, go!

'How many of you read self-help books?' I asked. It felt like a bold opener, going in for audience participation straight away.

I was amazed to see that almost all of them put their hands up.

'And how many of you think self-help is for losers?'

One old man in the corner and the young Bob Marley guy.

'Well, I am that loser,' I explained. 'I am that sad soul whose only company in bed is a copy of *Men Are from Mars and Women Are from Venus*, the one who has the *Little Book of Calm* on her messy desk . . .'

I got a few giggles at the mention of the names and then I relaxed a bit. I shared statistics I'd found about how self-help sales were booming: up twenty-five per cent in Britain since the 2008 crash. 'We all need guidance in times of uncertainty,' I explained, feeling very wise as I said it. I then made the argument that self-help was modern-day philosophy, dropping names such as Aristotle and Socrates, despite having read neither.

'And far from being American, did you know that the first self-help book was written by a Scottish man called Samuel Smiles in 1859?' I asked.

After what felt like one minute, a green light came on at the back of the room to signal I'd been speaking for five. Then a red light was telling me my time was up. There was applause and I rushed back to my seat, cheeks on fire, knees shaking, heart pounding.

I'd done it!

Afterwards over tea and ginger nut biscuits, everyone was very kind.

I was a natural! Engaging and funny! Was it really my first time? My head started to swell. 'You made eye contact throughout the speech, which most beginners don't do,' said Captain Birdseye. 'It's called the Lighthouse technique and is usually done by advanced speakers.'

'The first time I spoke I was so nervous I didn't even make it to the end of my speech,' he said. 'That man over there –' he pointed to Jammy Dodger man – 'wasn't able to get a word out, his lisp was so bad.'

'I couldn't hear any lisp,' I said.

'He's worked on it. He came four years ago when he had to do a father-of-the-bride speech and then he stayed. We have fun. It's a good bunch.'

And it was. There was a glow in the room, a glow of support and encouragement, a glow of people helping each other to face their fears. This crowd was the opposite of my usual night-life in some too-cool-for-school London pub where the only time people look at each other is to size up the competition.

At the end of the evening I was given an award for being the best newcomer. Jane, the president, called me to the front of the room.

'Usually we give chocolates but after Christmas I know that we're all watching our weight so I've got you this instead.'

She handed me a box of yoghurt bars.

'Only seventy-three calories!' she said.

'Brilliant!' I beamed.

Then I was given a certificate and my photograph was taken. It was pretty much the Oscars.

On the bus home I tried to get my head around the fact that it had gone so well. I wondered how many other things I might actually be quite good at that I'd always been too scared to try?

Maybe if I faced my fears instead of running away from them, I could be a whole different person. Maybe if I could get over my fear of looking like an idiot in front of other people, I could actually live life instead of always watching from the sidelines. And maybe if I didn't always have my guard up, waiting for people to judge me, I might realize that they are there to support and help . . . because deep down we're all as scared as each other.

As well as daily fear-facing, Susan says we should build up a library of inspirational books and tapes to listen to instead of the news. News is bad, apparently; it only brings us down. This was a bit of a technical hitch, seeing as I was a journalist who had started every day of her working life by reading the papers. Oh well.

As well as reading positive books, Susan recommends that you repeat affirmations throughout the day, such as 'I am alive and full of confidence!' or 'I can do anything I want!' The idea is that by repeating these statements over and over again, we drown out the more negative thoughts we usually have.

These affirmations should be in the present tense and be positive rather than negative; so rather than 'I will no longer put myself down', I was to say: 'I am becoming more confident each and every day.'

You can listen to recordings of these affirmations, repeat

them to yourself, or use the most valuable of self-help tools: the Post-it note.

Susan says the best thing to do is to write affirmations on Post-it notes and leave them everywhere – your bathroom mirror, by your bed, by your desk . . . on your dashboard.

'Go overboard,' says Susan. 'Be outrageous until your friends ask you what's going on.'

So instead of doing work, I channelled my newfound confidence and positivity into scribbling uplifting messages such as: 'I love and approve of myself', 'I love my life' and 'Money flows to me' on Post-it notes which I stuck on the wall behind my desk.

I put the 'It's all happening perfectly' Post-it – which is one of Susan's favourite catchphrases – on my bedroom mirror. Susan reckons that no matter what is happening – even if it seems awful at the time – events are unfolding just as they are meant to.

'The idea is that we replace our usual negative thoughts with positive ones,' I explained to Mum, who called in the middle of my scribbling.

'You mean you delude yourself?' she asked.

'No, you just try to focus on the good rather than bad,' I replied.

'You're not going to go all American, are you?'

'What do you mean?'

'You know . . . *happy*,' she spat out the word. 'People don't like that, Marianne. It's not real.'

Sunday 12th January. My day of nudity had arrived. On God's day, no less.

I sat under a bus stop outside the hall trying to psyche

myself up for yet another uncomfortable experience. The adrenalin that had carried me through so far had run out. I was tired. I didn't want to fight fears anymore. It was raining. Again. And it was dark. I called Sarah.

'What are you doing?' I asked.

'Watching *Sherlock*, eating a curry. What about you?'

'Getting my kit off for strangers.'

'Oh God, yes! How are you feeling?'

'Terrified and hungover.'

'Did you get a wax?'

'No, damn . . . I didn't think of that. I wasn't thinking of it like a date . . .'

'Don't worry about it, they probably like to keep things real.'

'I would pay a million pounds to be on the sofa watching telly with you, right now.'

'You were the one who wanted to get out of your comfort zone.'

'I know. Now I just want to stay in bed,' I said.

She laughed. 'You always want to stay in bed.'

And I did.

Sleep was one of my favourite things on the planet. I once wrote an article about a movement that was encouraging women to 'Sleep their way to the top' except instead of sex, it really was just campaigning for sleep. It was one of the best ideas I'd ever heard.

'Come on, it's exciting. Think of all the cool stories you'll have in the pub,' said Sarah.

'That's true.' Pubs were another of my favourite things. And so, I took a deep breath and got naked. Came home

and ate four slices of cheese on toast. As all the best
models do.

Tuesday 14th and I now had the most random to-do list in
the world:

- Stand-up!!! Where????
- Watch *The Exorcist*
- Book sky dive and spin class.

I could do with adding: 'Wash hair' to it.

And 'Do some actual paid work.' Fear-fighting seemed to
be taking up every waking hour. To kickstart the day I went
out for a power walk, muttering: 'I do it all easily and effortlessly . . .' I didn't know if this was a smart way to
reprogramme my subconscious mind or just a new form of
procrastination.

Thursday 16th and my head was reeling. Life had become
too weird.

I went to a spin class with Rachel, thinking it would be
an easy one to tick off the list. It wasn't. After twenty minutes my legs gave way. I sat motionless for the rest of the
class, while people with rock-hard calves went hell for
leather in expensive Lycra. It was humiliating, worse than
the naked modelling.

Rachel promised me it got easier and I promised her that
I had 'felt the fear' and gone spinning but I would never be
doing it again.

Afterwards I flopped out on the sofa and watched *The
Exorcist*. Despite the fact that I get scared by *Murder, She*

Wrote, I was not freaked out by the green puke and the flying furniture and neither did I get any satisfaction from ticking this fear off the list. Maybe because at the same time as watching the scariest film known to man I was googling open-mike comedy nights. A bit of demonic possession seemed like child's play compared to being heckled in a sticky-floored London pub. My life was starting to feel like a Japanese game show and I didn't like it.

I did no fear-fighting for the next four days. Instead I watched old episodes of *The Kardashians* (Kim having more Botox) and wrote an article on thermal tights.

The Positive Post-its on my bedroom wall kept falling down.

Monday 20th and I was forced to get back to fear-fighting with a hospital and a dentist appointment on the same day. Who says the universe doesn't have a sense of humour?

When I was eighteen, I found a dodgy mole on the inside of my left calf, which turned out to be a malignant melanoma – one of the most serious types of skin cancer. I was meant to be starting university but instead I was in hospital having a tennis-ball sized chunk of flesh removed from my leg while the words 'cancer' and 'chemotherapy' hung in the air. The kind I had is fatal in thirty per cent of cases.

The doctors believed the surgery was successful, but for five years I had regular check-ups to see if the cancer had come back. It was a scary time.

Every time I had to strip off and lie on a paper-covered bed, while a consultant felt for lumps and bumps, my chest would tighten and I would think: 'What if this is the time they find something? What then? I don't want to die!'

Fortunately I was given the all-clear when I was twenty-three and had – more or less – got on with life since. Then I'd noticed a dark spot on my back just before Christmas and so, in the middle of my fear-fighting month, I found myself walking through the same hospital reception as I had all those years before. As I lay on the same paper-covered bed and looked up at the same tiles in the ceiling, I remembered what it was like to be eighteen and not wanting to die.

Here I was, thirty-six and still not wanting to die.

I wasn't ready to go yet. I'd wasted too much of my life worrying! I hadn't done it right yet!

Why did I worry about small stuff that just didn't matter? Really, why? And why hadn't I learned that lesson the first time – when I was eighteen? Surely that brush with death should have left me with a 'life's short, seize the day!' mentality? But it hadn't. Instead it taught me that things can – and do – go wrong.

I was seeing a different consultant this time. This one looked ten years old.

'I can't say for certain until we do the tests but I'm not worried,' he said.

I was so grateful I wanted to hug him. Imagine having that job. Every day telling people whether they are going to live or die. Especially when you're ten.

I left the hospital feeling the same way I had after every appointment all those years ago – relieved but unsettled. I sat on a bench outside and had a little cry. I walked through the park and vowed to appreciate everything and not worry about stupid stuff anymore. I promised to be nicer to my mum and to be a better friend. I bought a cinnamon pastry.

After all that life-and-death stuff, the fillings were easy. I had three done with no injections. The dentist's assistant told me I was very brave. I had another cry.

I'd like to say that after the hospital appointment the thought of stand-up comedy felt like child's play – but it didn't. The upside of cancer is that you don't have to be funny about it. And, on the whole, people don't boo you.

But I didn't have cancer, thank God or whoever is up there. What I did have was a slot on a weekend comedy course, in a pub in Paddington. I had also arranged to do karaoke and eat offal during the same weekend in a last-ditch attempt to tick off as many fears as I could before the end of the month.

So at 10am on the last Saturday of January five of us congregated in the basement of the Mitre pub, hoping that comedy genius would strike amidst the smell of stale beer and Pledge.

Ian, our teacher, asked us to introduce ourselves and talk about why we came. First there was a Finnish guy whose wife had given him the course as a Christmas present ('She's telling me I'm not funny anymore,' he said), then there was a Greek Woody Allen who had booked the course while drunk, followed by a 'six-foot-five poof from Liverpool' (his words) and Jenny, an advertising manager from Manchester who had made a New Year's resolution to do more fun stuff. And then me.

Ian asked us to share who our favourite comedians were.

I struggled to come up with something. The truth was that I hated stand-up. Even the good comics made me uncomfortable. It's their neediness. Find me funny! Like me! Love me! I find the whole thing excruciating.

I didn't say any of this, of course. Instead I said, 'Joan Rivers.'

I gave them the whole fear-fighting spiel and they laughed. I told them about chatting up the guy on the Tube and about the naked modelling, they laughed again. I began to alter my views on comedy. Clearly I was a natural.

We were then asked to do an exercise called 'Rant and Rave' which involved finding five things that drove you crazy and ranting about them for three minutes. I prattled on about hen dos and being single at a wedding, like some sort of tragic Bridget Jones and then half-heartedly moaned about the phrase 'Let's put a date in the diary'.

'I work from home,' I said. 'I'm doing well if I leave the house most days . . . but everyone else is acting like they've got a schedule like Obama.'

It wasn't funny. My classmates were confused and I was embarrassed. I left at 5pm feeling like a woman with a death sentence to eat cow's brains with Rachel at St John – a restaurant described as every vegetarian's hell. I washed down the animal innards with buckets of wine so that by the time we got to the Bird Cage pub in East London, where I would be doing karaoke, I was in the perfect state of inebriation – still upright and able to read the lyrics but too drunk to care.

I got home around 2am, with 'Baby Don't Hurt Me' going around and around in my head. I woke up three hours later, half drunk, half hungover in a panic.

I had to write a comedy routine. I had to stand up in front of people and say it that night. The thought made me want to be sick. And so I was.

Back in the pub basement, the group agreed that I had some good lines but I had to work on my delivery. Ian asked me to speak with 'attitude' but I could do only one style of delivery: terrified.

He gave up: 'It's OK. Even if you deliver it as flatly as you have just now, you'll still get some laughs. Your desperation comes through. You've got that woman on the edge of a breakdown kind of vibe.'

Great. I was going for self-deprecating.

I practised my routine with Rachel before the show started. She didn't laugh once.

'I just feel bad for you,' she said. 'It really is hard being single at a wedding . . .'

I ordered a large glass of Chardonnay and paced back and forth in small circles by the bar.

I felt a strange numbness in my limbs and a high-pitched buzzing sound in my head.

I ordered a second glass of wine. The acid liquid landed in my acid stomach, making me feel even more nauseous.

I told myself that in an hour or two I would be home, on the sofa. Then I could watch television and eat some toast. Nobody was dying, nothing depended on this and, however badly it went, I could handle it.

The room filled up with paying punters.

My eyes were twitching with nerves and tiredness. My armpits were wet.

Greek Woody Allen was up first. He talked about his therapist asking the same questions every week. He figured it was a therapeutic technique but actually the guy had Alzheimer's. Jenny did a routine about a first date bringing out spreadsheets. And the tall guy from Liverpool pulled a blinder – turned out his dad was a Catholic priest who had left the priesthood when he met his mother! 'And look how God repaid him – with a giant poof!' he said. Comedy gold!

Then it was my turn.

The buzzing in my head returned.

I stepped under the white spotlight. I picked up the mike from the stand.

Bloody hell. You are actually doing this. It's happening. You're on a stage about to do stand-up comedy.

I took a breath and looked out at the silhouettes of heads in the audience.

I waited for a wave of panic to come but, well, it didn't. I was so tired I had gone past caring.

I started talking. I told them about my fear-fighting month.

I acted out the ballet poses I had done in the life modelling class. I could hear laughs. I told them about Mr Sweater making my arse look bigger than Australia and about Mum worrying that self-help would make me 'all American'. More laughs. Not uncontrollable give this girl a Perrier Award laughter, but real, honest laughter.

I talked about being put at the kids' table at a wedding. 'There's nothing like sitting with a bunch of teenagers playing Angry Birds to make you wonder where you've gone wrong in life,' I said. That got another laugh. It might have been a pity laugh but I didn't care.

And then, in a flash, it was over. My comedic debut, done. I floated back to my seat. Rachel looked amazed. 'It was funny!' she said. 'Really!'

I sat in dazed silence as people started to gather their things, ready to go home.

I went into the loo and looked at myself in the mirror.

My skin was greasy with sweat but my eyes were beaming. I'd done it. The most terrifying thing I could think of, something that most people would never in a million years do . . . I'd done.

In the cab home I told the driver.

'You didn't,' he said.

'I did, I swear.'

'Tell us a joke then.'

'It wasn't like that – I was just talking about my life,' I said.

'What, is your life that funny then?'

'Sort of,' I said.

I told him about my month and we ended up having a conversation about things that frightened us and he told me he hated going to parties since he'd split up from his wife. 'But it's all in our heads, isn't it?' he said. 'Cos, if I make myself go, it's all right and I wonder what I was worrying about.'

At the end of the journey he refused to take any money off me. 'I think what you're doing is great, love,' he said.

The thing is, so did I.

I had never felt prouder of myself in my whole life.

Compared to the stand-up, nudity and chatting up strangers stuff, I figured jumping out of a plane – my last challenge – would be quite easy. There was nothing I could fail at or be embarrassed about – my two main fears. And I wasn't going to be rejected – my other main fear. All I had to do was show up, strap myself to a stranger and fall through the sky. How hard was that?

The jump was at 7am in a Suffolk airfield, four hours

away, so I drove up (more motorways, tick, tick, tick) and checked into a local guesthouse the night before.

As I lay in the bath, the madness of the last month flashed through my mind like a video montage of a soap opera's best bits. The icy dip, the karaoke, the nudity . . . I'd done more crazy things in January than I'd done in a lifetime.

But had any of it helped me? Changed me?

Well, yes. I'd once read that our fear is not that life is short, it's that we don't feel alive when we live it. But during my fear-fighting, I felt alive. Exhaustingly alive. Every day felt like a day when something could and would happen.

I'd learned a lot too. By jumping in the pond, I saw that life begins the moment you decide to switch off the telly and get off your arse. With public speaking and the stand-up I learned that I was capable of way more than I'd realized. From karaoke I'd learned that life is much more fun if you just lighten up. And with the everyday things like parking, motorway driving and phone answering, I was surprised what a rush of confidence you can get just from doing the little things that you normally avoid. It was the opposite sensation to the energy-sapping worry and stagnation I normally lived with.

But I was aware there was stuff that I had not ticked off the list. I hadn't done anything about my fear of confrontation, I hadn't lost my temper or found out what people thought of me – but maybe the reality was that they were not thinking about me at all.

The next morning, I woke up at 6am and drove to the airfield. The sky was stony grey and the radio gave a storm warning but I was strangely calm as I signed the waiver saying that if I died it was not their fault. I was even calm when I got into the tiny aircraft that looked like it was made from tuna cans. I didn't bat an eyelid when our instructor started telling us to scream as we jumped because it would help us to breathe.

It was only when I was hanging off the side of the plane, the wind blasting my face, my legs dangling into the clouds, that I stopped being calm. Then terror hit me like a punch to the guts, but before I could tell them this had been a terrible mistake, it was too late, I was falling through the sky attached to a man whose name I could not remember.

The cold air and wind were a shock the like of which I'd never experienced. They made Hampstead Ponds feel like a jacuzzi. We were told that the actual temperature was minus fifteen degrees Celsius but with the wind chill it would feel infinitely cooler.

It was only then that it hit me: I was dropping through the sky at thirteen thousand feet. That's two and a half miles up in the sky.

No human body is designed to do this.

For forty seconds we fell. At 150 miles per hour.

It was like hell.

I honestly worried that I would have a heart attack. Surely people do have heart attacks doing this? But we kept falling, and I kept staying alive. Then we jolted upwards as our parachute opened. Our descent slowed. This was the part that most people enjoy, the peaceful bit where you look at the views around you and feel all at one with the beauty of the world. I looked at the muddy patchwork of fields and felt furious. I didn't need to jump out of a plane to see grass! I'm from Ireland, for God's sake. I was practically born in a field! Well, not really. I was born in Surrey near an A-road, but I'd spent every childhood summer knee-deep in cow dung.

Psychologists say that there are two sources to all our fears. The first involves our physical safety – so people are scared of heights, snakes and fire because they can kill us. The second source of fear is of social isolation, which is why we are so scared of looking stupid in front of people or of being rejected.

I realized while hurtling through the sky, that I got no reward from facing my physical fears. My fear of heights was a natural one and was not so extreme that it held me back in normal life – I didn't need to conquer it.

The first words on landing hard on my arse in a muddy field? 'I'm never doing that again.'

I didn't realize then, driving home through hailstones, that falling out of the sky would seem like a walk in the park compared to what was coming next.

2

Money, a Love Story, by Kate Northrup

'Our relationship to money is a direct reflection of how much we value ourselves.'

Pound notes are fluttering through the air and it's my job to catch them before they reach the ground. What if I don't get them before they hit the peach carpet? Or what if I drop them? What if I mess up this once-in-a-lifetime opportunity?

Sheila is there too. She is jumping up and down trying to clap the notes between her hands. Even though she is a year younger, she is taller than me and therefore has the advantage. This is grossly unfair – as are the facts that she always wins at Snap!, has silky brown hair (instead of frizzy ginger hair) and managed to escape freckles.

I jump onto the cream sofa to level the playing field. I try not to worry about what Mum will do if I leave a dirty footprint on it. My nine-, going on ten-year-old, mind knows that this matters more than getting into trouble.

I feel like I'm in a film or an episode of the *Crystal Maze* – remember that show where the contestants were stuck in a glass dome with a wind machine and they have to catch as many gold notes as they can while the clock is ticking?

Well, this is exactly the same, except it's happening in our living room, at 5pm on a school day.

Byker Grove or *Grange Hill* is probably flickering on the telly and we've most likely had spaghetti bolognese for tea, but I don't remember that. Nor do I remember if Helen, our youngest sister, was in the room. What I do remember is dad swooshing open the patio door, opening his wallet and throwing all the cash in it up into the air.

'You can keep whatever you catch – but as soon as it touches the floor it's gone,' he said.

Oh my God! The pressure of it all! There seemed to be millions of pounds flying around our living room, maybe even a trillion or a gazillion. Or at the very least fifty.

We sprang into action, grabbing and clutching and grasping for the green notes.

It couldn't have lasted more than a few seconds – but it felt like forever.

I have no memory of how many notes I was clutching in my little hands when the fun was over. All I do recall, nearly three decades later, is the end of the story. Dad announced that he was only joking, we couldn't really keep the money. We had to hand it back.

I remember a feeling of disappointment, then fury. Fury at the injustice of it all. Fury with myself for falling for it. Of course we were never going to get to keep the money! How stupid we were for thinking we would!

According to my self-help bible for February – *Money, a Love Story* – this memory was the key to understanding why I was the way I was with money. Namely: a total bloody disaster.

Overdrafts, credit cards – I had them all. Not only did I not take financial responsibility, I actively threw money away. You could have given me £100 and I would have found a way to spend it, lose it, drink it within the hour.

You know those couples who say they keep the romance alive by not seeing each other on the toilet – well, I was like that with my bank balance. I never looked. The only time I knew how much was in my account was when my card was declined. This meant I'd hit the bottom of my £3,000 overdraft limit.

So what did this have to do with the *Crystal Maze* memory?

Kate Northrup, my financial guru for the month, asks three questions in the first chapter of her book:

1) What's your first money memory?
2) What's your number-one financial frustration today?
3) Can you see a connection between your first memory and the financial situation you're in now?

Despite the fact that I had not thought about that moment since it happened, I realized that it had a profound effect on the way I'd approached money all my life.

I thought that money was: a) to be thrown around, and b) that you never get to keep it. Also anything to do with money, either having it or not having it, stressed me out. It made me feel the same tightness in my chest that I felt that day in the living room – which was why I was heading to forty with no house, no savings, no pension.

Kate was on to something. I read on.

I had procrastinated for two weeks before I finally opened *Money, a Love Story* on 14th February. In self-help land I believe they call this 'resistance'.

I knew I wanted to do a money book – well, wanted was the wrong word, 'needed' more like – but it was hard to decide which one.

When I typed 'money' into the self-help section of Amazon, 3,125 entries came up. There were books that promised to make me rich such as the snappily named *Get Rich, Lucky Bitch!* by Denise Duffield Thomas. Then there were books on how to budget, including *The Money Diet – The Ultimate Guide to Shedding Pounds off your Bills* (thank you, Martin Lewis for combining two reasons for most women's self-loathing – debt and the size of their bum). There were even religious get-rich-quick books such as *Pennies from Heaven*. Amen.

In this sea of fiscal wisdom and big promises there were a few classics that have stood the test of time. *Think and Grow Rich* by Napoleon Hill was published in 1937 and remains one of the most definitive books on wealth and success.

I put it on my Kindle but only got halfway through.

It was inspiring but not practical enough.

I also started a book called *Rich Dad, Poor Dad* by Robert Kiyosaki, which argues that the idea of working hard, saving money and retiring is a load of rubbish. Instead your aim should be to use your money to invest and to live off the interest. Seeing as I was in minus funds, this was a case of putting the cart before the horse.

Instead I opted for *Money, A Love Story*, by Kate Northrup, which was the bestselling 'personal finance book' that month. About my age, she was drawing on personal experience of how she got into – and out of! – $20,000 of credit card debt in her twenties.

Kate says that we all think that if we just had more money then we'd be OK, but you only need to look at all the lottery winners who are penniless within a couple of years to see that that's not the case.

She argues that just as crash diets won't work unless you understand why you overeat, no attempts at saving and budgeting will work unless you understand why you are the way you are with money and that understanding usually comes from looking at your childhood.

So if you grew up in a family that said, 'money is the root of all evil,' that's going to play out your whole life. And if you grew up in a house where money was being thrown around – in my case, literally – then that's going to have an effect too.

More importantly, Kate says that our relationship with money is a 'microcosm of the relationship we have with ourselves'.

She argues that if you love yourself you look after your money. People who don't look after their money – either by spending too much, getting into debt, or keeping themselves in the dark about how much they have – are not 'free spirits'; they are actually self-sabotaging.

Oh.

'You sure you don't want to come?' Rachel was applying lip gloss in the downstairs loo. It was Valentine's Day and she was going to a 'Trash and Treasure' party, where you each bring a single friend of the opposite sex that you don't find attractive – but who might be someone else's treasure.

'Yes, I'm sure.'

'You might meet the man of your dreams.'

'Highly unlikely.'

I walked into the kitchen, poured a glass of wine and opened my book.

Kate starts with a quiz to 'learn what's holding you back from the abundance you desire and what your current relationship with money says about you'. Self-help gurus love a quiz. They also love the word 'abundance'. Old-school self-help promised to help you get rich quick, the new self-help talks about 'abundance' and 'prosperity mind-sets'. That way you're not greedy by wanting more money – you're spiritual.

There are thirty-nine questions in Kate's book, so I started with the first one and worked my way through:

1) *Do you know how much you spent last month and on what within about $100.*
   No, I do not. I couldn't tell you in pounds either.

2) *Do you know how much you made last month within about $100?*
   Yes, next to nothing. I have been too busy engaging in full-time self-help.

3) *Do you have more than $1,000 in savings?*
   Very funny.

4) *Do you have at least one retirement account?*
   Oh, Kate, you're cracking me up!

And on and on it went, asking about real estates and stocks and shares . . . before I could finally answer some of Kate's questions in the affirmative:

Do you feel anxious when you think or talk about money?
Yes.
Do you lie awake in bed at night or wake up early worrying about money?
Yes.
Do you find yourself using the phrase 'I can't afford that' at least once a week?
Yes.
Do you avoid bank statements, credit card bills and other financial paperwork?
Yes, yes, yes.

At the end, I totted up the various yeses and nos and got a score of six out of a possible thirty-nine.

Kate's assessment: 'Your relationship with money has been tumultuous. It's not been a love affair in the past and you may be scarred. But that can change starting today.' I liked the word 'tumultuous'. It made me feel exciting. Perhaps this was part of the problem.

The next step for me and my six out of thirty-nine score was to write my 'Money Love Story', which meant writing out absolutely everything I'd ever done, felt and said about money.

This was the bit in a book I would usually skip but Kate says writing it out is crucial. So I dug out a notebook and started my secret teenage financial diary, by Marianne Power, aged thirty-six and a half.

I began with the floating cash memory and worked from there.

I grew up in a house of extremes. My Irish dad came
to London with nothing when he was sixteen. By the
time we came along he'd made a fortune in property.

As children there were trips to Harrods and Hamleys. Holidays to Disneyland and Europe.

For my ninth birthday I was taken to the Ritz for tea. My first alcoholic drink was a swig taken from a crystal decanter in the back of my dad's black Bentley. Always braver than me, Sheila preferred to actually drive the cars, starting at the age of fourteen.

Next thing we knew, there was an almighty bang and our gleaming green Jaguar was parked in our front hall. Sheila had mistaken the accelerator for the brake – and reversed into the house. Actually into the house.

Dad's response, upon seeing the relatively unscathed Jag? 'Good cars, aren't they?'

So in short – we were rich.

The kind of rich that can bounce back from a Jag being parked inside the hallway.

But as every poor little rich girl will tell you, it wasn't all perfect. Even as a young child I realized a few things about money (and flash cars):

People don't like people with money (and flash cars). When I was about nine we were in London traffic in Dad's Bentley and guys on the street were screaming 'Yuppie' at us. They banged on the bonnet. I didn't know what a Yuppie was but I could see the hate in their eyes. I asked Dad what it meant and he said, 'Young person,' but I knew that wasn't it. Dad was ancient.

Money (and flash cars) make you different. As a child all I wanted was to be normal. My greatest dream was to be called Sarah, have brown hair and to have a dad who drove a Ford.

Finally, having money (and flash cars) make you a spoiled brat. The world we were being brought up in

was a world away from the world my parents came
from. Dad grew up with nothing and was determined
to give us everything we wanted. Mum, on the other
hand, hated the level of excess we were growing up
with and made sure we knew it.

I learned to feel guilty about the money we had
and bad about the kind of people we were. Rich people.

So maybe it was just as well that soon enough we
learned another lesson: that money doesn't last.

When I was in my late teens, Dad's failing health
combined with the 1990s recession meant that the
money started to dry up quite spectacularly. When I
was seventeen Mum cancelled Christmas. By the time
we were in our twenties everything was gone – the
house, the cars, the money.

Here's what I learned about NOT having money:

First of all, anyone who's been there knows that
not being able to pay bills and facing the prospect of
losing your home is terrifying. Money might not buy
you happiness but it buys you security and a roof over
your head. When that goes, well, so does everything.
But somehow, you get through it. Life goes on. And
there are upsides. Mum says that we wouldn't have
worked so hard or done so well in our careers if
they'd kept their money. She also says that we've
turned out nicer people for it.

I glanced at the clock. It was 9.30pm. I'd been writing for
two hours. My wrist hurt.

Writing it all out like that – the cars, the holidays, the
floating cash – I could see for the first time how extreme it
all was.

Of course it was going to have an effect on me. How could it not?

I went to bed and watched *Graham Norton* on my laptop.

Bill Murray and Matt Damon were on. I found myself thinking that straight-old Matt was probably boringly good with money, while wild, wacky Bill would be a disaster. In my head all fun people had to be reckless with money. It was part of our charm.

Oh well, Happy Valentine's Day to me.

When I got up the next morning, Rachel was still asleep. Her thigh-high boots lay like slugs by the sofa. I headed out to Bread and Bean, one of my local coffee shops. I ordered my coffee and scrambled eggs and took a quick scan of the papers – flood warnings, an NHS scandal, something about Simon Cowell – before remembering that 'negative' media was not allowed in my self-help life. Instead I depressed myself with another story – my own. I started scribbling down how I was with money as an adult. I used 'adult' in the loosest sense.

> After graduating, I lived in London at the height of the Brit Pop era. It was the coolest city in the world but I was not cool, so I spent a lot of money trying to fix that by buying the latest Nike trainers, even though they looked ridiculous on me, and squeezing my beer-filled tummy into low-slung jeans. I was on a low salary and living beyond my means – shopping in Covent Garden for the first half of the month, living off cereal for the second.
>
> When I was twenty-nine, I got my first big job, as

features editor of a newspaper. My salary increased. Then the good times rolled! I used taxis like they were buses and ate out constantly. I bought designer clothes because I thought it was important that I looked the part now that I was a Hot Shot Newspaper Editor. I permanently looked as if I'd just stepped out of a salon. Because I had.

But underneath the bag and the hair and the dresses, I felt like a fraud. I was struggling to keep on top of my work so I quit the big job and the big salary to go free-lance. My spending got even more erratic. As soon as I got a cheque I'd be out celebrating, living it up, but then a week later I was broke and stressed. Every year I'd vow to be better with money, to grow up – but I never did . . .

I looked up. The coffee shop was packed full of couples and friends chatting. I felt shaken. How had I not seen what a huge part of my life money was?

I'd always thought my main issue was that I didn't have enough money but I could see now that, actually, no amount of money would ever be enough for me. I would be one of those people who ended up bankrupt four years after winning the lottery. 'I don't know where it all went,' I'd tell the tabloids, who'd picture me in my ten-bedroom house with indoor pool, hair salon and gold kitchen taps.

I paid my £14.75 bill for eggs and two coffees.

Rachel was in the kitchen, opening post. She wasn't afraid of brown envelopes like I was.

'So how was it?' I asked.

'Someone made Turkish Delight martinis,' she replied.

'What the hell are they?'

'I don't know but they were strong. I couldn't move my mouth for half the night. What about you – how was your hot date with your bank statements?'

'OK,' I lied. I felt too embarrassed to talk to her about money. She was so good with hers. She always knew what was going in and out. She was generous without being flash.

I went to my room and called Sheila.

I asked her what her first money memory was.

'I remember Mum going mental if we left lights on, or the heating.'

'And how does that connect with where you are now?'

'I'm careful with bills. What was yours?'

'That time Dad came into the living room and threw money around.'

'Oh yeah, I'd forgotten about that. But was that memory even real? Sometimes I think we made that up.'

'How would we both have made up a memory?'

'I don't know. So what does the memory mean for you?'

'It means I throw money around.'

'Who'd be a parent? Anything you do and your child can end up blaming you for ruining their life.'

But I didn't blame anyone but me for the way I was. I was an adult. I had choices. I just kept making the wrong ones.

Kate suggests that we write down our patterns and beliefs around money so I got out my notebook again and as I scribbled I discovered dozens of beliefs and patterns that I had had no idea were there.

First up was guilt. I felt guilty about having more than other people, so whenever I had money I gave it away – which is to say that I bought endless rounds of drinks and always shouted dinner. But there was something else going on: I could see that I'd bought people things as a way of making them like me. If I was paying, they were more likely to hang around. I wasn't the funniest or best-looking but I could be generous.

Philosophically, I considered meanness to be one of the most unattractive traits in a person. I thought it was boring, self-serving and greedy to be concerned by money. I was better than that! Sitting on my bed, scribbling, I had an unsettling realization: I treated money as if it was beneath me.

I also hadn't grown up when it came to money. I was scared of it. Kate says that a lot of women are waiting for a man (in the form of a husband) to come and fix their situation; she calls it the Prince Charming Effect – was that what I was doing? It made me cringe to think that might be the case but I'd definitely spent my life playing the victim when it came to cash. I didn't look after it, then I played 'poor me' when I was 'broke' and suddenly couldn't afford the bus fare. I'd lost count of how many times Sheila had had to bail me out.

Finally, to tie in with my first money memory, I believed that money comes and goes, so I don't get attached to it, look after it, or make plans with it.

Kate says to think of ways of looking at your story and understanding (as Susan Jeffers says in *Feel the Fear*) that it all happened perfectly. This is the 'love' bit in which you learn to love yourself and the lessons you've learned.

I wrote about the fact that I might have blown a lot of money but I'd had fun. I was glad I'd had that experience of going on fancy trips to New York, buying designer handbags and eating in fancy restaurants. It was a moment in time and I'd made the most of it. I'd also come out the other side and realized, as clichéd as it sounds, that stuff doesn't make you happy – it just makes you look better as you paper over the cracks of your life.

Kate says nothing is as bad as the insidious fear that comes with keeping yourself in the dark about your finances and so my next task was to gather six months of bank statements in order to get what Kate calls 'cash clarity'. She warns that it's going to be hard. She was right.

The next day was the kind of miserable Sunday designed for the sofa but instead of slobbing out I got the train to my mum's to go through my financial paperwork.

Looking at the numbers was horrific.

Four hours after I started, the reality of how much debt I was in began to emerge.

I added it all up for the first time and realized that I was £15,109.60 in debt. There was £6,000 owed to Sheila, a £7,000 overdraft on my business account and £2,109.60 on my current. I felt physically sick to see the figures. How had I been so irresponsible? How had I not known I was in this deep?

Fifteen thousand pounds in debt. And that's with no mortgage, no kids. It was inexcusable. Fifteen thousand. The number kept going around and around in my head.

Kate says that you can't beat yourself up for what you've done – that it doesn't help. But I *was* beating myself up. I felt so angry with myself. And ashamed.

I could no longer see the upside in my spending or the philosophical lessons. Looking at my finances was like looking through a massive magnifying glass. I could see all that was bad about me: I was reckless, stupid, vain, careless, deluded. A spoilt brat.

I locked myself in the bathroom and cried on the loo. Then I ran a bath. I poured in the oil I'd bought Mum for Christmas – Pomegranate Noir, Jo Malone, £40 – and cried some more. That bath probably cost me £5.

Monday 17th. Still pissing down outside and teary inside. More than anything I wanted to stick my head back in the sand. But I couldn't. I had to see this through – rip the Band-Aid right off.

Kate suggests looking through your statements to find the sources of what she calls 'financial energy leaks' – spending that makes you feel bad rather than good. The aim is to cut down on these leaks.

Looking through my statements, it was clear that I may as well have had no kitchen. Or even a kettle. About fifty per cent of it was Starbucks, Costa, Caffè Nero, Strada, Wagamama, some pub or other, another pub or other . . .

Then there were the beauty-maintenance transactions. Blow-dries at £25 a pop, nails another £25, £42 at Boots for God knows what, £22 in Holland and Barrett for stupid vitamins, £70 facials, £60 waxes. I was a classic example of the 'I'm worth it even if I can't afford it' generation. At the time I'd told myself that these were investments; I thought that if I looked good, I'd feel good and then . . . and then what? I'd meet the man of my dreams? Get promoted?

And I hadn't even got to clothes yet. I didn't buy lots but when I did, I didn't buy cheap. £150 on a sweater which I'd end up being too lazy to hand-wash, so it would spend its life lurking at the bottom of my laundry basket.

Looking through the statements, I also discovered that

my average phone bill was £143 a month. £143. I didn't even like talking on the phone!

Then there was £14 a month for a magazine subscription I wasn't getting, a couple of direct debits that I couldn't identify and which had probably been coming out of my account for years, and finally the mystery cash withdrawals: £100 here, another £100 there – I had no idea what it got spent on. It may as well have vanished into thin air.

After years of earning good money, I'd blown it all on high heels, hangovers and endless stupid coffees. It made me feel sick, embarrassed and ashamed. What a fucking idiot.

The whole time I was going through my bank statements I had Mum on my mind. She didn't spend £150 on cashmere sweaters she was too lazy to wash. She managed to look a million dollars shopping at TK Maxx. She knew the price of everything. 'Do you like my top?' she'd ask. 'It's a hundred per cent silk – £20, down from £60! And the trousers? Pure linen – £15, down from £45!'

She didn't go out and spend £2.50 on coffee she could make for pennies at home. She only bought food at the end of the day when it was discounted. She probably ate for a week on what I'd spend on stupid avocado on toast in some stupid hipster coffee shop . . .

That night, she knocked on the door of the spare bedroom I was in, surrounded by papers.

'Are you OK? Would you like a cup of tea?' she asked.

'No, thank you.'

'How's it going?'

'Not good.' My voice cracked. I started crying. 'I've been an idiot.'

'How bad is it?'

'I'm not telling you. But it's bad.'

'You've been living a life you can't afford, Marianne,' she said.

'I know,' I cried.

'You always say, "I know," but you do the same thing time and time again.'

'I know.'

'You'll feel so much better if you cut down your spending. I get more of a kick out of saving now than I do shopping. Security is a nice feeling. You have to take control.'

'I know,' I said. But actually I didn't know. I had never felt secure when it came to money and I had never learned how to take control of anything.

Gemma called.

'What's wrong?' she asked.

'Nothing,' I said.

'Don't give me nothing,' she said. 'I can hear it in your voice.'

I gave her the short version – without the numbers.

'I feel like a bad person,' I told her.

'You're not a bad person, you're a generous person and that's a good thing but maybe cut back a bit now,' she said.

I could hear baby James crying in the background and I felt ashamed to be taking up her time when she had a newborn to look after.

For the second night in a row, I cried myself to sleep.

The next day I felt calmer – the kind of calm that only comes when you no longer have the energy to feel sorry for yourself. And I had to give myself some credit for facing the monster in the attic. The important thing now was to keep going.

Kate says it's important to organize your finances into 'strong containers'.

She recommends red folders – according to Feng Shui red is the colour of affluence – and labelling everything prettily with a 'label maker'. She also suggests 'bedazzling' your folders with sequins.

I skipped the sequins but I went to Paperchase to buy four clean white ring binders. £4.50 each.

'Can you not just use some of the folders you already have?' asked Mum.

'They have to match and look good so that I feel good about them and will use them every day,' I replied.

She said nothing.

I got home and put all my Barclays statements into one folder labelled 'Beautiful Barclays'. I got another folder for HSBC statements – and labelled it 'Happy HSBC' – and put all my tax documents into a folder with little hearts drawn around the letters HMRC. I felt like I was in a remedial art class but it was oddly therapeutic.

Kate also says that you have to look after your physical money – no shoving it in pockets or throwing loose change at the bottom of bags, as I had always done. She keeps all her notes in order of value, facing forward in her wallet. I thought that was a bit much, but I looked through pockets, drawers and the bottom of bags and managed to source £22.53. I arranged this money carefully in my wallet. Money for nothing.

I headed back to London feeling shaken but stronger. During Feel the Fear it had never occurred to me that money was one of my fears – but it was a big one and, just as Susan said, facing the fear felt empowering. Now I had to keep facing it.

Kate says that there are two things I had to do every day to keep my finances on track. First I had to check my bank balance every morning and then I had to think of three things I was grateful for. Kate reckons that what you focus on expands. So if you focus on your debt you'll get more debt, if you focus on all the great things you do have – a cheque on its way, kind friends, a good cup of coffee, etc. – you'll get more great things. I didn't really understand how this worked but I was prepared to try.

She also says thinking nice thoughts every time you look at your bank balances creates a kind of Pavlov's dog thing – you associate your bank with happiness. Even when your Barclays account is minus £2,211.03. For example.

So when I got back to Rachel's, I looked at my balances – all in negative – but gave thanks for the fact that I had biscuits with my tea and there was heat coming out of the radiator. And just that simple act felt big. I never checked my bank balances. Ever. But seeing the number felt good. At least I knew where I was.

The next day my editor emailed asking me to write about a £100 'super-vitamin' supplement that Elle Macpherson had just launched, containing forty-five ingredients designed to 'support nutrition at a cellular level and optimize the functioning of all eleven systems of the body'. Buy this and you too could look like a supermodel. The old me would have bought two packets. The new me was just grateful to earn money writing about it.

On 22nd February I had a major blip. It was Sarah's birthday

and after all my good behaviour, I figured I was allowed a
night out. The only problem was that it wasn't just a night
– it was an eighteen-hour spending spree.

A bunch of us met for brunch in King's Cross. Price for
coffee, eggs and bubbles? £22.50. Then Sarah wanted to go
to Oxford Street to buy something to wear that night. She
found a top in Topshop that cost £29 and looked fantastic
on her. I bought a stupid leopard-print sweater in Whistles
which cost almost three times as much at £85. I didn't even
like it that much, but I felt fusty in my boring grey sweater.
I could see all the clever ways my mind justified the spending. *It's important to look good. You never know who'll you meet.
And it's Sarah's birthday – it's nice to make her day fun – don't
be a spoilsport.*

I felt guilty instantly but I drowned that feeling with red
wine over late lunch in Cote.

'Come on, let me get this,' said Sarah when the bill
arrived. I refused.

'It's your birthday,' I insisted. 'I'll get it.'

'Yeah, but you don't have it, it's OK.'

'No, I've got money coming in,' I lied. 'Please, I want to,
it's my treat.' And even as I handed over my card for £50, I
worried that it would get declined.

Why did I do that? Insist on paying? Kate says that if you
want money in your life you have to learn to receive as well
as to give. She says that if you refuse things such as compliments, or letting your friend treat you to dinner, you are
'blocking the flow of abundance'. That language made me
cringe but maybe there was something in it. I always refused
compliments and wanted to pay for things.

Then we got our nails done, £25, went home, got
changed and met the gang at Shoreditch House.

I hate Shoreditch House. It's a stuck-up pretentious members' bar designed to make anyone who steps inside feel inferior. A feeling that can only be alleviated by: a) acting like a stuck-up twat, or b) spending lots of money. I opted for b). Crumpled receipts in my pocket showed me that I'd spent £79.85 on four coffee martinis and a bottle of prosecco – drinks I have little memory of ordering. What I do recall is feeling fat and ugly in my stupid leopard-print top and hating everyone at the bar. I remember thinking, 'Just go home now, call it a night and go,' but I didn't. I threw good money after bad, hoping to make the night a success. Then I spent £25 on a taxi home. Grand total spent in one day: £246.35.

The next day I felt disgusted with myself.

In my old life I would never ever have totted that up and would have had no idea that that was what I got through on one social Saturday. I thought about how many times I had spent money on clothes I didn't like, just to try and feel good. I thought of all the nights trying to buy fun in pretentious bars that made me feel like crap.

I spent the day in bed watching people at their worst in *House of Cards*. A bit like Shoreditch House but with fewer coffee martinis.

'What's going on?' Rachel looked alarmed. 'Are you OK?'

'Yes, why? I'm fine!' I snapped.

'OK.' She stood by my bedroom door looking in at the chaos within. Clothes in piles. Shoes angrily jutting out of Tesco bags.

'What time did you get up?'

'I don't know. Early.'

I'd got up at 6 on Monday morning, on a mission to do

penance for all my financial sins – starting with hand-wash-
ing every item of clothing languishing at the bottom of my
laundry basket, followed up with a clear-out of my wardrobe. Kate says we must sell everything we don't use
because it's a source of cash and also in Feng Shui clutter is
bad because it blocks our capacity to get new things.

So I piled my old, unworn clothes on my bed.

When I say old, that's not really true. There were dresses
that still had labels on them, bought for occasions and never
worn. There were a couple of Topshop jeans bought in a
size too small, in the hope that I would slim into them and
a pair of Marni heels I'd bought in a sale that were always
too big and fell off every time I wore them.

I knew I could probably get more for them on eBay but
I was too lazy so I took them to a local second-hand shop,
feeling quietly confident that they'd be delighted with my
collection. I envisioned them telling me what nice taste I
had, that they couldn't believe I was getting rid of such
beautiful things.

It didn't go that way.

'We don't do Topshop,' said the shop assistant with
straightened, bleached hair, when she picked up the jeans at
the top of the Ikea bag full of clothes.

'There's a pull in this seam,' she said, pulling at the hips
of a spotty dress from LK Bennett.

'This has a stain,' she said, pointing to a hardly noticeable
bit of foundation just by the neck on another dress.

Then she picked up a green silk evening dress which I'd
worn to the IFTAs, the Irish equivalent of the Oscars. It was
the most expensive thing I'd ever bought at £700.

'It's not the right time of year for black tie,' she said,
tossing it aside. 'Bring it back in November if you want.'

'This we can take,' she said, of a peach-coloured dress I'd bought for a wedding and the too-big Marni shoes.

Shows what crap taste you have, I wanted to shout. That dress was horrible! I bought it out of desperation!

'We'll try the shoes at £50 and the dress the same. We keep them on sale for five weeks, if they haven't sold after four, we put them on discount and if they don't sell then, they go to charity. We take fifty per cent.'

So my designer life was worth £50. Tops.

I gathered up my rejected clothes and left with my cheeks burning.

By the time I got home, I was fuming.

'Stupid stuck-up cows!' I ranted.

'Who are?' asked Rachel.

'In that shop. They didn't want any of my clothes.'

'So, put them on eBay or come do a trunk sale with me. You'll make more money that way.'

'That's not the point!'

'What is the point? Why are you letting some woman you don't know get you so angry?'

I thought about it and realized that the woman in the shop was not the problem. I was.

The truth was selling my old possessions felt beneath me and the fact that they didn't even want them added insult to injury.

I felt demeaned and embarrassed, stripped of the status I usually had when entering a shop as a customer. And I hadn't realized how much I liked that status, the status of going into a shop and buying a cashmere sweater while the assistant wraps it up nicely. The status of being able to flag a cab when it's raining, instead of standing by the bus stop.

The status of eating out instead of bringing in a packed lunch . . .

I didn't like what any of this said about me.

'I've made a mess of everything,' I said.

'What do you mean?' asked Rachel.

And for the first time ever, I shared my dirty money secret. I told her just how much I was in debt and how stupid I'd been. I told her about how much money we'd had growing up and how it had all gone. She made me a cup of tea and squeezed my hand.

'Now you know the situation, you can fix it, can't you?'

I nodded.

And Rachel was right. I could fix it. Things would change. Starting now.

I celebrated the end of my money month with something Kate calls a Financial Freedom Date.

Kate says it's important to sit down weekly to track expenses and earnings – and that putting on nice music, a special outfit and lighting a candle will make the whole thing enjoyable. It becomes a ritual. A money love-in. She even has a play list for the occasion on Spotify – there's a lot of country music on it, which didn't make sense to me. Country music is so miserable it makes me want to go shopping. Mind you, I could say that of a lot of things.

I opted for Kanye West's 'Gold Digger'.

I didn't burn a candle because after years of literally burning money with over-priced candles, I was going cold turkey. Also, I didn't want to put the heating on (tick, tick!), so I was not wearing a little black dress – I was wearing two sweaters.

To start I had to go through my bills, which Kate refers to as 'Invoices for Blessings Already Received'. Kate says that instead of focusing on the money going out, we should give thanks for the service we got for that money. So I looked at my last crazy phone bill and thanked it for the lovely conversations I had with wonderful friends.

My most sincere gratitude and all-out love went to Netflix. For just £5.99 a month I got hours of entertainment (more hours than I'd care to admit), not to mention a faithful bedtime companion. I sensed it was a love that would last.

Next I counted my earnings. This was a short task. I'd written one article that month. Usually I'd be writing two articles a week. Self-help was taking up too much of my time.

Finally, I did some financial housekeeping. I phoned up the magazine company I had been paying money to every month. It was a *Vogue* subscription from three years ago, sent to a flat I hadn't lived in for two years. Instead of beating myself up – I let it go. I phoned *The Times*, to whom I was sending £17.99 a month for, it transpires, the uber de luxe iPad package. I did not have an iPad.

I called my phone company and asked them why my bills were so high. Turned out that every time I called Gemma in Dublin, to discuss something major like whether she'd watched *X Factor*, it was costing me about £20. I was informed that there was a £5 a month package I could buy that would allow me unlimited minutes to Irish phones.

'Why didn't you notice this sooner?' asked the guy on the phone.

'Because I'm an idiot,' I said.

'I'm as bad: it's in one pocket, out the other,' he said.

It struck me, as The Notorious B.I.G.'s 'Mo Money Mo Problems' came on my playlist, that so many of us have money issues that we never talk about.

That night Rachel had friends around for dinner. One told me she'd knocked up £40,000 of credit card debt in her thirties.

She'd broken up with the man she thought she was going to marry and went into a spiral. 'I'd stay at home, order takeaway, drink wine and buy clothes online. I didn't even open the packets half the time – the clothes would arrive and I'd throw them in the bottom of the wardrobe.'

And that's the thing. Kate says that any time we are out of control with our finances, whatever it might look like, we are not having fun; we are actually self-destructing. And that self-destruction can be because of different demons, but in her world all those things come down to one thing: not loving yourself enough.

I found it hard to get on board with the whole 'love yourself' stuff because it's so abstract but there's some truth in it. I grew up with extreme habits around money, which I replicated. But my sisters were not in the same financial state that I was, which meant there was something else going on. As clichéd as it might sound, I thought it came down to this: I never felt good enough.

I never felt pretty enough, so I'd spend on clothes. Despite all the promotions, I never felt I was good at my job so I squandered my earnings instead of taking pride in them. I didn't really see why people liked me, so I'd try to buy them things. When I didn't know what else to do, I would go out and spend to find happiness. But all I found was a bigger overdraft. I then used my debt as another reason to beat myself up and hate myself more – the spiral continued.

Kate says that if we're worrying about our money we are not 'fully present' in other areas of our life. If you wake up at 2am worrying about money (as I did), you are not going to think creatively or work effectively. Those niggles in the back of your mind mean that you can't enjoy anything properly. It's so true. I thought worrying about money was the norm. I didn't realize there was an alternative.

But there was. Kate's book had helped me see that. It had also made me understand that it was going to take a lot longer than a couple of weeks to sort out my money problems. It would, I suspect, take years.

A part of me wondered whether I should stick with the book for another month, just to follow through on what I'd learned. I could spend March really getting on top of things. I would sell that stuff on eBay, maybe even draw up a budget . . .

3

The Secret,
by Rhonda Byrne

'Whatever you dream of can be yours'

Except I didn't. Sell the clothes on eBay, that is. Or create a budget. Instead I picked up a book that told me I didn't need to sell my dresses, I had to buy new ones. A book that suggested only losers cry over bank statements, winners write themselves pretend cheques and imagine money flying through the letter box. A book that told me I could have anything I wanted, and more, without doing anything at all . . .

This book argues that there is a 'Great Secret' that has been passed down between the best minds in history – people such as Plato, da Vinci, Einstein . . . and, er, Australian daytime-TV producer, Rhonda Byrne. What is this secret?

You can have anything you want in life if you just believe.

The man of your dreams, the house of your dreams, the job of your dreams, millions of pounds . . . all yours, if you just think positively enough. No need to work, study or do anything, really – just wish for it.

I know, wonderful, isn't it? What the hell have we been making life so complicated for?

And in case you are sceptical (you cynic!), according to

The Secret, it's all down to something called the 'law of attraction', which states that 'thoughts become things'. So, if you think about money, you're going to get lots of money. Think about debt and that's what you'll get more of.

'Thoughts are magnetic and thoughts have a frequency,' says Byrne. 'As you think thoughts, they are sent out into the Universe, and they magnetically attract all like things that are on the same frequency.'

Hmmmm.

I'd had a flatmate who was obsessed with *The Secret*. She used to fall asleep watching the DVD (it started life as a film) and gave copies of the book to all her friends, including me. I'd never got past the first few pages; I objected on aesthetic grounds. I hated the stupid brown pages, which looked like they'd had coffee spilt on them and I hated the stupid scrolly font that's trying to make everything look old and scholarly but actually makes everything look naff and crap.

And, even though I hadn't bought it, it really bothered me that the price of this small, ugly book was £14.99. Rhonda Byrne had clearly uncovered the secret to getting rich. In fact, her bestselling book is reported to have grossed around $300 million internationally, selling to 19 million people and sprouting a series of sequels called *The Power* and *The Magic*. Which begs the question: if *The Secret* answers the mysteries of our time – why do people need to buy the other books?

And it wasn't just me who had an allergic reaction. Concerns were raised about the materialistic message in these books – in which happiness always comes in the form of money and cars. Greater criticism was levelled at the idea that, according to the law of attraction, anything bad that happens is your fault.

Then Byrne fell out with two of the main contributors, Esther and Jerry Hicks, and in 2011 one of the so-called experts in the book, James Arthur Ray, was charged with 'negligent homicide' after three people died in a sweat lodge at one of his retreats.

It was all deluded and dangerous nonsense – the very worst of self-help.

So why was I doing it?

Because ever since I'd started the project people had one of two reactions: either they looked at me blankly or their eyes got bigger and they asked me if I'd read *The Secret*, before telling me how their life had changed since reading it.

One friend reckoned *The Secret* got her pregnant. She'd been trying for five years with no luck. They were just about to go through their third and final round of IVF treatment when her mum gave her the book. She went on to have twins nine months later.

'Something just clicked,' she said. 'I had total faith that it was going to happen – and it did.'

Another swore blind that the flat she was living in was one that she visualized, to the inch, five years earlier. 'I used to draw out plans for my ideal home – the size I'd like the living room to be, the kind of bedroom I wanted with a window overlooking a garden. It was *The Secret* – absolutely,' she said.

A former colleague believed that she got proposed to because of *The Secret*. She had been single for years when one New Year's Eve, at home alone, having been given the book for Christmas, she wrote a list of everything she wanted in her life. Top of that list was 'Be engaged by the end of the year'. It happened sooner than that. She met a guy the weekend after and he proposed within two months. Unfortunately, it didn't work out. 'Next time I'm going to specify the kind of guy I want to be engaged to – so not an alcoholic head case,' she said.

I scoffed when I heard these stories. There was always a more realistic explanation. I think Jo got pregnant because she was more relaxed and therefore everything worked better. Or maybe it was just her time. Lucy got the flat not because of the powers of the Universe but because her grandmother died and she inherited enough for the deposit. As for Sam, she met someone because she was looking.

But, believe it or not, the idea of the law of attraction has been around for more than a century – featuring in *The Science of Getting Rich* written by Wallace Wattles in 1911 as well as Napoleon Hill's *Think and Grow Rich* and Norman Vincent Peale's *The Power of Positive Thinking*, published in the 1950s.

It's even backed up by science, according to Byrne, who argues that the law of attraction is 'a law of nature' and supported by quantum physics.

'The discoveries of quantum physics and new science are in total harmony with the teachings of *The Secret*,' she explains. 'I never studied science or physics at school and yet when I read complex books on quantum physics, I understood them perfectly . . .' I didn't do physics at school either, Rhonda, so I'll have to take your word for it.

But as far-fetched as it all sounded, a little tiny part of me couldn't help but wonder . . . What if we really could have anything we wanted just by changing our thoughts? What if there are forces at work that I don't understand?

For all my cynicism, deep down I wanted it to be true. I wanted to believe that all my problems could vanish in an instant. That I could get everything I wanted, and more. I wanted to believe in the magic.

I also needed a bit of light relief.

It had been a high-octane start to the year, followed by the tears and shame of money month. That phrase, 'You can't handle the truth!' kept going around in my head. Too bloody right I couldn't. I didn't turn to self-help looking for the truth.

So at the start of March, given the choice between continuing to face financial reality or sticking my head back in the sand . . . I chose sand. Lots and lots of sand.

I picked up my old copy of *The Secret*.

I once read an article that argued that all self-help books promise to tell you one of three things: how to get laid, how to get rich, or how to lose twenty pounds. A book that could combine all of those – well, it was guaranteed to be a best-seller. Cue *The Secret*.

The book's basic formula is this: Ask, Believe and Receive.

First you should 'Ask' for what you want. Then you must absolutely 'Believe' that it is on its way to you. And hey presto! Before long you are 'Receiving' untold men, money and a supermodel body.

Having spent the last month in tears over my finances – my ambition for March was simple: it was time to get stinking rich. Apparently this is really very easy.

The book tells the story of a guy who used to get lots of bills in the post until, one day, he decided to imagine cheques coming through the letter box instead. Then, what do you know, within a month the cheques came flying in.

So on Monday 10th March, instead of writing an article

I'd been asked to write about the magic power of goji berries, I closed my eyes and tried to imagine cheques flying through my letter box rather than bills and takeaway pizza leaflets. I pictured them shooting onto the doormat, like coins coming out of a slot machine. There were so many of them they formed a little paper mountain.

This felt ridiculous, obviously. But also quite nice. I mean – who doesn't like a little get-rich daydream?

Next I downloaded a blank cheque from 'the Universe' that I found on the *Secret* website. You just fill out the amount you want and then that amount will magically come to you in real life.

As it chugged out of the printer, I debated how much to ask for. The book says, 'It is as easy to manifest one dollar as it is to manifest one million dollars,' but I didn't want the Universe to think I was greedy. Nor did I want to miss my opportunity. I decided on £100,000. The number scared me. 'Who do you think you are?' thoughts came into my head but still I wrote the six figures in the box and filled it out in my name. I looked at it and for a second I felt a flutter of excitement. Imagine if it was true . . .

Rhonda says I needed to believe it was going to happen and to 'feel the feelings of having that money now'.

She also says that for the next thirty days I should look at everything I wanted to buy and say, 'I can afford that! I can buy that!' I went on Net-a-Porter and had a browse. Did you know that jeans could cost £300? Me neither, but they can. And according to *The Secret*, I could afford them. So I pictured myself in a pair of high-waisted Victoria Beckham jeans and a floral blouse . . . Then just for fun I visualized myself being skinny in these over-priced jeans.

Visualization is important because 'When you are

visualizing, you are emitting a powerful frequency. The law of attraction will take hold of that powerful signal and return those pictures back to you, just as you saw them in your mind.'

And to make sure the Universe gets the message, *The Secret* suggests I also doctor my bank statements to let them show the amount of money I wanted rather than the reality of what I had. I took out one statement that informed me that my account was minus £1,238.00 and changed it to plus and Tippexed out the point so that it read £12,380.

By the end of the day I still hadn't finished the piece that could have actually earned me some real money but I had picked out a fantasy wardrobe for my fantasy life. I did not check my real bank balances. I figured it would lower my frequency.

It was just a week after my financial reality check and already I was going back into La-La Land.

As if she could sense the slippery slope I was on, my mum rang.

'I've just written a cheque to myself for £100,000,' I told her.

'What?'

'The book I'm doing this month says you should write yourself a pretend cheque and imagine it coming to you, and that if you believe it will come, the money will appear.'

'Oh, for goodness' sake.'

'I know, it's silly.'

'We all have a genie in a bottle, do we?'

'Yes! Actually *The Secret* says that in the original story Aladdin didn't get just three wishes, he got unlimited amounts.'

'Right, so when is this money going to land?'

'Rhonda says our dreams only come true if we really believe – and if they don't come true it's because I don't believe.'

'That's convenient,' said Mum.

'And she says that "time is just an illusion".'

'I bet she does.'

Silence on the line.

'You don't really believe this, do you?' she asked, after a long pause.

'No, not really but loads of people swear by it. And maybe it's good to think positively instead of always imagining the worst. Who knows, maybe I will write a bestselling book, earn millions and move to an LA beach house? Then you'd want to come and visit, wouldn't you?'

'Do they have earthquakes in LA?'

'I don't know.'

'Well, at least when you get too big for your boots you'll be able to afford new ones . . . You could celebrate by getting your roots done. Or get your teeth sorted.'

I didn't know which was better – Mum's cynicism or *The Secret*'s magical thinking. But I knew which one was more fun.

That night I fell asleep watching a YouTube clip of young Jim Carrey being interviewed by Oprah. He was talking about writing himself a cheque for $10 million when he was a broke actor. He put it in his wallet and a few years later he was paid $10 million for the movie *Dumb and Dumber* . . . And I know it sounds nuts but as I watched it I thought, why not? Why shouldn't something like that happen to me? To all of us? I mean – what makes people who achieve different to the rest of us except that they believed that they could do more? What's that Henry Ford quote? Something along the lines of 'Whether you think you can or you can't, you're probably right.'

I thought about how nice it would feel to be out of debt, to have £100,000 in the bank, to have my own flat and a sense of security. I could take a plane anywhere, to see my sister in New York, or to see my friend in Spain . . . I'd be a really nice rich person. I'd give to charity and be very down to earth despite my fabulous wealth . . .

When I was at school our gym teacher had an old Mercedes sports car in blue. I loved it and have always wanted one. *The Secret* says that if you have a dream car you must take it for a test run just to help you believe that it's yours. After my night listening to Jim Carrey I was willing to believe there might be something in it.

I found a garage in East Finchley that had one for sale and asked Sarah if she wanted to come. We met at the station.

'It feels like I haven't seen you for ages,' she said.

'I know, I'm sorry, it's been hectic.'

'How's it going? Are you feeling new and improved?'

'I don't know. I scared myself witless in January and cried over bank statements in February – but it's been good. More full-on than I was expecting but definitely not boring.'

'So what does *The Secret* say?'

'It says we can have anything we want in life if we just believe.'

'I think that's true.'

'Do you?' I was delighted. I was now hungry for proof.

'Yeah, I think if you set your mind to things, make a plan and work hard – you can do anything.'

'The book isn't about working or making a plan, it just says you have to decide what you want, believe it's going to happen and then the Universe magically delivers it to you.'

'So you don't do anything at all?'

'There is one reference to the fact that you might have to take "inspired action" but they reckon this doesn't feel like work – it feels "joyous" – so no, the idea is that it just comes to you.'

'So if I want a big house in Hampstead I just sit there and imagine it?'

'You don't just imagine it, you have to believe it's already yours. If you don't believe, it's not going to happen.'

'How can I believe that a house that's not mine is mine?'

'I don't know, you just do. You have to have faith.'

'And I can just sit at home waiting to win the lottery, can I?'

'Yes.'

'I don't even have to buy a ticket.'

'Well, you might be inspired to joyously buy a ticket . . .'

'And what happens when I don't win the lottery?'

'That's because you didn't really believe it was going to happen; therefore it didn't.'

'That's bullshit.'

Even though I knew Sarah was right, I felt defensive.

'I can just ask for bigger boobs, can I?' she continued. 'And what happens when bad things happen? Everyone in Syria asked to be in a war zone, did they? Those people in concentration camps just weren't thinking positively enough?'

'That's kind of what the book implies,' I admitted. Actually it says: 'Imperfect thoughts are the cause of all humanity's ills, including disease, poverty, and unhappiness.'

'That's disgusting.'

'I know.'

We walked in silence until she repeated the question that Mum had asked: 'You don't really believe in this stuff, do you?'

'No.' And I didn't. Not really. Just a bit. Maybe. Oh, I don't know.

We got to the garage, a 1980s temple of chrome, glass and black leather sofas.

Gary, the salesman, walked us to the showroom, where the sky-blue Mercedes was parked. I asked him how many miles were on the clock, just to be convincing. He gave me a number and I had no idea whether it was high or low but he assured me it was 'Very rare for a car this age.'

I nodded as if I knew what he was talking about. I felt bad. I was wasting Gary's time. I guessed he was on commission.

'I'm afraid you can't take it out today, but would you like to get in and see how it feels?' he said.

Sarah and I got into the car, while trying to keep a straight face. It felt like being fifteen and getting served in the pub.

The door was reassuringly heavy and the cream leather interior reassuringly soft.

'Ooh, this is nice,' said Sarah, stroking the mahogany dashboard.

I put my hands on the steering wheel. It *did* feel nice. Very nice.

I moved the wheel around like I did when I was a child, then I stopped in case Gary saw me.

'So do you believe the car is yours?' asked Sarah.

'Weirdly, yes. Why not?' And I did. Sitting in that car, it felt like I was meant to be there, meant to be driving it.

'Well, tell him you'll take it, then,' she said. 'Write him one of those cheques from the Universe.'

'Ha, ha,' I said, sarcastically, as we got out of the car and made our excuses to Gary.

'I'll think about it,' I said. 'It's really lovely, but I'm looking at another one next weekend.'

I could feel myself going red.

Sarah and I went for an Italian around the corner. We both ordered the cheapest thing on the menu – spaghetti with tomato sauce.

'I'm broke,' she said.

'Me too, but we're not allowed to say that. If you say you are broke then you are attracting more broke-ness to you,' I replied.

She rolled her eyes but I kept going: 'The more positive you are the more good stuff happens, so we should be repeating affirmations like, "I'm a money magnet."'

'I'm a food magnet,' said Sarah, taking a big bite of garlic bread. 'I am eating everything in sight. I wish I could be one of those people who stops eating when they get stressed . . .'

She started talking about how crazy work was and how her boss had buggered up her holiday.

'She said she didn't get my email asking for dates in June and now she's booked those off, which means I can't go.'

'Maybe she didn't see the email.'

'I get a notification when messages have been opened.'

'Maybe she opened it and then got busy and forgot to put it in the calendar.'

'No. She does this kind of thing all the time . . .'

The Secret says that you cannot talk negatively about anything. It says that you should not complain because if you are complaining the law of attraction will give you more things to complain about. You must, instead, replace negative thoughts with positive ones. You must think loving thoughts about everyone and be grateful for everything because that creates a vibration that attracts more good things. If you keep moaning about what you have now, you are giving off a signal of not enough and that's what you'll keep feeling.

And if your friends start to complain you should change the subject or leave. But this was a problem. For years this is what all my friendships had been based on: moaning and drinking. But I was no longer allowed to moan. And, for once, I didn't even want to. I thought about how much time I'd wasted complaining about things, getting angry and bitter with people.

'I'm going to Camden to meet Steve and his friends; do you want to come?' she asked.

'No thanks, I think I'll head back.'

She looked hurt. Usually I'd have gone out and it would have been a four in the morning job.

'Are you OK?' she asked.

'Yeah, fine.'

I got the bus home.

For the next few days I replayed my conversation with Sarah. Of course, she was right. This was all nuts. But then maybe it wasn't . . . I mean, it was good to be positive, wasn't it? And miracles happened all the time, didn't they? And why did so many people love the book if there wasn't something in it?

I decided to investigate further by trying to get the body of a supermodel while eating carbs. Suckers go to the gym and eat well but people who know *The Secret* don't bother with that. According to Rhonda: 'Food cannot cause you to put on weight, unless you *think* it can.' So if you want to lose weight, simple! Eat the Mars bars but think skinny thoughts.

This is Rhonda's three-step plan for weight loss:

> Ask: Visualize yourself at the weight you want to be. If it's a weight from your past then take out an old picture and keep looking at it, otherwise find a picture of someone who is your perfect weight and look at that.
>
> Believe: Believe that you are that weight already. Write out the weight you want to be and put it on the scales, over the real number.
>
> Receive: Feel good about your weight now. Rhonda says: 'Think perfect thoughts and the result must be perfect weight.'

I dug out the dusty scales from the cupboard under the bathroom sink. I took off my jeans and shoes (every little helps) and stood on the grey plastic square. The dial hovered then settled on a number. 11 stone 9 pounds – I was more than half a stone heavier than the last time I'd stood on scales. This was why I didn't weigh myself; it was too depressing. Fat and ugly thoughts started to flood my mind but I stopped myself.

Think of Elle Macpherson's legs. Imagine you have Kate Moss's bum. Heidi Klum's flat stomach . . .

I went to my room and found the sticky white labels I'd used on my financial folders and put one on the plastic window of the scales. So how much did I want to weigh? Maybe lose two stone? I wrote '9 stone 9 lb' in blue marker.

I looked at the scribble and felt worried for myself. The

front door opened and Rachel shouted hello. I shoved the scales back into the cupboard so she couldn't see what I'd done.

'If we eat this and think thin thoughts it won't make us fat,' I said that night, eating risotto.

'How does that work?' she asked.

'*The Secret* says that you only get fat by thinking fat thoughts, it has nothing to do with calories or cream or Parmesan.'

I helped myself to some more cheesy risotto but Rachel said she'd had enough. She had an outdated approach to staying slim – she just didn't eat too much. You could never sell a book on that.

I looked up at a woman with perfect white teeth and brown hair, hair that was so straight and shiny that I knew that we could never be friends.

'That book changed my life,' she said. I was in Bread and Bean, working (looking at Facebook), and the book was out on the table.

'Last year I broke up with an arsehole and a friend gave me it. I wrote a list of everything I wanted in a man. I forgot about it until I moved house and found it in the drawer. The guy I'm going out with now is everything I listed except one thing – he doesn't dive! But he can learn.'

Why did everyone have a story like this?

'Are you single?' she continued, clearly flouting all English rules about not talking to strangers.

'Yes.'

'Have you written down exactly what kind of boyfriend you want?'

'No, but I've spent the last two days clearing space in my wardrobe and making sure I sleep on one side of the bed.'

The Secret quotes a woman who, like me, was always single. This woman had done lots of visualization of what she wanted her 'perfect partner' to be like, but he wasn't turning up. Then one day she came home and realized – duh! – the reason she was single was because her car was parked in the middle of the garage.

'She realized that her actions were contradicting what she wanted. If her car was in the middle of the garage there was no room for her perfect partner's car!' says Rhonda.

So she not only moved her car, she cleared space in her wardrobe for her 'perfect partner's' clothes and stopped sleeping in the middle of the bed, all to leave room for her 'perfect partner'. Then she met the man of her dreams and lived happily ever after . . .

Shiny-haired woman smiled. 'Oh, I didn't do any of that. I just wrote it all down – the man I wanted, the kind of house, the job, the travel . . . Then I did a Vision Board with pictures of things I wanted to attract. Have you done a Vision Board?'

'No.'

'You should.'

'Do you really believe this stuff works?' I asked.

'I *know* it does, but you have to believe,' she said.

'But how do you make yourself believe in something you don't believe in?'

'Fake it till you make it.'

So that weekend I set about creating a Vision Board, which is basically a big pinboard or piece of card on which you stick pictures or words that depict your dream future. I was determined to take this seriously. I was going to suspend my disbelief and really put my heart into it. No more cynicism – otherwise known as reason.

As I sat down with a pile of magazines and a pair of scissors, the first problem quickly became apparent. I did not know what I wanted from life beyond a vague idea about being skinnier, richer and more successful. I had never thought about what I wanted because: a) how was it going to happen, and b) who do you think you are?

'Most of us have never allowed ourselves to want what we truly want because we cannot see how it's going to manifest,' writes Jack Canfield, author of *Chicken Soup for the Soul*, who is quoted in *The Secret*. To which Rhonda answers: 'How it will happen, how the Universe will bring it to you, is not your concern or job. Allow the Universe to do it for you . . .'

So if there were no obstacles – otherwise known as reality – what did I want?

I decided to start off with a fancy house.

John Assaraf, 'metaphysician, marketing specialist and author', says he cut out a picture of a giant mansion from a magazine for his Vision Board and five years later he found himself living in it – the exact house.

Ever since I'd gone to LA to report on a Zumba convention a year before, I'd dreamed of living there. With that in mind, I went online to do some imaginary house shopping. I couldn't decide between something in the Hollywood Hills or something by the beach. Spanish bungalow or uber modern and glassy?

Then I spent twenty minutes looking at bathroom tiles for a house I didn't have, in a country I didn't live in. Aqua or green? Purple or blue? I did the same with cushions for my non-existent beige sofa. I kid you not, this got me stressed. What if I made the wrong choice? How much money was I spending on all this? Was I already bankrupt in my dream life?

As I looked at hundreds of pictures of perfect people in their perfect houses I got that familiar feeling of not being good enough. I wasn't pretty enough to live in LA! Who would I be friends with? I'd be lonely in a big house on my own.

I found a picture of the old Mercedes I'd sat in but that didn't inspire me either. A car wasn't going to change my life.

I made myself some tea and cheese on toast and realized that perfect bendy skinny LA girls don't eat carbs. I was failing my dream life already! I didn't want to pick a future that meant cutting out cheese on toast.

By the time Rachel came home she found me half a bottle of red down, surrounded by mountains of paper at the kitchen table.

She sat down and picked up a picture of a house in the Hollywood Hills.

'What's this?'

'My future home.'

'Really? It doesn't seem very you.'

'Why not?'

'I don't know, it just doesn't. Why do you want to live in America? You don't know anyone over there. Why can't you be happy here?'

It was a good question. Why did I always think that happiness had to be somewhere else, with me being someone else?

I'd always thought that happiness had to come in the form of stacks of money and nice clothes and a fancy house, but maybe it didn't. Maybe there were other ways to be happy? I didn't want my life to be a giant shopping list.

Bloody hell, I really was changing.

I decided to change tack. Time for a new vision! The new me wouldn't be money-obsessed and skinny – she would be happy and free and fun! I pinned up pictures of Indian temples and Moroccan tiles (not for my designer bathroom, but to symbolize a trip to Morocco). I added a picture of an old desk by a high window where future me would write wonderful, fabulous words. I put on a picture of a woman meditating, another doing yoga, a glass of green juice (the future me drinks green juice) and a cour-gette salad. There was a woman doing a handstand. I have not done a handstand since I was eight – but I liked her. She looked joyous in her upsidedownness.

Next to me Rachel was pinning pictures of picnics in the sun, country cottages and people around a table laughing. Her Vision Board looked like her life right now, full of simple pleasures, good food and good company. Not a designer handbag in sight.

'Now we have to find a man,' she said.

I went through a pile of Sunday supplements to go man shopping. It should have been a fun job but I kept looking at lovely smiley men and imagining them thinking, 'Dream on, love, as if I'd go out with you.'

I started cutting out a picture of the man who designed the new London bus. There was an interview with him and he seemed clever and modest and funny. And he had nice curly hair. I googled him and learned he had a wife. I can't have another woman's husband on my Vision Board.

'You're over-thinking this,' said Rachel.

'I know, but it doesn't feel right,' I said.

'So what do you want in a man?' she asked.

'I don't know. Someone nice.'

'OK. What else?'

'Someone kind, clever, funny . . . and twinkly.'

'What's twinkly?'

'You know – just got a twinkle about him. And he has to be down to earth and successful but not too successful. He can't be a dickhead.'

'Why do you look so scared?'

And it was ridiculous but I was scared. It felt scary even *thinking* about what kind of man I would like because he wouldn't like me back – why would he? He could do better than me and then I'd be rejected and hurt and what was the point in all of that? Better not to want it at all.

I was rejecting myself even in my fantasy life.

But this was exactly the problem – if you don't think you deserve good things, you will not allow them to happen.

Gemma always talked about the time I got chatted up in a pub. The man probably ticked every box on my dream list – at least in the looks/job department – he was tall, dark hair, blue eyes, smiley and an architect. So what did I do when my future husband started chatting to us and asked me if I'd like a drink? I said, 'No, thanks.'

I'd just come from a twelve-hour shift at work and looked rubbish – greasy hair, no make-up, dodgy office outfit – and couldn't believe that a guy like that could seriously be interested in someone like me.

'He's drunk and trying it on with everyone,' I said to Gemma.

'No he's not, you're an idiot,' she replied. I was. I am.

Rhonda says: 'When you feel bad about yourself you are blocking all the love and all the good that the Universe has to offer you.'

I had been blocking a lot of things for a long time. It felt safer that way. Better not to dream at all than to dream and be disappointed. I had to get over that.

I started to google 'Smiley handsome beardy men' and passed a good twenty minutes looking at generic bearded men online. Then I remembered the email Sarah had sent a few months ago with THIS IS THE MAN YOU ARE GOING TO MARRY in the subject line. It was a link to an interview with the lead singer from a band called Snow Patrol. He was talking about being rubbish with the opposite sex and drinking too much. And he lived in LA. We were pretty much spiritual twins. I printed off a picture of him and stuck him on. And it made no sense but it felt so exposing to do this – to stick up a picture of a man and say that I might like one in my life.

After dinner I propped the Vision Board on the floor by my desk. As I lay in bed I looked at it. My dream life. And it looked nice. And the more I looked at it over the next few days the more I started to believe that these things were possible.

Maybe that's what this book's secret really is; it gives us permission to daydream about our futures in a way most of us don't do after the age of five, when we would announce with no self-consciousness that we wanted to be astronauts or ballerinas or ambulance drivers. It stops us from making excuses and hiding behind so-called 'reality', something we start to do as soon as we hit our first teenage disappointments.

It was actually scary to dream big because it meant opening yourself up to disappointment when/if your dreams didn't become reality. But it felt good to become much clearer on what I really did want. I had thought it was the car and big house stuff, but really what I wanted was peace of mind and friends and travel. Although, let's be honest, I wanted the pots of cash too. My cheque for £100,000 was also pinned on my board. And the more I looked at it, the less ludicrous this dream life (even the cheque) seemed.

The Secret says that it's not our job to worry how things are going to happen, but the whole glossing-over of the idea of 'work' still made me uncomfortable. I didn't believe a genie in a bottle was going to work magic; I believed I would, with enough positive thinking and hard work.

Athletes believe in their success and visualize the moment they cross the finish line, but then they train every day to make that vision a reality. I remember watching a documentary about Usain Bolt. He might make his record-breaking sprints look like fun runs but the film showed him training so hard he vomited.

Was that 'inspired action' and the law of attraction? Or was it old-fashioned hard work?

Then something strange happened: four days after doing the Vision Board, I got an email from my editor asking me if I'd like to write an article about kale being cool. I had to eat and drink nothing but kale for a week and report back – presumably from the toilet.

Days after putting up a picture of green juice on my Vision Board I was getting paid to drink green juices! I wrote about health stuff all the time, so the kale story wasn't completely out of the realms of normality . . . but . . . two days after that the same editor asked me to

write about a yoga class which involved hanging upside
down . . . Universe, is this a sign? Maybe the magic does
work. Now, if someone would just send me a cheque for
£100,000 . . . then, I'd be convinced.

4

Rejection Therapy,
with Jason Comely

'You must be rejected by another person at least once, every single day.'

I was eight years old, traipsing around the playground. I can't recall where my best friend or, indeed, my other friends were – but that day I was all on my own.

The lunch hour stretched ahead like a Sunday afternoon.

It had been raining that morning and the grey concrete was damp. Clouds sat heavy in the sky, another downpour was imminent. The world felt ominous.

Groups of girls were scattered around the yard. Some were hanging upside down, on the climbing frame, their navy pleated skirts tucked into their knickers. Others were playing hopscotch on squares painted in banana yellow. There was a group skipping too. *Eggs, bacon, chips and cheese, which would you rather please . . .*

I scanned the playground for anyone I could play with, someone else on their own, maybe. A safe target. But there was nobody. Instead I saw two girls from my class sitting on a bench, talking. Their legs were crossed in the way that they'd seen their mothers do. One was eating crisps and the other a little box of raisins. I envied their snacks. I was only ever allowed fruit and today's banana was mushy. I knew them a bit but we'd never played together before. I walked over to them and hovered.

'Yes?' asked the girl with the crisps, whose name was Lucy T. There were four Lucys in our class. Lucy S, Lucy W, Lucy J and Lucy T. Lucy T was clever and had an older sister at school, which gave her a certain status. Her wild mousy curls were so thick she couldn't even wind her hairband around more than once. She was with Lucy J, who had silky brown hair and spoke very softly. She also had big sisters and she had foreign stationery from Italy and France. This gave her double status. Continental notepads, with their tiny checked pages, were the height of glamour in our classroom.

'Can I play with you?' I blurted out. I worried as soon as I said it that it sounded desperate and babyish. I was eight. Too old to 'play'. Why didn't I say, 'Can I sit with you?' or 'Can I talk to you?' My mistake hung in the air. The girls looked at each other.

'We'll need to think about it,' said Raisin Lucy.

'Could you please walk a few steps away while we talk about it,' said Crisp Lucy.

I walked a few steps away and pretended to look at a giant oak tree. Last term we had taken leaves from its branches and traced around them in class before putting them in a book to dry. We'd drawn acorns and felt its bark. I wished I could just play with the tree.

'You can come back now,' said Raisin Lucy.

I walked back.

'You can't play with us today,' said Crisp Lucy. Clearly. Decisively.

'But maybe tomorrow,' said Raisin Lucy, with a weak smile that suggested she felt bad about this state of affairs.

'OK, thank you,' I said. I'm not sure why I thanked them. I guess for taking the time to consider it.

As I walked away from them, looking down at my grey Clark's shoes, I could feel my cheeks getting hotter and my eyes beginning to sting. Don't cry, don't cry, don't cry. But I did cry. I went into the toilets, closed the door and cried until the bell rang.

That is my first conscious memory of rejection and even though I haven't thought about that day much since then, I have probably spent most of my life avoiding that moment when you ask someone to play with you and they say 'no'. That two-letter word which can make me feel eight years old again.

'Are you nuts? That sounds like self-harming,' said Sarah, when I called her at work to tell her about my next self-help challenge.

'People who have done it say it changes their life – and anyway I need to keep my feet on the ground after all *The Secret* stuff.'

'This isn't just keeping your feet on the ground, it's nailing them there,' said Sarah.

My mission for April was an extreme form of self-help called Rejection Therapy. I was bending the rules slightly in that this was a game, not a book.

The aim is simple: I had to get rejected once a day by another human being. Not *try* to get rejected – but *actually* get rejected. When I first heard about this masochistic form of self-development a couple of years earlier I had thought it seemed insane. I mean, who would do that to themselves? Life's hard enough! But it had stayed in my mind, niggling away, and after a month of fake cheques and fantasy, I felt it was just what I needed. A cold shower of reality. And if the last few months had taught me anything, it was that the less I wanted to do something the more I probably needed to do it.

'But I don't understand how getting rejected every day is going to help you,' said Sarah.

'The idea is we're all living our lives in fear of rejection. We don't do half the things we want to do because we're scared people will say "no". But with this you learn that it might feel horrible to get rejected but it won't kill you. And people who have played the game say that it's much harder to get rejected than you think it is – lots of times you get a "yes" when you think you'll get a "no".'

This was the experience of the Canadian IT guy named Jason Comely who came up with the game after his wife left him. He had been spending his days and nights alone in his one-bedroom apartment, becoming more and more isolated. He realized that what was holding him back now – and what had always held him back – was a fear of rejection and so he made it a challenge to get rejected every day.

Jason had flipped the rules of life. He made rejection something he wanted rather than feared.

Without realizing it, Jason had used a tool of psychotherapy called exposure therapy or flooding. This is when you force yourself to face your fears so that eventually you become desensitized. It's used to treat phobias of snakes and heights.

Jason kept seeking out rejection. He started asking to cut in line at the supermarket, friend-requested strangers on

Facebook, asked for discounts in shops. He even went on Canadian *Dragons' Den*.

More often than not, people would say 'yes', leading to encounters and opportunities he would never have had otherwise.

'So are *you* going to do *Dragons' Den?*' asked Sarah.

'No! God, no!' I snapped.

'I was joking. Don't get stressed.'

'But I am stressed. It's stressful doing all this stuff. I'm tired.'

'So why don't you take a break? Come over to mine this weekend and we'll go out and drink too much and spend Sunday hating ourselves on the sofa,' said Sarah.

'I can't. I need to get organized and make a list of ways to be rejected.'

'Can't you take a weekend off? I feel like I hardly see you anymore and you've already done so much.'

'I haven't really.'

'You have and it's amazing, but this can't be good for you, all this chopping and changing. A few days ago you were road-testing cars and now this . . . It's like you're swapping diets all the time. Doing Atkins one month, then going vegan the next – Damn. Sorry. Gotta go –'

And with that she rang off. Her boss must have come back into the room. I pictured Sarah in the normal world of work and emails and colleagues . . .

I sat at my desk and felt very alone as I looked out of the window at clouds. Next-door was having work done and the drill was getting on my last nerve. I wanted a drink. I looked at my phone – it was only just past noon.

I didn't want to do Rejection Therapy. Not at all.

I didn't know where to start. I mean, practically speaking. Should I walk down the street now and ask people to give me a tenner? Or go to the pub and ask for a free drink? I'd wanted to ask Sarah for ideas but what I was doing felt ridiculous next to her real-life stresses so I put a request on Facebook for suggestions.

Here's what I got:

> Go to Claridge's and ask to have a quick nap in one
> of their rooms – for free!
> Phone Buckingham Palace and ask to go to the
> garden party
> Audition for *X Factor* or a West End show
> Go into Chanel and ask them if their bags are fake
> Go to a model agency and tell them you want to
> sign up
> Ask to interview Kate Moss

I decided it wasn't too early to drink.

Three days later, having spent the weekend either drunk or in bed, I gave myself a good talking to and wrote a list of sixteen rejection scenarios to get through by the end of the month:

1) Ask for a discount in a shop
2) Ask for a free coffee
3) Ask for a free meal
4) Smile at every person I see for a day
5) Say hello to five strangers on the street
6) Ask a stranger on a date
7) Ask for a stranger's number

8) Ask to cut to the front of a queue
9) Ask to join a stranger at a bar/restaurant/cafe
10) Ask for credit card interest/bank charges to be reduced
11) Contact three new magazines to work for
12) Ask a bank to give me £100 for no reason
13) Ask someone I admire to meet me for a coffee
14) Ask a stranger to be friends with me on Facebook
15) Ask for a free room at Claridge's
16) Ask for a free bag in Chanel

Jason suggests starting small with your rejections, by asking for a free coffee. My regular cafe in Tufnell Park was one of those tolerant places that lets freelancers like me spend hours on laptops while sipping only one or two coffees. So on 3 April, I did my work (an article about how you can blame your postcode for your frizzy hair – from tap water to exhaust fumes, where you live affects your looks . . .) before going up to the till to pay.

'Did you get much done today?' asked the owner.

'Yes,' I lied.

'You're ready to pay?'

'Not really,' I said, with a smile. 'Can I have it for free?'

He laughed.

I laughed back.

'No, really, can I have it for free?'

He continued to laugh but I got the sense that he no longer found me funny.

I felt horrible but I persisted: 'So I CAN'T have it for free?'

He gave me a sad, tired smile. He rubbed his bald head.

He didn't really understand what I was playing at but his expression suggested he'd like the game to be over.

'It helps if you pay. We're very quiet today . . .' he said, looking out into the cafe.

We both gazed forlornly at the semi-deserted premises. There were three people hunched over their laptops with empty cups. One woman with a long purple cardigan was hugging up against the radiator. She didn't have a laptop, just an old newspaper and a glass of tap water on her table. It looked like she'd been there all day without spending a penny. A young girl with orange hair and Doc Martens boots was reading Mary Wollstonecraft's *Vindication of the Rights of Woman*, scribbling furiously into an A4 notebook. Then there was a twenty-something guy I'd seen there before – black t-shirt, black jeans and giant headphones on. He was shooting people from his computer.

The owner was too nice. This was no way to do business.

'Why is it so quiet today? Do you think it's the rain?' I asked.

'I don't know. Maybe. There are so many new places opening, maybe they go to Costa across the road.'

'People are stupid, this place is much nicer than Costa.'

'Thank you. It's hard to compete. When Costa comes into the neighbourhood, all our rents go up. Soon everything will be a Costa. A Costa or a Starbucks.'

We both stood in silence, contemplating this coffee-shop apocalypse.

'How much do I owe you?'

'£1.60, please.'

I put down £2.50 and left, feeling awful for having tried

to deprive him of his livelihood. I had insulted him. Note to self: do not do Rejection Therapy in small businesses.

In the name of fairness, I went across the road to Costa and asked them for a free coffee.

'I buy a lot of coffees here and just wondered if you did any of those cards, you know where you get the stamps and get a free coffee?'

'No, we don't do those,' said the teenager behind the counter, perfectly pleasantly.

'So could you just give me a free coffee?' I asked.

'No. We cannot give you free coffee. Would you like to *buy* a coffee?' she said, again, perfectly calmly. Like she got this kind of request every day.

'No, thanks!' I said, with a smile.

I flounced out. Take that, Big Business! I'm fighting for the man! Or against the man?! I never really understood those phrases . . . But my point was made. Sort of.

After the incident I felt too ashamed to go back to that independent cafe. I spent the rest of the month writing in Costa.

The next day I popped into the phone shop.

I'd lost my charger and needed a new one. I picked one off the shelf and took it to the till where a spotty guy of about eighteen was waiting.

'Hello,' I said. 'I'd like to take this please –' I handed over the charger.

He went to scan it in.

'I don't know what I do with them,' I continued. 'I've lost count of how many I've bought. I keep leaving them places.'

He kept looking at the till, with an expression that seemed to say, 'Madam, I could not care where you leave them, why are you talking to me?'

'Anyway,' I ventured, 'I'm a really good customer, is there any chance of a discount?'

This time he looked up from the till. He looked confused. He wasn't expecting this. He paused for a second and looked around for his colleague, who was busy.

'Er, unfortunately I'm not able to do that, madam.'

I grinned. 'Are you sure? I'm a really, really good customer. My bills are crazy every month . . .'

He gave me a look which suggested that not only were my bills crazy, I may be crazy and he might have to call his manager soon. 'Er, sorry, no.'

'Not even £1 off?'

'No.' He looked alarmed. His big brown eyes darted from the till to his manager. Then I remembered that I didn't need to keep this going – the whole point was that I got a rejection.

'OK! Thanks. No worries!' I said, still grinning, wildly.

He looked relieved. I handed over my card and tapped in my PIN number. He smiled, nervously. I smiled manically. The end.

I felt bad that I'd put the guy in an awkward situation. That's the thing with rejection: it's painful for both sides.

With one rejection under my belt, I headed to a job – blissfully unaware of the rejection that lay ahead. Superdrug had relaunched various make-up products from the 1960s and I had been asked to compare the old-fashioned foundation sticks and pressed powders to today's hi-tech serums and highlighters, with the help of a make-up artist.

I told her what I'd been doing so far that year.

'You're so brave!' she said.

'Oh well,' I said modestly.

'No really, I think you're so brave! Tash, have you heard

what she's doing?' She started chatting to the photographer's assistant about my year of self-help.

So I told them all about it. The best bits – stand-up comedy and public speaking. The worst bits – jumping out of a plane and looking at my bank statements. They ate it all up and I ate up the fact that they were eating it up. All year I'd been waiting for people to recognize how brilliant I was but so far my friends and family had been spectacularly underwhelmed. Maybe it took strangers to see your profound and breathtaking bravery.

I gave them both a lecture about how important it was to get out of your comfort zone, how the minute you do something – *anything* – scary you feel stronger and how I no longer sweated the small stuff . . .

'I mean, imagine what we'd go for if we weren't scared of rejection!' I was saying once I'd told them about this month's challenge.

Then Tash started saying words that made me wish I'd never opened my stupid mouth.

'Me and my friend are queueing up for *X Factor* auditions the week after next, you should join us!'

'Oh well, um . . .'

'Can you sing?' asked Tash.

'No.'

'Perfect! You'd get rejected! The doors open on Saturday but the queues start on Friday night, so we're going to meet at midnight and head there. Where do you live?'

'Archway.'

'I'm coming from Peckham but we can meet somewhere that works for all of us,' she said.

What? No! Don't make travel plans around me! I'm not going to do this!

I couldn't audition for *X Factor* – I'd be an actual public laughing stock . . .

But just as strong as my feelings that I could not do this was my certainty that I had to. I mean, what were the chances of being offered such a perfect opportunity for brutal and public rejection in the very month I was supposed to be doing Rejection Therapy?

'Is that a yes, then?' asked Tash.

'Um.'

'Go on . . .'

'OK.'

I went to the loo and put my head in my hands as my normal life went down the bend.

That night I drank a bottle and a half of red while Rachel calmed me down.

'I'm going to be one of those acts that gets laughed at for being so deluded. I'll be like a Ginger Jedward. But on my own.'

'No, you won't. There'll be thousands of people there, you'll end up singing for two minutes to some producer in a back room.'

'Are you sure?'

'Yes. You'll never get on camera. They only do that if you're really bad or really good. So just be average bad and don't wear anything stupid.'

Ten days to *X Factor*. Woke up with a hangover and googled 'worst *X Factor* auditions'. Took two Night Nurse and slept all day.

Nine days to go – pure panic. What should I sing? 'Manic

Monday'? Was that too old? Or Tracey Chapman's 'Fast Car'? Wrote a text to Tash to cancel but didn't send it.

Eight days to go – the only way to get through this was to pretend it was not happening. I would focus on other rejections, starting small: smiling at strangers on the Tube. I gave a middle-aged couple a half-hearted smile on the Northern Line. The woman gave me daggers before glaring at her husband: 'Do you know that woman?' she demanded.

Seven days to go – went out for a walk. Said 'hello' to three strangers on the street on the way to the Post Office. One older man smiled and said 'hello' back, which was nice but two women looked at me as if I was nuts. I felt like a freak. Seriously, what is wrong with us human beings that we don't just say hello? Why are we all so suspicious of each other? And what damage was this doing? Studies have found that every time someone blanks us in public – even someone we don't know – it makes us feel disconnected and this feeling of disconnection is linked to depression, high blood pressure and dementia. We're all killing each other with our aloofness. Gandhi might have told us to be the change we want to see in the world but that was thankless work when you were saying hello to strangers in Archway.

Back home I went back to scrolling through songs in my head. What about the Cranberries? That singer had a voice that wasn't too high.

Six days to go – I visited a friend and her eighteen-month-old daughter, who screamed, 'No, no, no!!!!' when I walked into the room. Maybe I'd sing Alanis Morissette's 'Ironic'.

Five days to go – I went to the Post Office with a plan to ask to skip the queue but I looked at all the old people waiting for their pensions, and mums trying to keep their kids in line, and I couldn't bring myself to do it.

Four days to go – spent the day near tears as I learned all the words to Adele's 'Someone Like You'. In the evening – OK, 4pm – I went to Tesco to buy a bottle of wine. The guy behind the counter asked me for ID to prove I was over eighteen. I was just about to tell him that it was the nicest thing to happen to me all week when he looked up and said: 'Oh don't worry, I didn't look at you properly.'

Three days to go – did not sleep a wink. This did not feel like self-improvement. It felt like some sick joke. Kept reminding myself that Rachel was right. They would not be filming me. I would be one of a gazillion. I'd be in and out. Another silly experience to add to the list. The phone rang. It was Sarah.

'You sound stressed,' she said, sounding concerned.

'I'm about to audition for X Factor, of course I'm stressed!' Jesus – why didn't anyone understand what I was doing here and the toll it was taking on me?

I could hear her take a breath.

'Angel, you don't have to do it if you don't want to do it.'

For a second I softened at her term of endearment – a term that always made me smile, always made me feel better – but then I pulled myself together. This was not the time to relax. I had to focus.

'The whole point is to do things that make me uncomfortable. I can't wimp out,' I said, my voice brittle.

'I thought the whole point was to be happier and it doesn't seem like this is making you happier.'

'Yes, it is!' I snapped before hanging up and singing Adele while pacing my room.

★

Two days to go and I woke up with a now familiar slanging match in my head.

I can't do this.

You have to do this.

I don't want to.

Tough. Stop being such a fucking wimp.

I checked my phone and saw three missed calls from Mum. She was in Ireland for a wedding and it was unusual for her to call. As soon as she went away she treated her phone like it was radioactive – she couldn't touch it or look at it for fear of coming home to a £3,000 bill.

'Your uncle has died,' she said, in tears when I got through.

My mother's much-loved younger brother had left the family wedding early because he wasn't feeling well. A few hours later he had a massive heart attack and died. He was just fifty-nine.

So the next day, instead of preparing to travel to Wembley to give Adele a run for her money, I flew to Ireland for the funeral. In that one phone call all of my stupid fears about singing for a stupid television show felt, well, stupid.

The church was so full there were people standing not only at the back of the building but outside it. We walked the coffin the four miles from the church to the cemetery, along an old coast road. There was silence except for the sound of black shoes, walking.

The wake was at the house. My cousins sat in the kitchen, pouring endless cups of tea and glasses of whiskey while they talked about their dad.

My uncle Gerald had been a farmer but his main occupation was smoker and tea-drinker. He was always at his kitchen table, cup in one hand, cigarette in the other, looking out of the window and listening to the radio. In between hours of daydreaming and silence, he'd make declarations about the modern music scene. Statements such as, 'That Lady Gaga's getting more like Madonna every day,' were funny delivered in a thick Irish accent, even funnier when you took in the outfit of muddy Wellington boots, battered jeans and forty-year-old sweater.

My cousins talked about the day he drove through the fields on his tractor, shouting, 'No, no, no . . .'. They were wondering what he was shouting at. Turns out he was singing the Amy Winehouse song: 'They tried to make me go to rehab, I said "No, no, no . . ."' Then there was his knack of acquiring cars with something wrong with them. One was a car that hooted every time he turned the steering wheel. We had fits of giggles imagining him on roundabouts effing and blinding as the horn went 'beep, beep, beep.'

He was so loved that, long after his children left home, their friends would still call around to see him.

He'd listen to everyone and greet any problem with a cock of the head and a tut that seemed to say, 'Sure, what can you do?' It was a nod that put everything in its rightful place. In a world that was changing and moving he remained resolutely the same, a constant.

In the pub that night, I got talking to a second cousin who'd made his fortune in America.

'This is what's real – your family, your friends – none of the rest of it matters,' he said, looking at the mourners.

I agreed.

'Are you still doing the journalism?' he asked.

'Yeah, a bit but not so much.' I told him about the self-help. 'I was meant to be auditioning for X Factor now,' I said. 'As part of Rejection Therapy.'

He looked at me with concern.

'Was your life so bad that you had to do all that?' he asked, softly.

As soon as he said it I felt ashamed.

Of course my life wasn't bad – by anyone's definition it was good, beyond privileged. Standing at my uncle's funeral, my whole year seemed absurd.

Gerald hardly ever left his kitchen and yet, somehow, he had touched hundreds of lives with his kindness and patience. He listened to people. He was there. Didn't that make him more of a guru than any of the authors of the books I was inhaling? I should be more like him, not Rhonda Byrne. Just be a nice person. Do my best. Be grateful for what I had.

When I got home, I did no Rejection Therapy. I couldn't face it. I was sick of self-help and sick of myself.

Sarah called but I didn't pick up. I didn't know what to say to anyone anymore.

5

Rejection Therapy, Take Two

'From now on, think of comfort as the enemy of your personal progress.'

By the end of April normal service had resumed. I went back to spending my days working, sleeping and watching television. I was not being rejected, not repeating affirmations and not looking at my Vision Board. I was also not waking up wondering if today was the day I should request a free room at Claridge's, ask George Clooney on a date or try to be on the cover of *Vogue*. It was a relief.

'So are you quitting self-help?' asked Rachel. There was hope in her voice.

'Dunno. I'm just taking a break. I'll see,' I said and continued to slowly dig my way back into the old rut until the second week of May, when I found a piece of paper tucked in my diary.

'Comfort is highly overrated for individuals who want to progress in life . . .' it read. 'Your comfort zone may be more like a cage you can't escape from than a safe place you can retreat to. From now on, think of comfort as the enemy of your personal progress . . .'

It was something I'd printed from Jason Comely's website at the start of April. I surveyed my room, where I'd spent the weekend watching crap on telly – glasses of water everywhere, dirty jeans on the floor, half-empty coffee cups . . . my messy cage.

I kept reading: 'The fear of rejection keeps us from breaking through to our true potential . . . it turns into regret and lack.'

This was true. Self-help might be self-indulgent and ridiculous, but how was opting out and slobbing out any better? I didn't want a life full of regret and lack. I wanted to live to my potential, whatever that was.

Jason's final words were a rallying cry: 'Choose your master. Obey the fear and deal with feelings of regret for the rest of your life or choose rejection.'

I chose rejection. Again.

'But if you hated it why don't you just move on to another book?' asked Rachel over breakfast.

'The fact I hated it so much is a sign that it's a big thing for me and I want to tackle it.'

'Rejection is a big thing for everyone,' said Rachel.

And of course it was. I'd learned that in Feel the Fear. We're hard-wired to fear rejection because in our caveman days we needed to be accepted by the group to survive. Rejection in those days meant death and it still feels that way even if it's just two girls who don't want to play with you or a boss not emailing you back.

But now this fear wasn't saving my life, it was stopping me from living it. It was time to change that.

———

On Friday 9th May I went out with my youngest sister Helen and her friend Jim for drinks at the Queen's Head in Islington. I texted Sarah to see if she wanted to come but she replied that her boiler had broken and she was waiting for an engineer to come and look at it. There were no kisses at the end of her message and I had the queasy feeling that she was annoyed with me for not picking up her three last calls.

So far Helen had been keeping her distance from the whole self-help extravaganza. She's more of a 'just get on with it' kind of person. Go figure.

Jim, on the other hand, was enthusiastic. 'You should ask them if you can play one of their instruments,' he said, pointing to the jazz band who were playing plinky-plonky music in the corner.

'Nah, they'd never let me,' I said.

'That's the whole point,' said Jim.

'Oh, yeah, I keep forgetting that.'

So when the music stopped, I walked up to the floppy-haired bassist.

'Hi,' I said.

'Hello,' he replied, not quite looking me in the eye.

'I was just wondering . . . um . . . I've never played the double bass and always wondered what it would feel like. I know it's a random request, but could I have a go?'

I was just about to start saying, 'Don't worry if you don't want a stranger playing your very beautiful and probably extortionately expensive instrument . . .' but before I could even get that out, he shrugged. 'Sure, if you want.'

Oh! Just like that! He passed over the silky wooden instrument and I wrapped myself behind its curves. It was taller than me but lighter than I expected. I plucked the thick strings and felt the sound vibrate with a thrill.

'What do you think?' asked Mr Double Bass.

'I love it!' I said. 'Is it heavy to carry around?'

'More awkward than heavy but you get used to it. The Underground can be tricky.'

'I really love it!' I said, plucking again.

'Good!' he said. He smiled this time. 'Do you play anything?'

'No, I got to Grade One piano and Mum made me give it up because I sounded so bad.'

'Oh.'

'I'm not very musical. I mean, I love listening to music, but I can't play. I only came up because of a challenge I'm doing.'

I told him about Rejection Therapy; his eyes widened.

'Try being a musician,' he said. 'You get used to rejection . . .'

And then he started telling me about how tough the music business was, and how he would be better off following his other dream, which was to open a coffee van.

'I'd buy coffee off you,' I promised.

'Would you?' he asked.

'Yeah, of course.'

His face lit up and I went back to the table.

'So you didn't get rejected, then?' said Jim.

'No, he was really nice!'

And while I wanted to take some time to celebrate my brave break from social norms – Jim was staying on task.

'Your next challenge is to ask the barmaid if you can pull your own pint,' he said.

I looked at the bar. The woman behind it was all eyeliner and aggressive cleavage and I figured she would definitely

say 'no'. I didn't want to put her in that position of power
but I went up anyway . . .

The music had started up again and the pub was noisy,
so there was a bit of confusion when I started my spiel. 'I've
never pulled a pint before and I'd really like to know what it
feels like . . .' I said.

'You want pint?' she demanded, frowning. She was not
English and the language gap wasn't helping.

'Yes, but I'd like to pull it myself.'

'You want pint? Beck's? Foster's?'

'Yes, but . . .' I now made gestures of me pulling the pint.

She frowned and her angry-eyeliner'd eyes got angrier.

I kept doing more pulling motions and pointing at the
beer taps and then at me.

Then she seemed to get it because, before I knew it, she'd
opened the heavy wooden flap built into the bar and was
motioning for me to come to her side. I ran around and was
excited to discover that the bar staff was on a raised level – I
had gone up in the world! Angry eyeliner lady grabbed my
hand, put it under hers on one of the pumps and suddenly I
was pulling! Pulling my own pint! Yay!

'Like this?' she asked.

'Yes! Thank you!'

We both grinned at each other. She wasn't angry eyeliner lady, she was fun, sweet lady!

'Did you see that? She let me pull the pint!' I said as I sat
back down, giddy with excitement.

Jim high-fived me and then pointed to a group of
women in the corner of the bar.

'Now your mission is to ask to sit down and join them,'
he said.

So I did it. I walked up to the three women who were

deep in conversation and stood at the end of the table until they looked up at me. I gave them my best smile and said, 'My friends are boring me, do you mind if I join you for a while?'

'Yeah, sure! We were just talking about what it's like having sex the first time after you've had a baby,' said a woman with a magnificent cleavage.

Two of them were new mums and this was their first night out. They'd been celebrating with prosecco and had just ordered sticky toffee pudding.

And so I ate dessert with my new friends and learned, in graphic detail, what happens to a vagina after giving birth.

'They were lovely!' I said to Jim back at our table. 'Isn't it so stupid that we don't all talk to each other all the time? Why don't we? Why do we all stay in our little groups talking the same old crap to our friends?'

'I don't know,' he said. 'Not everyone is as confident as you, I guess.'

'I'm not confident.'

'You are more confident than you think you are.'

'Why do you say that?'

'I would never do the things you're doing.'

'Yeah, but that's because you're sorted – you've got the wife, the house, the kids – you don't need to do all this stuff. You're happy.'

He looked at me, then knocked back the rest of his pint. His blue eyes were bloodshot and glassy, his shoulders slumped.

'I get up every day and know exactly what's going to happen – you wake up every day and *anything* could happen. Make the most of that.'

Helen walked back from the loo. We gathered our things

and headed out into the mellow night. It was getting warmer. Summer was on its way. The lights of expensive clothes shops were casting their glow onto the road. Couples walked home, cuddling in to each other and speaking softly. A gang of friends brushed past us, cheering and jeering.

I still hadn't been rejected, so when we passed a young man parking his motorbike, I spotted my opportunity. 'I've never sat on a motorbike before . . .' I said. 'Would you mind if I sat on yours for a minute?'

He grinned. 'OK!'

I swung my legs over the cushioned leather seat and sat down. It was surprisingly comfortable.

'I like it!' I said.

He grinned again. 'I just got it yesterday.'

He talked about engine sizes and speeds; happy to be talking about his new baby. He told me he was seventeen.

'What does your mum say about it?' I asked.

'I paid with my own money so she can't do much about it,' he said.

'Will you take me for a quick spin?' I asked.

'I don't have a spare helmet.'

'So you can't?'

'Nah, sorry.'

Hurrah, rejection accomplished.

Lessons learned?

1) Rejection Therapy is easy when you're drunk.
2) People are lovely. It is our own fears that make us think they are not. I told myself the guys in the band were stuck up and the woman behind the bar was scary. Neither was true.

3) It's much easier to stay safe in your pub (life) corner but the second you do something silly, like ask to join the band or pull a pint, life becomes more fun – it feels like an exciting game rather than an endurance sport.

4) Embarrassment doesn't kill you. It passes quite quickly, actually.

5) I now loved Rejection Therapy.

The next morning, I woke up, hungover, to a conversation going on in the neighbour's garden. It was between the little boy, who was probably about four, and his dad.

'Daddy!'

'Yes!'

'Daddy!'

'Yes, Nate.'

'I LOVE YOU,' said the childish voice.

I smiled under my duvet.

'I love you too . . .' said his dad. 'Do you want a hug?'

The little boy seemed furious at the suggestion: 'NO!'

Rejection . . . it's everywhere.

I was back in the game.

Monday 12th May, the sun was shining and all was well with the world. My night in the pub had changed how I felt about Rejection Therapy – and my whole project. I kept thinking about Jim and what he had said. For the first time I didn't feel like a failure because I didn't have what he – or all my friends – had. I didn't have a husband, a house or savings, but I did have freedom and adventure. And I was going to make the most of it. For the first time since Feel the Fear,

I felt proud of what I was doing. It wasn't self-indulgent and narcissistic (well, not entirely) – it was brave and brilliant!

I jumped out of bed and went for a walk around Hampstead Heath, wearing the leggings I'd slept in. On the way I smiled at everyone. I smiled at dogs and children. Old men and trees. I even smiled at stuck-up skinny women. The trees and the skinny women didn't smile back but most of the others did. I was winning friends and influencing people!

On the way back, I walked past a basketball court, where two teens were shooting hoops in hoodies and trainers. They looked like they should have been in school but I decided not to ask. Instead, I asked if I could join in.

'Yeah, sure,' said one. They spent the next ten minutes coaching me, positioning my hands on the ball, telling me about angles and how to bend my knees. Their names were Steve and Leon.

I told them about Rejection Therapy. They looked at me as if I was a crazy old lady who might well have slept in her leggings but they kept talking.

'Try being a guy,' said Leon. 'You get rejected every day. You go up to a girl and you get blown out and then you have to walk the ten steps back to your mates . . .'

'Does it bother you?' I ask.

'Nah,' he mumbled, looking down at the floor.

I told them that one of my challenges was to ask out a man.

'There's no way a guy would reject you,' said Leon.

I beamed.

'Cos, you know, a guy'll say "yes" even if he doesn't like the girl, cos, like, why not? You might get some . . .'

Charming.

We kept talking. Me and two sixteen-year-olds swapping chat-up techniques.

As I walked off the basketball court Leon shouted: 'What are you going to do now? We didn't reject you.'

'Could you lend me a tenner?' I asked.

'Nice one,' he smiled.

'Is that a no?'

'Yeah, it's a no.'

'But what has any of this got to do with your real life? It's not like you applied for jobs you wanted and got rejected –'

'I pitched to other magazines,' I lied. I hadn't really pitched to other magazines. I was hardly doing any work at all.

'And what happened?'

'They didn't reply.'

'Did you chase up?'

I was on the phone to Sheila. I'd called her with news of my daring deeds, in the hope she would tell me how brilliant I was. It wasn't happening.

'I don't really see what the big deal is about asking someone if you can play his instrument. You were in a pub. That's the kind of thing you'd do anyway,' she said.

'No, it's not – when have I ever done that?'

'I just think you need to do things that affect your real life. If those two boys had said, No, you can't play basketball with us – would it have ruined your week?'

'No, but I would have felt embarrassed and the whole point is you get used to being uncomfortable with small rejections so then you feel stronger when it comes to the big ones.'

'Yeah, that's my whole point. When are you going to do the big ones? The only thing you did that involved real rejection was when you chatted up that man on the Tube and that was months ago.'

I hung up feeling furious . . . *Screw her! I'd like to see her jump out of planes and ask teenagers to play basketball . . . Why can't anyone be more supportive? Why is everyone so critical? I need new friends, new family . . .*

I tried in vain to stay angry and avoid the fact that Sheila was, as usual, right – seeing straight through me like the light you hold a dodgy £50 note up to.

Jason says that we should start with small rejections before 'graduating to more emotionally and socially meaningful rejections', but I hadn't faced meaningful rejection by friends, nor had I faced rejection from the opposite sex and I had definitely not pushed the rejection stuff enough with work.

As a freelance writer I should have been constantly sending ideas to different publications but I didn't. I had colleagues who had done great things not because they were better than me but because they knocked on doors and hustled. I didn't do that because I didn't want to get rejected. And I didn't want to get rejected because I would take that as a confirmation of all the insecurities I had in my head – that I was a rubbish writer, that I had been lucky to get even this far, that I would never work again.

That's the thing with rejection – it can hurt more than the event justifies because it confirms all our worst thoughts about ourselves. But rejection isn't always a sign that we're not worthy. There are dozens of famous rejection stories: *Harry Potter* got knocked back by twelve publishers. Almost every record label turned down the Beatles; Walt Disney was fired because he lacked imagination – the list goes on . . .

And so I pitched ideas to editors at the *Telegraph, Grazia* and the *Irish Independent.*

The first reply was to the point: 'This has been done before.' It didn't feel liberating to get that rejection – it felt rubbish – but then I got two more replies. One was another 'no' but came with the message: 'Please do send more ideas, I always enjoy your articles and I'd love to commission you.' She always enjoyed my articles! She'd love to commission me! She knew who I was!

Then came the third email, which was in response to my most daring suggestion – that I write a regular column about the tiny habits that can make us happier. 'Send me a few examples,' said the editor. Yay! I potentially had a column! An actual newspaper column!

In my last week of Rejection Therapy, I was given my Big Moment. A make-or-break, do-or-die opportunity.

I was writing in a coffee shop in Soho when a good-looking man walked in. When I say good-looking, he was my current version of good-looking – scruffy, beardy and intellectual-looking.

And it wasn't the first time I'd seen him.

He'd been at the same coffee shop a couple of months earlier, the only other time I'd been there. He looked clever and serious and I imagined him writing a brilliant book or a screenplay. I had been so smitten I'd told Rachel about him when I got home.

'You should have said hello,' she said.

'Yeah, right,' I said sarcastically. I would never in a million years do that.

Now he was back. I was doing Rejection Therapy. It was a sign.

A sign that I should completely and utterly panic and freeze.

Even though I knew rejection was the name of the game, and that crashing and burning would be a success, I stayed stuck to my seat.

First there was the practical challenge of the act itself – chatting up a stranger. How would I do it? Just go up to him and say, 'Hello'? And then what? He says 'hello' back and there's deathly silence and I walk away?

People in American sitcoms could handle those situations, I couldn't.

Then there was the emotional challenge of being rejected by a member of the opposite sex, which I found devastating. Even though I knew that his lack of interest in me would not change my life, it would feel like a blow, the kind of blow that could get me on a self-doubt spiral for weeks.

And so I just sat there stirring my coffee and staring at him.

At one point my staring must have become obvious because he looked up from his laptop and smiled. I panicked and looked away. A guy I liked smiled at me and I blanked him. I was so bad at this stuff!

After another half an hour he smiled again, and this time I smiled back. I felt my cheeks burn. It's such a tiny thing – this smiling business – but it felt like I was wearing a t-shirt that said 'I'm single and lonely, please like me! Do you like me? I bet you don't like me. Of course you don't like me . . .'

I went back to studying my Facebook feed.

Then disaster struck. A friend joined him. After a few minutes the friend turned around to look at me. This was so embarrassing. They must have been talking about the weirdo that was staring all afternoon. I fixed my gaze on my laptop.

I looked at the time – it was 6.10pm. Jason Comely says that when it comes to Rejection Therapy we must live by the three-second rule, an approach strategy conceived by pick-up artists, which says that when you see someone you like you must approach them within three seconds. Any longer and fear starts to creep in. 'Remove time, and you remove fear,' says Jason. I had not removed time. I had been in the coffee shop for four and a half hours – no, I'm not exaggerating – FOUR and a half hours, nursing cold coffees and trying to get the courage to talk to a man.

I was due at a work drinks thing at 6.30pm. I thought about texting Sarah but felt guilty about my lack of contact and figured she'd still be at the office so I texted Rachel.

> Me: *'Am in Soho coffee shop and my good-looking guy is here with a friend and I am paralysed. He is smiling, I am smiling. We are getting nowhere. Ugh!'*
> Rachel: *'Rejection therapy remember! Tell him he has a nice smile – v cheesy but if he likes you he won't think so!!! XX'*
> Me: *'Ughhhhhhhhhhhhhhh. I am so crap at this.'*
> Rachel: *'Shut up and do it.'*
> Me: *'I am too scared.'*
> Rachel: *'You don't have to see them ever again. If you make a fool of yourself so what? You have done speaking in public, stand-up comedy, posed naked . . . you can do this.'*

But I really couldn't, so at 6.20pm I left the coffee shop to go to the launch of a new mattress. Seriously, this is what the drinks were for.

As I walked out, I berated myself. *You coward. Why didn't you even say hello to him? Just hello. You bottled it. You bottle everything.*

At the door of the fancy furniture shop, a man holding a tray offered me a glass of prosecco, I took one and stood by a four-poster bed hating myself.

Why are you such a fucking idiot when it comes to men? What is your problem? Would it have killed you if he hadn't said hello back?

There were about twenty people there, well-dressed magazine women and a couple of suited men, who I guessed were from the mattress company.

'Well, if you saw him before you'll probably see him again – don't worry about it,' said Liz, who was organizing the event and therefore only half listening.

But I knew that life doesn't work like that. It is rare to see the same person twice in the centre of London. I'd already been given a second chance, which is more than most people get. I had a choice – I could either stay with the warm prosecco and mattresses – booze and bed, a fitting representation of my comfort zone – or I could face my fear of rejection and head back to the coffee shop.

'I'm sorry but I have to go,' I said to Liz, thrusting my half-empty glass into her hand and marching towards the door before I could change my mind. Once outside, I crossed the road, darting in and out of cars, feeling like the heroine of a romantic comedy.

Am I doing this? Am I really doing this? Oh my God, I am . . .

Then I got to the coffee shop doors and froze. I could see him through the window, still chatting to his friend.

Keep going, don't stop. Come on . . .

I pushed the door open and walked up to his table with no idea of what I was going to say. Before I knew it, I was standing right next to him. He looked up. His friend looked up. I froze.

'Hello,' I said – or rather croaked. Something weird had happened to my voice.

'Hello,' they both said.

I felt like I was looking down at the scene from the ceiling.

Say something, Marianne. Say something!

Then the friend, quick as a flash, announced: 'I was just leaving. Would you like my seat?'

I said 'yes' and sat down. My guy looked a bit surprised but didn't miss a beat.

'Can I get you a coffee?' he asked.

I said 'yes' – even though more caffeine was probably the last thing my system needed.

I looked at him as he walked back from the counter with our drinks. I couldn't tell how tall he was – was he taller than me? – but I noticed he stood very upright. Like he was taking the world square on. Not in an arrogant way, just a 'here I am' way. Nothing to hide. I liked it.

He put down the coffees and held out his hand to introduce himself.

His name sounded Greek, so I asked him if he was Greek, and he said yes. He asked me if I spoke Greek and I said no.

'But I went to Athens once – it was very hot. I basically sweated my way around the Acropolis,' I said.

Why the hell are you bringing up how much you sweat, you moron?

My hand was shaking the coffee cup.

'I went to university with a Greek girl and she used to say something when it was raining, I think it translated as "We are not made of sugar, we will not melt," I said. I was manic and talking through my nerves but he laughed with me, not at me.

Then we were properly chatting.

Turns out he wasn't a great author, but a PhD student studying something to do with psychology and he divided his time between London and Greece.

'Do you have plans for the evening?' he asked.

'No, not really . . .'

'Would you like to get a glass of wine?'

'Yes, sure. That would be nice,' I said.

The voice that came out of my mouth was, I hoped, cooler than the one in my head, which was screaming *Bloody hell, this is happening! You walked up to a man in a coffee shop and now you are going on a date!*

We walked out and I felt self-conscious. We were about the same height but he was lean and I felt chunky next to him . . . *Pull yourself together, Marianne, stop doing this to yourself.*

The streets were busy with after-work drinkers, so we ducked in and out of them. We looked like a couple. A couple going for a drink, as normal couples do . . .

He led the way to a wine bar I'd never been to before. It was busy but not too busy, fancy without being pretentious. He ordered the drinks while I sat on a squashy leather sofa by the window.

'Cheers,' he said.

Our glasses clinked.

He looked into my eyes and I felt shy.

'Well, this is an unexpected surprise,' he said.

We both laughed. Nervously.

'I know,' I said.

There was a second of silence.

'I was stunned when you came to the table,' he said. 'And then when I went to the counter to get the coffee my heart was beating and I was worried that I'd get the wrong kind of coffee.'

'You seemed very relaxed to me,' I said.

'I wasn't,' he said. 'I'd noticed you and I would have gone home angry for not having had the courage to talk to you. I am bad at approaching women.'

'So am I – well, not women, men . . .'

'So you don't make a habit of going up to men in coffee shops?'

'No!'

I told him about Rejection Therapy.

'But I didn't reject you,' he said.

'That's true.'

So I asked the barman if he could give us free drinks and he said he'd love to but he'd get into trouble with his manager. No worries. Rejection accomplished. It could not have hurt less.

'If a woman smiles at me three times, I take it as a sign that she is interested and I will try to say hello,' he said. I'd never smiled at a guy three times – I was too proud and scared and embarrassed. I'd spent my whole life thinking other girls get guys because they are skinnier and prettier, but maybe they were just smiling more.

He said he had been single for the last three years after coming out of a long-term relationship.

'What about you?' he asked. That standard first-date question that I hated. I cringed as I confessed that I had been single for most of my life and my relationships hadn't lasted more than a few months.

'Why's that?' he asked.

Such a simple question – *the* question really – and I didn't know how to answer it so I took a sip of my drink and changed the subject.

He told me about his life: he was brought up between Greece and New York, his dad was a musician and travelled a lot. He was an only child.

After the bar closed he walked me back to my train.

'You coming up to me like that is the loveliest thing to happen to me in a long time,' he said.

I looked at my feet.

He laughed and leaned in to kiss me. It was a sweet kiss. A tender kiss.

I felt toe-curlingly awkward. Why do I feel like that? Why do these moments terrify the hell out of me?

When he stepped away we both smiled.

'That was nice,' he said.

'Yes, it was.' I laughed.

'I am going back to Athens on Friday but I will be back in London in a few weeks.'

'OK.'

'My dad has not been very well, so I need to go home and help my mother,' he said.

'I'm sorry to hear that.'

'That's OK. It's been going on a while. But would you like to meet again when I come back?'

'Yes, that would be great,' I said and got on my train home.

Rejection Therapy had been excruciatingly hard at times. I felt uncomfortable with the fact that the game asks you to get your rejection kicks at other people's expense and I was shocked by how hurtful it was to smile at someone and be greeted by a steely downturned face – but I had gained so much from it. Not only had I had some small but heart-warming interactions with strangers, which made the world seem like a friendlier place, but I'd had some big wins too. After sending three examples of my work, I was given a newspaper column. Well, column might be stretching it. It was the size of a matchbox – but it was mine! Media domination, here I come!

I'd also had a date.

Mostly, however, I had come away with one profound, life-changing realization. I had learned that for all my fear of rejection, I'd hardly ever been rejected in reality because I'd gone out of my way to avoid it – at work, with friends, in love.

At the start of May, I'd come across this quote from JK Rowling: 'It is impossible to live without failing at some-thing, unless you live so cautiously you might not have lived at all. In which case you have failed by default.'

I had been failing by default, rejecting myself by default. And that had to stop.

As I rattled away on the Northern Line, looking at tipsy couples and students, for once I felt like I belonged with the happy people around me. I thought about the fact that your entire life could change just by saying 'hello' to someone.

6

F**k It: The Ultimate Spiritual Way, by John C. Parkin

'If you're feeling stressed about something, say "Fuck It" and you will feel instantly better.'

Sarah's text landed when I was at the Wetherspoon's in Gatwick Airport. *'Are you OK? What's going on? We haven't seen each other in weeks and any time I suggest meeting you don't seem to want to. Have I done something wrong? Sx'*

It's true. I hadn't set out to distance myself, but it had just kind of happened . . .

We were in different worlds. She was in the real world of work and broken boilers and I was . . . well, chatting up men in coffee shops and repeating affirmations. Even though nobody had said anything to this effect, I had started to get paranoid that my friends were secretly mocking me. Before January, I had been able to laugh at my extra-curricular Oprah-endorsed reading habits but now, by the beginning of June, six months into my self-improvement mission, I didn't want to hear anything even vaguely critical of it or me. Self-help no longer felt like a laughing matter; it felt very serious.

It was no longer a hobby – it was my life.

Pushing myself out of my comfort zone was taking up my every waking thought – and quite a few sleeping ones too. And it was changing me. I didn't want to talk about work dramas the way I used to. I didn't want to bitch about people and talk about stupid, unimportant stuff. I was trying to stay positive, trying to be a better person!

I looked around. Next to me was a sixty-odd-year-old man with long hair and a Hell's Angels t-shirt. He was wearing sunglasses indoors and downing his pint like it was last orders. On the other side of me, a young couple, so perfectly tanned and buff they looked as if they were made of plastic, drank rosé. It was just gone midday.

F**k it. I ordered a glass of Chardonnay. Large.

As I drank the wine my guilt hardened into something new: defiance.

The old me would have said anything to make it OK with Sarah, apologizing profusely for everything I'd ever done or not done, but F**k It. I was so fed up of apologizing. I took another drink.

My phone beeped. It was a message from The Greek.

'Have fun!☺*'*

I hated smiley faces. Do PhD students really use smiley faces?

I texted back: *'I will!'*

I overuse exclamation marks instead of smileys. It's not something I like in myself.

I looked at the information board. Ryanair flight to Ancona BOARDING.

I downed the last of my wine, put my phone in my bag and made my way to the gate. I'd reply to Sarah when I got back.

On the plane I looked out of the window and opened

my book. As we climbed higher into the air, home life vanished. It was just me. Nobody to think about but me. F**k It all.

A few years earlier, another stressed-out Brit had run away from his life. John Parkin was a London advertising executive when he had a life crisis. In his book, *F**k It: The Ultimate Spiritual Way*, he writes: 'For the first time in my life I lost all sense of meaning. Every single moment I felt in pain . . . it was simply the pain of being alive.'

Things got so bad that one day he found himself lying in the gutter. Literally. 'I lay in the gutter and curled up like a little boy and starting moaning. And that was the high of the week,' he writes.

Who doesn't love a dramatic rock-bottom moment?

After that John read every kind of spiritual book known to man, in order to find the source of his misery. He gave up his job and got into yoga, t'ai chi and shamanism before packing up all his belongings into a camper van and moving, along with his wife and two young sons, to Italy, where they set up retreats for other burnt-out executives.

It was at one of these retreats that an off-the-cuff comment ended up spawning a self-help movement. John was working with a thirty-year-old woman who was stubbornly refusing to relax despite a week of breathing exercises, yoga and visualization. Just as she was leaving to go home, with as much mental baggage as she had started with, John suggested that she just say fuck it to everything she was worrying about.

She wrote back a few weeks later to say that she had indeed said 'fuck it' and this simple profanity had changed everything. She no longer gave a fuck and life was much better as a result.

John recognized he was on to something. He wrote a book declaring that 'F**k It' is the perfect Western expression of the Eastern spiritual ideas of letting go, giving up and relaxing our hold on things'. He realized that the moment we say 'F**k It' we stop obsessing about things which are not important.

'F**k It' is an expression that says that – ultimately – nothing matters that much. Which, of course, it doesn't. I knew this, intellectually, but in my day-to-day life everything mattered a lot. What people thought of me, how I was doing at work, how fat I was, how bad my hair was, my overdrafts and credit cards, my future, my love life, or lack of . . . it all swam around in my head in a giant soup of self-created misery.

*F**k It* was going to be the antidote to that – my way out.

I'd read the book years ago and liked it. But I am Irish, so anything with swearing works for me. It's spiritual without being smug, new agey but full of common sense.

It's self-help for people who don't like self-help.

But the main reason I had decided to pick this book up again was because it came with a holiday attached. Week-long F**k It retreats take place in Italy. Soul searching in the sun . . . now that was something I could get on board with.

Mum had an issue with it, though.

'Can you afford to go away?' she asked.

'Not really, but I need a holiday.'

'Marianne, we all need a holiday. Last week you were crying at your credit card bills.'

'That wasn't last week, that was months ago – and I've been working a lot recently. I should be OK.'

I lied. I hadn't been working a lot. And the reason I hadn't been crying over my bank statements recently was because I hadn't been looking at them – not even to draw on extra zeros.

I tried to ignore the uncomfortable feeling that everything I was doing was self-indulgent nonsense. My sixty-eight-year-old mum worked full time as a teacher and her only holiday was two weeks in rainy Ireland every summer. When life was falling down around her, she just lay in bed and gave herself a good talking to. I was about to pay hundreds of pounds to fly to Italy to do it by a swimming pool.

I put it on the credit card. Obviously.

I fell asleep on the plane and woke up with dried dribble on the side of my mouth, as Ryanair's tannoy system boasted about how many flights landed on time. The midday wine had knocked me out and so did the wall of heat that greeted us as we stepped off the plane. My jeans and cotton sweater, which had felt daringly summery in London, now felt like ski gear.

A couple in their sixties were standing in silence next to me, waiting for their luggage. She looked miserable. He looked red-faced and resigned. I hoped they weren't on the retreat.

Across the carousel a tall, tanned blond man was picking up a North Face bag while a woman with dark curly hair stood next to him, pointing at a silver wheelie case. He picked it up for her and they walked out. They were a good-looking couple, clean, shining skin, with slim, fit bodies . . . off, presumably, for a romantic mini-break. I felt fat and sweaty and began the usual stream of thought about not having a boyfriend . . . but then I remembered The Greek and smiled. Maybe we would end up being one of those good-looking, mini-breaking couples? I could visit him in Greece and we could holiday on the islands . . . after I'd gone on a diet.

At the taxi rank I showed the address to a man with dark hair in a ponytail and a shirt that was a bit too open. It was as if the Italian tourist board had sent him especially from central casting. We climbed away from the coast and the white plastic rosary beads hanging from the rear-view mirror swayed as the roads got windier. Twenty minutes later we pulled onto a dirt track which cut through vine-yards and olive groves before arriving at our destination.

'Eez here!' said the driver, pointing to the old stone building in front of us.

I got out of the car and stood for a minute, taking in the long terrace and a turquoise pool whose water seemed to spill into the green hills surrounding it. It was so much more beautiful than anything I'd been expecting.

I was taken to my room, which was in a stone cottage in the gardens, overlooking a small church. I jumped up and down and squealed in delight at the huge bed, flat-screen television and marble wet room . . .

I thought of Sarah and of Mum. I felt a pang of guilt that I did not deserve to be here in paradise when I had a neglected friend and an ageing mother slaving away at work but then I heard a splash of water and shrieks from the pool and I quickly got over it.

*F**k It. F**k It all . . .*

I took off my clothes and lay on the crisp white sheets in my underwear. I closed my eyes . . .

When I woke up the Italian sun was casting a deep orange glow though the shutters. It was 7.10pm. I'd slept for two hours and was due to meet the others. I threw on a blue jersey dress, scraped my hair up into a bun and walked to the terrace where a dozen or so people were sipping drinks.

I spotted the good-looking couple from the airport.

'Are you a fellow Fuckiteer?' asked a smiley woman with a brown bob.

'I suppose I am!' I said.

'Join us.'

There was one seat free, next to Mr Airport, who was wearing shorts and a blue t-shirt that both looked box-fresh. His girlfriend was at the other table.

'I'm Geoff,' he said, with a Northern Irish accent and brown eyes. He stood up as he held out his hand. He was so tall. Up close he looked like something out of a Gillette ad. My tummy flipped. I took his hand and worried that I'd gone too hard on the handshake and that my hands were sweaty.

'God, this is stunning,' I said, looking at the pool.

'It is. I was expecting shared dorms and mung beans,' joked Geoff.

'Me too, that's exactly what I was thinking!' I said, too loudly.

'So you haven't been here before?' he asked.

'No, but I've read the book . . .'

I always know when I like a guy because one of two things happens. I either go mute or I start to talk much more loudly than I usually would, aware of every sentence and the need for it to be funny or impressive. And so I put on a show.

He looked a bit worried for me as I did my one-woman self-help act and I felt disloyal for transferring my affections so quickly after meeting The Greek.

Before I could dig my hole any deeper a man in trendy dark-rimmed specs, floral shirt and Birkenstocks walked out onto the terrace. I recognized his face from his book cover. It was John, our guru for the week. Except he didn't look like a guru. There were no flowing robes or wooden beads. Not even a sarong. Instead he looked exactly like a middle-aged man who used to work in advertising.

Behind him a tall, stern woman cast her gaze over the group as if she was scanning our souls. She looked like a fierce German yoga teacher.

Once John had said hello, he introduced this woman as his wife, Gaia. She smiled and, as she did, her eyes crinkled shut and her whole face lit up. She was no longer a fierce yoga teacher, she was a beautiful wise lady!

'We don't have a set plan, each week we do is different, depending on what feels right for the group,' said John. 'There'll be no 5am chanting or meditation. We believe everything is spiritual – drinking, laughing, scoffing chocolate cake . . . we meet around 10 most mornings, although Gaia is always late, and then we go through till about 1pm, when we break for lunch, and then you can lie around by the pool or do whatever you want.'

Over dinner we drank wine and began to swap stories.

The next morning the stories continued in earnest, when we sat on cushions arranged in a circle on the floor of a sunlit room. John asked us to share our names and why we'd come. My nerves started to build as I listened to the others.

There was a combination of divorces, deaths in the family, illness and a lot of work stress. People were disarmingly honest.

As my turn approached, my heart pounded. I felt like an imposter. My parents hadn't died. I wasn't getting a divorce. I didn't want to tell everyone about my self-help challenge in case they thought I was a bit nuts, and so I said: 'I spent all of my twenties working like a crazy person and I always thought that my problem was work stress. I thought if I could just work less I'd be OK but then I quit to go freelance and I realized that it wasn't work that's the problem, it's me . . .'

I looked at the floor while the person next to me started talking.

'Every time we do a retreat, a different theme emerges,' said John. 'This week it seems that we have a lot of burnout – you are like good soldiers, you keep going no matter what and this is a positive thing in a lot of ways but it can end up in exhaustion and unhappiness. This week we can look at what it would be like if you let go and stopped trying so hard.'

There was a collective release of breath.

At lunch I sat next to Geoff.

'That was intense,' he said.

'Yeah, it's like AA or something,' I said. I looked around for the girl with curly hair but could not see her.

'Where's your girlfriend?'

'Huh?'

'Aren't you with the girl with curly hair? I saw you together at the airport.'

'Oh yeah – no, we just got talking on the flight. I'd never met her before.'

I tried to suppress the grin breaking out on my face.

Play it cool, Marianne.

That afternoon we all lay on loungers by the pool. I had the *F**k It* book with me, but it lay unopened next to my sunscreen. I fell asleep the minute I lay down.

The next morning we learned how to say F**k It, with the help of a Werther's Original.

We were told to get into pairs and hold one arm out while our partner grabbed hold of it. We then had to try our hardest to get our hand in our pockets (to grab an imaginary sweet) while our partner tried to pull our arm in the opposite direction.

I partnered up with Janet, a Glaswegian nurse. She was about five foot with a childlike nervous energy and a huge smile. Turned out she was a reformed party girl who was now addicted to the spiritual stuff. 'I see them all,' she said, 'healers, psychics, shamans, channellers . . . I do chi gong, meditation, Buddhism. I'm exhausting myself trying them all! I need to chill out from trying to chill out!'

She was surprisingly strong. The harder I tried to get to my pocket, the harder she gripped against me. After several minutes of wrangling, I got nowhere near my imaginary sweet. Then we were told to take a different approach. The sweet was still in our pocket and we still wanted it but we weren't that bothered if we did or didn't get to it. We were told not to force the issue, just relax our arms and see what happened. I wiggled and twisted my arm, as if I was just shaking it out for fun and it got to my pocket straight away.

Janet, who was trying to stop me, looked confused. 'I was really trying,' she said.

John explained that F**k It doesn't mean doing nothing – it just means not caring so much about the outcome. You can go for the sweet (or the job, or the man, or the house) but you do it with a relaxed attitude and accept that what will be will be. And in fact, if you're too tired to go for the sweet (or the job, or the man, or the house), then sod it – don't. Have a nap. Take a year off. Take your life off.

All easier said than done, of course. Most of us have been brought up with the message that we have to work hard, push ourselves and never give up. No pain, no gain. We wear the exhaustion of our twelve-hour days in the office like a badge of honour. But why does life have to be so hard? Really, why? Should life be punishing? Or should it be enjoyed? And why did the thought of enjoying life feel so naughty? So bold?

John believes, 'If we find the courage to loosen up our hold on things . . . to stop wanting so much . . . to stop working and striving so much . . . something magical happens . . . we naturally start getting what we originally wanted but without the effort . . .'

He admits that it's confusing to get your head around the fact that to get what you want you must give up wanting it, but he describes it like this: 'Any form of desire and striving involves some form of tension. When you let go of the desire, the tension goes. And the relaxation that replaces it tends to attract good things to your life.'

I have no idea why that is true – but it is, isn't it? It's why the guys you don't like like you – because you are relaxed and being yourself. It's why people fall pregnant after years of trying just when they give up. It's why when you decide to quit your job you actually start enjoying it. You just take the tension out of everything and it goes much better.

John reckons that 'When you say F**k It, you carry out a spiritual act . . . because you give up, let go, stop resisting and relax back into the natural flow of life itself . . .'

After the sweet exercise we went for lunch and settled in for another afternoon of spiritual pool lolling. I fell asleep again. I seemed to slip into a mild coma every time I was horizontal. Back in the room, I saw that The Greek had texted. *'Just saying hello,'* he wrote. *'Hope you are having a nice time in the sun* ☺☺☺.*'* His keenness was putting me off. I replied quickly, *'Having great time!'* before running to dinner.

I was late and the only seat left was next to a woman who I'd so far managed to avoid. She had a conspicuously good posture. Look at me good. I-got-up-at-6am-to-do-yoga good. And she talked too loudly, as if everyone in the room was her audience. She flaunted her happiness. And she was wearing her hair in plaits. I mean, please. Who does that over thirty?

I sat down with a fake smile – and she mega-watted me back.

'I'm Daisy,' she said. Loudly.

'I'm Marianne.'

'I know! I overheard you talking on the first night about your project and I've really wanted to talk to you!' she said. 'I've read a *lot* of self-help . . . Have you read *Women who Love Too Much*? Or what about *I'm OK, You're OK*?'

'No, but I've heard of them,' I said.

'What about Esther and Jerry Hicks and *The Law of Attraction?*'

'No, but I did read *The Secret* and it did my head in.'

'You really want to read Hicks – that's the real thing. Then you'll get it. I have manifested so many things into my life!'

'Like what?' I asked.

'Oh, so many things!' She swept her arms like she didn't have the time to go into details.

Then she smiled at me. One of those smug and enlightened 'you don't understand the higher powers of this universe in the way that I do' smiles. I couldn't tell if I wanted to punch her or be her.

On the third day we learned how pretending to like things you don't makes you feel sick and tired.

We were told to hold out our arms and say out loud something we really liked. So I held out my arm and said, 'I like pasta, I like pasta, I like pasta . . .' Janet tried to push my arm down with all her strength while I tried to keep it up. She pushed for a couple of minutes but got nowhere. Conclusion: 'Aye, you really like pasta.'

Then we had to hold our arms out and tell a lie. I held mine out and said, 'I like mushrooms, I like mushrooms, I like mushrooms.' I really don't. When I was younger I was given a mushroom vol-au-vent at a friend's house. I'd never seen a vol-au-vent in my life and I didn't yet know that I hated mushrooms. The second the small puff of pastry hit my mouth I started to gag. I coughed up the brown mush into my hand, which then went in my pocket, where it sat, getting wetter and colder as the day went on . . .

While I declared my love of mushrooms, Janet easily pushed down my hand. 'Aye, you really dinnae like mushrooms,' she concluded.

The idea was that when we're telling the truth – in a broad sense, being true to ourselves – we are strong. When we're pretending to be something we're not, to like things we don't – we become weaker. Physically weaker.

Along the same theme we did another exercise. We were each led to a random spot in the room by our partner, who then had to try to move one of our legs off the ground. Janet had me face a wall and was able to pick up my leg easily, even though I was trying very hard to keep it on the ground.

Then I was to choose my own spot. I moved to a place in front of the big glass doors facing the garden. I stood still. I looked out of the window at the trees and soft hills which rolled into a deep blue sky. A tractor tootled around a field. A bird danced in the sky. Swooping, dipping, rising. Janet could not budge me. I felt like I was being pulled down by roots. I wasn't trying. I wasn't doing anything. The world wanted me to be in just that spot and it was keeping me there.

Conclusion: if you're in the right place, doing the right thing, you have amazing strength. If you're somewhere you don't want to be, somewhere that someone else has chosen for you (a job, a relationship, etc.) it will make you sick and tired and weak. This is how most of us spend our lives.

And so the days went on with funny revelations about life, love and everything – based on fictional sweets and where we were standing in a room. I continued to sleep and to eat everything in sight, including the cake on offer at breakfast – not cake pretending to be muffins, or croissants but actual cake. We were living in Eden, cut off from the rest of the world, cut off from the bullshit.

With each day that passed we started to look lighter and softer. We settled into a soothing routine: group work in the morning and sleeping by the pool in the afternoon, while evenings were spent eating prawn linguine, cheesy gnocchi and pizza washed down with wine . . . On the third night I found myself sitting next to Geoff, who it turned out was a film director.

'What kind of thing?' I asked.

'Oh, you know, a few shorts, nothing big – but I'm hoping to get my first feature off the ground in the autumn.'

'Sounds cool.'

'I have to do some corporate stuff I don't like to pay the bills but yeah, it's cool.'

I listened to him talk about a job he was doing that summer, following an Indie band around the States. He might have talked about 'creativity' a bit too much – and used the phrase 'seminal artist' more than is ideal – but I liked him.

After dinner we sat on the veranda under fairy lights and stars and shared our life stories.

The Greek was fading into a distant memory.

On the fourth day we were told to lie on the floor and breathe for an hour. We would each pick a partner who would sit next to us and watch us as we breathed, holding us if we felt we needed it. It sounded boring but there was something in John's voice that made me nervous: 'This can bring up a lot of emotions for people,' he warned. 'But that's OK. Just surrender and go with it.'

The air became heavy with nerves. We all sensed something big was about to occur. I started to panic. I didn't want to surrender! And I didn't want to bring up emotions!

I was sitting between Janet and Geoff. So far I had done all my exercises with Janet, but maybe it would be good to Feel the Fear, embrace the potential rejection and ask this handsome man with immaculately ironed shorts if he would watch me breathe for an hour?

'Shall we?' I asked.

'Sure, OK,' he said.

'I'm scared,' I said.

'Why?' he asked.

'I don't know.'

'You'll be OK,' he said.

I lay down. I closed my eyes and tried to look beautiful and peaceful, as if I had deep thoughts flowing through my mind, deep thoughts that he would desperately want to understand . . . I was pleased that I'd left my hair down that morning and hoped that it was creating a flattering fan around my head. The effect I was going for was Ophelia, but, you know, less dead.

The music started – it was loud and tribal. John told us to breathe deeply so that our tummies went up and down; we were to feel the oxygen and energy travelling around our body . . . then he was telling us to breathe faster and faster with no pause between the inhale and the exhale. . . it wasn't long before my hands, feet and legs started to tingle. The music got louder. I kept breathing – faster and deeper. I felt like my whole body was being pressed into the ground.

I knew I had to just go with it – to let go – but I didn't want to. I was scared of falling down a black hole – that was the image I had, that if I let go I'd fall down a black hole. I realized, as I lay on the floor doing nothing more than breathing, that this was a feeling I had through all of my life – that if I just relaxed for half a second I'd fall into a black hole and . . . then what? I didn't know but I just knew the black hole was bad. And it was always there. But why did I feel like this? Why did I always feel something bad was going to happen – that I would be punished if I relaxed in any way and maybe let myself feel happy for a moment?

The tears came thick and fast. They ran down my cheeks and then down my neck. Geoff put his hands on my arm and shook me gently. This made me cry more. I was not used to a man being nice to me and I was not used to letting my guard down in front of one. Why did I spend my life terrified of men? Terrified of everything?

The music changed from deep and pounding to something higher. It felt like light was being showered down on me, each note a warm, golden drop.

But I was still standing by the black hole. I was scared of falling into it but I was also scared of leaving it. It was familiar.

You have a choice, you have a choice. It's not your black hole. You don't have to go down it. Move away. Move away, said a voice from deep within me – the same voice that came at me at 3am, asking me what I was doing with my life.

Then another voice joined in. This one was real. It was Gaia, whispering into my ear.

'You are powerful,' she hissed with urgency, her hot breath on my skin. 'More powerful than you know. You are an animal . . . Be in your body, feel your body, enjoy your body . . . you spend all your time in the mind but you have a body too, a body of sensations . . . you are an animal, a tigress. Feel it, feel the power.'

My cheeks burnt. I felt embarrassed at this discussion of my dormant animal nature while Geoff was in earshot. Gaia moved away and then it was over. The weird trip into my self had ended. I felt like I'd just taken a load of drugs but all I'd done was lie down and breathe.

'How was that?' asked Geoff.

'Strange. I felt there was a black hole that I was going to fall down and I realized that, every moment of my life, that's how I feel: like I'm going to fall down and that it's my fault. But it's not my fault. I'm not a bad person and I don't know why I always feel like I am . . .'

Geoff nodded like this was all totally normal.

'I'm not a bad person, am I?' I asked him. I had no idea how he'd know if I was a bad person or not but I wanted reassurance.

'No, you're not,' he said, looking right at me. I bit my lip.

Then it was Geoff's turn to breathe and cry and my turn to hold him. I wanted to rock him gently, in the way he had done with me, but I felt scared and embarrassed. It felt too intimate. What if he didn't want me holding him? What if my hands were too sweaty and gross?

Pull yourself together, Marianne. For fuck's sake.

He lay waiting, expectant, peaceful with eyes closed, blond eyelashes fluttering slightly as he breathed. After a few minutes I put my two hands on his left arm and I rocked him ever so slightly, distracted by the sounds coming from around the room, the sounds of sobs and wailing. Middle managers, civil servants, music industry hipsters all crying like lost children. It was the sound of pain. The pain of being alive, as John put it.

Then the music changed pace again and Geoff was smiling, beaming even. His face glowed and I glowed too. I felt connected to him, honoured that he was trusting me in this moment.

Across the room a young woman was sobbing and her boyfriend was cradling her like a little bird. Her howls filled the room. He looked like he would sit there forever with her, just stroking and rocking until her pain was gone.

When the exercise was over, Geoff looked over at them. 'If I was a woman I'd want to go out with someone like that,' he said.

'I know,' I said. But his comment annoyed me. I wanted him to be thinking about the connection we'd shared, not about the couple across the room.

'Thank you for asking me to share that exercise with you,' he said. 'I felt very paternal towards you. Very protective.'

This made me furious! Paternal? I didn't want him to feel paternal, I wanted him to fancy the pants off me. I looked over at the beautiful couple and I felt jealous. No man would ever love me like that. I was not delicate and pretty and vulnerable. I could never let go the way she was letting go because I knew there was no one there to catch me.

'I have to go to the loo,' I said to Geoff. I walked into the blue-tiled bathroom, looked in the mirror and cried. I looked at my sweaty puffy face. I didn't look like a pre-Raphaelite, I looked like a wonky Picasso.

Of course, he wouldn't fancy me. Why would he?

This was why I didn't like feelings. They hurt and they made you look like an idiot.

I walked into lunch late and Geoff had saved a seat for me. I shook my head and pointed that I was going to sit next to Janet. I didn't eat anything. I felt like a gaping wound. That afternoon I lay on my bed and cried until I fell asleep. Outside my room a statue of an angel with wings outspread looked out into the hills.

The next day our breathing exercise was relocated to a small indoor pool in the fancy spa area, where we were to float in warm water while another person supported us. Geoff found me by the entrance.

'Do you want to partner up again?' Geoff asked.

'I said I'd go with Janet this time,' I said.

He looked surprised and I felt petty and victorious.

The pool was surrounded by bronze tiles and the blinds had been drawn so it was dark. Amazonian music echoed across the hard surfaces. I floated while Janet's fingers propped me up. It was meant to be like going back to the womb and it sort of was. Though I doubted Mum's uterus had Amazonian music playing on an iPhone.

We were told to breathe gently and with every breath to feel light coming into our body. There was no black hole this time – just white light flowing everywhere and surrounding my heart. I could feel Janet's love and patience coming through her fingers and I felt connected to her and to everyone in the water. Like we were all one life force. To trust another person and lie there while they looked after me felt almost unbearably beautiful. I saw there, in that pool, that I never trusted people. Never relaxed with them or believed that they would be there for me. I was always braced for people to let me down, to laugh at me, hurt me and leave me.

I cried like a baby again but this time it was not a release

of pain it was just a release. Of love. Of emotion. Of the
magic of being alive. My feelings were so intense they hurt
but it was a good hurt.

This is what it must be like to fall in love, I thought.

Then I saw so clearly that of course I had never been in
love before, because I had never let my guard down long
enough to feel anything like that. I had never surrendered
before – I always shut down or ran away just at the point
where I could get hurt.

But I surrendered in that pool. For a few minutes I could
feel deep in my heart the beauty of life and people and the
cosmos. I was part of something bigger that me, something
magical.

Something spiritual.

On our final night, before dinner I shaved my legs and put
on lotion. My hair, which had been up in a bun most of the
week, was down and had gone good frizzy rather than wild
woman frizzy. I put on a long black-and-white dress and my
sandals with a chunky heel. I looked in the mirror. My eyes
were bright and clear. My face was glowing and I was smiling. I felt pretty.

When I walked into the dining room Janet squealed.
'Look at you!'

Geoff looked up and smiled. 'You look nice,' he said.

'So do you,' I replied and felt the heat rising in my cheeks.
He was wearing a white linen shirt and had picked up a
tan. He held my gaze.

I looked back. His brown eyes steady. I was scared out of
my mind.

After dinner we went for a group walk through the vine-yards and olive groves. Bare, tanned shoulders gleamed in the moonlight as we walked in pairs and threes, chatting about anything and everything. We were strangers six days ago but now we were old friends. At ease. Open. Teasing. Geoff and I were walking side by side at the back of the group.

'I don't want to go home,' I said.

'I'm ready,' he said.

'What time is your flight tomorrow?'

'Ten past nine, so I'll be gone early. What about you?'

'It's later, maybe 3pm. I need to check.'

We kept walking, the sound of our feet crunching on gravel. My foot wobbled against a pothole and I stumbled, banging into him. I felt the warmth of his arms as he caught me.

I wanted him to keep his hand on me, but he moved it away.

We kept walking. The moon shining down on us, nature giving us about as romantic a setting as it's possible to get.

I willed him to kiss me. To just stop, turn to face me, and kiss me.

And then he did. He did! He stopped and looked at me.

This is it, this is it, this is it . . .

'I nearly forgot!' he said.

'Forgot what?'

'England's playing France tonight,' he said.

'What?'

'The football. It's England v. France.'

Seriously? This is what is happening? I felt like I'd been slapped in the face.

I walked ahead.

'They might have it on in reception,' he was saying, a couple of steps behind me.

Back at the main house some of the group watched the football while a few of us drank by the pool.

'So . . . ?' asked Janet, eyes glinting.

'No, nothing happened. He talked about the football.'

'What?'

'I'm not imagining it, am I?'

'I dinnae know, babe. These places are strange. We're here telling each other everything, it's like rehab. Has he mentioned meeting up when you're back?' asked Janet.

'No,' I admitted.

She shrugged and poured me a glass.

'F**k It! It's the last night, let's have fun,' she said, raising her glass.

'F**k It!' I said, banging mine against hers.

Daisy appeared, panting: 'I've been hugging trees! Come on, you have to do it, it's so healing!'

I looked at Janet, who jumped out of her seat. 'F**k It! Let's do it.'

We took off our sandals and walked barefoot across the inky blue grass.

'I'm not telling people at work about this – they already think I'm mad,' said Janet.

And maybe we'd all gone mad – but it didn't feel like it.

I opened my arms and wrapped them around the warm, smooth bark which glinted silver in the moonlight. I looked at Janet and Daisy doing the same a few steps away and we laughed at the ridiculousness of it all. I hadn't laughed that much since GCSE history, when someone made a joke and giggles spread around the class like a virus, leaving everyone, including the teacher Mrs Fisher, doubled over in pain.

But then as my arms stayed wrapped around the tree, the laughter stopped.

For a second everything stopped. Nothing mattered. Geoff. The Greek. Sarah. The stillness of the tree became my stillness. I felt wisdom, peace and love emanating from its bark. I felt its roots pulling into the earth and I felt its depth. I felt my own depth. An energy hummed between us. Everything felt right. Things were exactly as they should be.

That week had been nothing like I expected. I'd thought it would be sweary and boisterous but it had been much more profound and moving than anything I had experienced before. At certain moments, I felt a glimpse of something big. Was it God? Or energy? Or beauty? It didn't matter. I just knew that everything would be OK. That I was OK. That the world was beautiful, that my worries were nonsense, not reality. *This* was reality, connecting with trees and sky and clouds and people.

My eyes filled with tears at the perfection.

7

The F**k It Fallout

'And that's what F**k It does . . . some part of you just gives up caring. The thing that mattered so much, somehow doesn't matter anymore. And the freedom that comes from that is a blast and a half.'

The tears continued when I got home. Adverts for building societies, a YouTube video about a remote tribe meeting people for the first time, Bob Dylan's 'Blowin' in the Wind' on Radio 2 . . . everything set me off.

Having spent most of my life thinking that feelings were for weak, indulgent people, I was now feeling feelings all over the joint. In fact, feeling my feelings had become a full-time job. I certainly wasn't doing my other one. Instead I spent the rest of June walking around parks, taking in the exquisiteness of everything. One morning, walking through Hyde Park, I found myself crying at the beauty of squirrels. Seriously. Squirrels!

Geoff had sent a couple of texts so as well as crying at squirrels, I was spending a lot of time thinking about him. He was in America for the summer but I felt sure we'd meet up when he got back.

'What about The Greek?' asked Rachel.

I felt guilty. The Greek was still in Greece. He had been messaging about coming over in July to see me but I'd told him I was probably going to be away for most of the summer.

'I thought you liked him,' said Rachel.

'I did. He's lovely – I just don't know if I *fancy* him, fancy him – not like Geoff. And it's not a good time for him to come back to London – his dad is sick and he's looking after him.'

'That can't be easy.'

'No.'

'He sounds like a good man,' said Rachel.

'Yeah.'

Rachel opened her mouth to say something then closed it again. Why did people keep doing that around me?

'What?' I demanded.

'Nothing,' she said. 'Just don't mess him around. If you don't like him then tell him.'

'I know.'

'And what's happening with Sarah?'

'Don't ask.'

In the days after coming home the Sarah situation had turned into, well, a situation. When I got back from F**k It I'd decided to F**k It and tell her the truth. I was fed up of trying to please everyone, of doing things I didn't want to do! It was time to embrace an era of honesty and openness! She'd thank me for it. I was sure. Friendship needed truth.

And so I sent an email:

Hello,
    I'm sorry I haven't been around and I am sorry that
I haven't been picking up your calls. This whole self-help

stuff is taking up a lot of my head space – I can't explain why but it is . . . I don't really want to go to the pub and moan and rant anymore – which seems to be what we do when we're together. I'm trying to be less negative and less drunk! But let's have a coffee?

Love

Marianne.

Turns out she wasn't that thankful for my moment of honesty.

Her reply:

Well that was quite an email. I didn't realize that all these years you thought we were 'moaning and ranting'. I thought that we were listening to each other and helping each other. I'm pretty sure I've been there for you every time you've needed a shoulder to cry on. I didn't know that all that time you thought I was such a negative bitch. It's good to know where we finally stand.

I replied:

I don't think you are a bitch! I wouldn't be friends with you if I thought that – I love you! I was just trying to be honest about what I was thinking.

Her reply:

Well, if it's honesty you want – here goes. Self-help is not making you better, it's making you self-obsessed. You are not the only one going through changes, other people have things going on, too, not that you'd know that because you no longer pick up the phone. You've changed and I think it's best we don't talk to each other for a while.

I felt sick to my stomach. I never argued with friends. It felt horrible to fight. Horrible to hurt someone. But then all the self-help books talk about the importance of ditching negative people from your life and maybe that's what she was. A negative person.

'Sarah's one of the least negative people I've ever met,' said Rachel, when I told her what happened. 'She's been cheering you on through all of this.'

'We just don't have much in common anymore,' I replied. 'I want to talk about proper stuff – deep things, important things – not complaining about some girl in the office.'

'But, Marianne, that's what we all talk about. It's what *you* used to talk about. What you're doing is –'

'What?' I snapped.

Rachel took a breath before speaking: 'What you're doing is intense and you can't expect everyone else to be on the same wavelength.'

'All the books warn that when you change, some people won't like it and there's nothing you can do about that,' I replied.

'So you're going to fall out with one of your best friends?'

'I don't know but right now we're going different ways.'

It was becoming clear I was now going in a different way to most people in my life.

The whole point of this project was that I would change – but what I hadn't expected was how much it would piss off other people.

Mum's main concern seemed to be focused on my

decision to say F**k It to worrying about my appearance. The Saturday after I came back, we met for our monthly lunch and wander around the shops, where Mum looked at prices in Whistles and informed me how much something similar would cost in TK Maxx. It was always £16.

'You're looking very Bohemian,' she commented when she met me by the station.

She was waiting in slim-fitting grey trousers, a grey trench and a cream silk scarf. Her hair was tonged perfectly into place. You could put that woman in a war zone and she'd emerge from the trenches with perfect creases in her trousers and lipstick on.

'What's that supposed to mean?'

'Nothing – it's just your hair, it's looking wild. And you're a bit pale. Are you sick?'

'No, I just didn't put any make-up on today.'

'Oh, you didn't lose your toiletry bag, did you? Marianne, you're always losing things . . .'

'No, I just didn't feel like putting make-up on.'

'Oh.' She moved on to looking me up and down, weighing me with her eyes.

'Did you eat a lot of pasta?' she continued.

'Yes, Mum, I did. And I ate cake for breakfast,' I said, daring her to say more.

'Oh well, you'll lose it when you get back to normal.'

'Lose what, Mum? I'm hardly the size of a house.'

'I didn't say you were!' she said, surprised at my reaction.

'I'm fed up of always worrying about my weight and my appearance. There are more important things in life than being skinny and pretty, you know! Half the world is starving and here we are worrying about calories.'

'OK,' she said.

'And anyway, the guy who held our retreat said that if we said F**k It to dieting and forcing ourselves to go to the gym, then we'd all be a lot healthier. We'd let our body get back into natural rhythms, instead of always trying to control it. Then we'd find that we want salad sometimes, or want to take a run . . .'

'So do you want to get a salad for lunch?' she asked.

'No, I want pasta.'

'More pasta?'

'Yes!'

We walked to an Italian deli near the square and I ordered spaghetti carbonara with red wine while Mum had a chicken ciabatta and coffee. As I shovelled pasta into my mouth I continued to articulate my hastily assembled views on patriarchy and body image.

'Someone shared a study on Facebook the other day where researchers asked men and women to take an intelligence test. They performed exactly the same until they had to do the test in their swimwear. Then women couldn't think straight because all their energy was going into worrying about what their bodies looked like. Think how much energy we waste worrying about our appearance! If I hadn't spent my life worrying about my hips I could have been prime minister by now!'

'You want to be prime minister?' Mum snorted.

'No. That's not the point, I'm just saying that I'm done with worrying about my looks. There are more important things in life.'

'Fine! Let it all hang out! You'll be burning your bra next!' she said, laughing at her own joke. I forked more pasta into my mouth and said nothing.

When she'd finished eating, Mum opened her handbag,

looking for her lipstick, which she applied with a mirror. I never had a mirror or lipstick in my bag.

'I just think it's nice to take care of your appearance,' she said. With perfect lips. 'It always makes me feel better.'

I didn't know what to say. She was right. It was nice.

We walked to Cos and she tried on a few things that all looked great on her Twiggy legs. I tried to suppress the uncomfortable feeling that my F**k It approach to eating was not doing me any favours as I tried on silky green palazzo pants which showed every dimple on my arse. Oh well, F**k It.

For the rest of the month I continued to say F**k It to being nice to my friends, F**k It to my appearance, and an even bigger F**k It to work. My career had taken a back seat since I'd started my period of self-discovery, but now I had downed tools completely. After years of being a workaholic, I was no longer even pretending to be interested.

'I don't want to write about mascara and anti-cellulite cream or why I hate fake tan,' I said to Rachel one evening, after a day spent watching squirrels do their thing.

'We all have to do things we don't want to do,' said Rachel.

'But why? Why do we all have to do things we don't want to do? When we landed back in Gatwick, everyone looked just so miserable. All these grey faces on the Tube – but why do we do it?'

'To pay the bills.'

'There has to be more than just working and paying bills and buying crap we don't need,' I said.

'So what? We all quit our jobs? Do nothing?' asked Rachel.

'Why not? John says that our problem is that we fight the natural rhythms of life and that sometimes we need to rest. So, yeah, you might quit the job you hate, go to bed for a week – even a month – but then one day you'll wake up and want to do something. And that something will lead to something else and then you're off on a new path. A path you *want* to be on rather than a treadmill . . .'

'And what about money?'

'John says that we're all too obsessed with money. When we don't have it we think it will solve everything, when we do have it we worry we are going to lose it – but the reality is that most of us are not going to starve in this country. Even if we did lose everything we'd find a way to go on.'

It was 10pm, she'd been working all day.

'I'm going for a shower,' she said.

I could hear her walk up the stairs, her feet heavy and weary.

I was pissing everyone off. I knew it. I didn't care. For the first time in my whole life I didn't care.

Everyone around me seemed to be living a lie. A half life. I didn't want that. I wanted something more, something different.

Underneath all this F**k It stuff was the idea that we have to let go and surrender and trust that it's all going to be OK, that there is some sort of force that will look after us – whether that's God, or the Universe or something else.

And I was starting to believe that. For the first time in my life I felt I could just let go, and it felt great.

———

'You did what?'

'You heard me.'

'You did naked yoga?'

'Yes.'

'Yoga with no clothes on?'

'Yes.'

'In a room with other people?'

'Yes.'

Helen looked at me with one of those 'have you lost your actual mind?' stares.

'So just to get this straight – you were doing downward dogs with your head in someone's bum?'

'No, the teacher had arranged the mats in a way that meant you were never looking directly at anyone. And the lights were very dimmed, so I only saw half a willy.'

'Gross.'

'It wasn't like that. It wasn't pervy,' I said. Lying.

It was the only yoga class I'd attended with more males than females. And there was a distinct frisson in the air. I got through the class by keeping my eyes closed for ninety per cent of it.

I wasn't going to tell Helen that though.

'It was all about learning to love your body, and accept the way you are. . .' I continued, feigning a 'I'm now a free-spirited woman of the world' tone.

'I just don't understand why you did it. You don't even do yoga with your clothes on.'

'I heard about it and I thought F**K It, I'd try it.'

Helen finished her drink and reached for her coat: 'I just think there's a line and you're crossing it. What next? Are you going to become a Scientologist? Join a cult?'

But neither Helen, nor anyone else, could bring me down. I loved F**k It with all my heart and soul. And if my friends and family didn't get that – then F**k It.

Besides – I'd made new friends.

By the end of my week in Italy, I'd decided that Daisy wasn't so bad. At least she was open minded and thinking about the big things in life.

She'd been texting since we'd come back, asking if I wanted to go to various talks on subjects such as 'Embracing the Light Within' and 'Saying "Yes" to All There is'. I was amazed to find how many of these events existed, let alone the fact that hundreds of people went to them. It felt stimulating and exciting to sit in halls full of smiley-faced, hugging soul-searchers.

By the end of June, I was seeing Daisy most days. From what I could make out she was taking a sabbatical from her job so she had time on her hands, which suited me. She was my gateway into a new world – a world of meditation groups and expressive dance classes where I pretended to be totally at ease with grown women crouching on the floor in foetal positions, and men running around flapping their arms like birds, squawking over the house beats.

The crazy dancing was a bit much, actually. I kept trying to catch Daisy's eye during the class, to share a smirk at the mad scene before us, but her eyes were closed. She was lost in the music. For a second, I wished that Sarah was here. She'd have squawked and flapped with the best of them while wetting herself with the ridiculousness of it all. Then we'd have gone to the pub to dissect just what was going on with the old guy in the teeny tiny shorts and the girl making monkey sounds. We'd have drunk too much and laughed till we cried.

But Sarah was not here and these were my people now. Weren't they?

8

Unleash the Power Within,
with Tony Robbins

*'There is a powerful driving force inside every
human being that, once unleashed, can make any
vision, dream, or desire a reality.'*

Nine o'clock on a Thursday night and seven thousand
people are chanting 'YES! YES! YES!' in an East London car
park. It's pitch black and the ground is damp. Our bare feet
are going numb on the cold, hard concrete.

A drum pounds in the distance and we keep step with
the beat. It feels as if we're on our way to a ritual killing.
Maybe our own. We've already signed waivers warning us
about potential 'serious injury, including burns or other
physical or mental damage' . . . and we've spent the past
half-hour being told how to avoid hospitalization.

The crowd keeps pushing me forwards until the drum-
ming stops and a hush fills the air. Our fate glimmers grey
and red in front of us: lanes of burning coals, which we are
to walk over. I want to run away but I don't. I have spent
hours preparing to do this. To put my feet on those hot
coals.

Two men wearing bandanas tip a wheelbarrow of

burning embers on top of the existing coals. Red sparks fly into the night sky. A figure appears out of the darkness and grabs my elbow, pulling me forwards.

'Are you ready?' he shouts in my ear.

'Yes! Yes! Yes!' shout the throng behind me. A crowd cheering at the gallows.

No, No, No! shouts a voice inside my head.

But 'no' is not an option.

We've been told that once you overcome the fear of walking on thousand-degree coals, you can 'conquer the other fires of your life with ease'.

And that's what I want. A life without fear. A life as the best me. The Outstanding Me.

I take a deep breath and let out a roar – a primal, warrior sound. Then I take a step . . .

My transition from naked-yoga hippie to potential cult-member came much more quickly than even Helen – or I – had expected when Daisy asked me to go with her to a Tony Robbins event.

'When you walk over the fire, it's like . . .' She looked up to the heavens for the right words. 'It's like one of those moments that just changes everything.'

She spoke with the fervour of someone who had discovered God and sex on the same day, which I soon found out was how all fans of Tony's talked. Even the men. Perhaps especially the men.

According to his website, Tony's Unleash the Power Within seminar would help me 'discover how to identify what it is you really want, permanently break through any barriers that might be holding you back, dramatically increase your energy and mental clarity, and infuse passion into your life'.

Daisy had already gone to two of his events – one in Palm Springs and the other in London the year before.

'Go on, get a ticket, he's only in London once a year,' she said.

'How much is it?'

'It's totally worth it,' she said.

'Yeah but how much?'

It turned out that tickets started at £500 and went up to £1,200 – but £500 for four days that promised to 'Revolutionize your body, your emotions, your finances and your relationships' was a bargain, surely. And given that Tony's book *Awaken the Giant Within* was 500-odd pages, I figured this was the quicker way to get a Tony fix – and, let's face it, time is money.

The credit card came out again.

I met Daisy at the entrance to the ExCeL Conference Centre in Docklands. The Tube had been packed and I was hungover and had a cold coming. I was not in the mood to be surrounded by perky women with perky hair and perky smiles, chatting to men who looked like they lived on protein shakes and sheer determination – but this seemed to be the demographic.

'I need a coffee,' I told Daisy.

'You can get one after we register,' she said, so excited she was literally bouncing. It was driving me crazy.

As we queued to register, volunteers in black t-shirts marked 'Crew' tried to high-five us. Anyone new to the

Tony Robbins experience looked embarrassed and confused, while the old-timers, including Daisy, high-fived back.

'Can we get a coffee now?' I asked, once we'd signed in and got our wristbands and workbooks.

'Why don't we get a good seat first and then you can go out and get one?'

I rolled my eyes and followed Daisy towards the sound of booming electro-pop coming from the main arena. More high-fiving from strangers. The smiles were getting manic, the music louder and louder.

We snaked past a bank of what looked like telephone kiosks. Each had a sign with a language: Russian, Chinese, Polish, Spanish, Hebrew . . .

'That's where the translators go,' shouted Daisy. We were told later that Tony's words were being translated into thirty-two different languages via headphones.

Once we got into the main arena it was a scrum. People were running to get to seats as close to the stage as possible. Daisy grabbed my hand and pulled me forwards, darting towards the area marked Gold.

'Is this OK?' shouted Daisy over the music. She'd got two seats on the edge of a block. 'This way we can dance in the aisles *and* we have a good view of the screens.'

On stage, crew members were dancing and clapping to 'I Gotta Feeling' by the Black Eyed Peas. They looked to be a cross between children's television presenters and IT managers on an office night out. In the audience multiple Daisies were bouncing up and down like cheerleaders. This was too much.

'I'm going to get a coffee.'

When I got back Daisy was dancing with a man wearing

a paisley cravat. I sat next to a woman who was sitting with folded arms. I smiled but she didn't smile back. I looked at my phone and ate a chocolate muffin and thought about how ridiculous this all was and how much I hated it.

Then Rihanna started playing and I got up to dance. I'm a sucker for Rihanna.

A couple of songs later, the big moment – and the big man – arrived, bursting on stage dressed in black t-shirt and long black shorts, with a wireless microphone across his face. With his Hollywood tan, white teeth and lantern jaw, he looked like something that a Mills & Boon writer would dream up. And just to add to the effect, his chiselled face was blown up to God-like proportions on massive screens behind him.

The audience exploded.

It was like the Beatles and the Messiah had landed in Docklands on a Thursday lunch time.

Seven and a half thousand people jumped up and down as music blared and lights flashed on and off. People were high-fiving each other. Daisy hit me so hard my palms stung. I turned to the woman on my other side.

Her hands remained crossed on her chest.

I had a choice – I could either sit with Mrs Misery for the next four days or go with the madness.

'Are you ready?' yelled Tony, with a voice so deep it sounded like it came from the centre of the earth.

'YES!!' I screamed back, along with everyone else.

'Who wants an amazing, extraordinary quality of life? Life on YOUR terms? SAY AYE!!!!!!!"

'AYE!'

And then he was off . . . firing words like a sexy motivational machine gun from 1pm to 9pm. No tea breaks, no lunch, just one inspiring slogan after another: 'Love is oxygen for the soul!' 'Energy is life!' 'Trade expectations for appreciation!'

Tony's message is that anything is possible if we just get our minds and bodies into the right state. He says we are all defined by our limiting beliefs and if we get rid of them, then 'The Impossible just gets done'.

To prove the point, he told the story of an eighty-four-year-old nun who ran triathlons: 'It's not your chronology that counts – it's your psychology!' he shouted and I found myself scribbling that down. It seemed important.

Then he pulled out a woman from the audience who said she was depressed. He asked her if she was depressed while having sex and she smiled. Apparently not. And then, and before we knew it, the depressed woman was faking an orgasm in front of seven thousand people while Salt-N-Pepa's 'Let's Talk About Sex' blasted from the stereo.

She beamed! So did we! Her depression was gone!

Tony explained why this woman was depressed – and it wasn't because of her chemical make-up or her life experiences – it was because she liked being depressed! According to Tony – who was fast becoming the love of my life – there are six human needs that drive absolutely everything we do.

The first need is for Certainty / Comfort – this is our need to feel in control and secure. The second is the opposite: our need for Variety and Uncertainty. The third need is Significance. We all need to feel important and unique. Tony explained that some of us get a feeling of significance from our work, some achieve it by having a flash car or by getting a thousand Twitter followers. Tony said that you can even get significance by committing crimes – sounds strange but if you hold a knife up to someone you are suddenly very important in their eyes. Need four is Love and Connection. Need five is Growth – 'If you're not growing, you're dying,' according to Tony – whether that's growing your business, your relationships, your education, etc. And the final need is for Contribution – 'Life's not about me; it's about we,' says Tony.

Any time we find ourselves in a seemingly undesirable situation it will be because it actually satisfies some of these needs. The depressed woman admitted that her condition allowed her comfort and security because it gave her a reason to stay in bed and not push herself. It also gave her significance because she became special when she talked about her illness. Finally, it gave her love and connection because it meant her family had to look after her.

Wow! This made a lot of sense. Tony explained that we all prioritize these needs differently. For some of us, certainty will be key; for others, the desire to feel special and significant will be the most important.

We were told to talk to somebody we didn't know about the needs we prioritized.

'For me it's security and love!' said a Norwegian accountant in the row behind me. 'I have been in the same job since university. I married my girlfriend from school. It is very safe but very boring.'

'We are opposites!' I said, excited by this lightbulb moment with a stranger. 'I value uncertainty and significance, which is why I am a freelance writer who never has savings or a plan and am constantly looking to feel good enough through my career!'

We grinned at each other.

The music changed and we all danced again.

Daisy was air-guitaring in the aisles with a muscle-man who looked like he belonged on the cover of *Men's Health* and I did the mashed potato with the Norwegian accountant.

Then we were taught how to get into a 'peak state' by thinking of the best moments of our lives, the moments we felt strongest and most at peace.

I thought of sunny beaches, getting my degree even though I'd been in and out of hospital because of the cancer scare – and the fact that I was an actual paid journalist.

Each time we had these thoughts we were told to 'make a move', so every time we made that move in the future, these memories would come flooding back.

I pumped my fist in the air, again and again and again.

The theme from *Chariots of Fire* blared from the speakers, then 'Life Will Never Be the Same Again' – and that felt right. Life would never be the same again! It really wouldn't be! I wanted a life of orgasms and triathlons! Until I was a hundred!

By the end of the first day I was in the aisles with the others, dancing, shouting, roaring. The Norwegian accountant was now wild-eyed and wet with sweat. 'I think I am in love!' I shout. 'Me too!' he replied. We both looked up at the screen, at Tony. Our God.

F**k It had been replaced by F**K YEAH!!

Poor John didn't stand a chance.

And so it went for four days.

Every moment of Tony's life was spun into motivational gold. His terrible childhood, his abusive mother, the fathers that came and went . . . they all helped him become who he is today – which was rich and successful. And we were in no doubt as to how rich and successful Tony was because he kept telling us.

Every story was littered with sports cars speeding down the Californian coast or involved him hopping on private jets to visit his private resort on Fiji where he hung out with the most powerful people in the world. But somehow he said it in a way that made us feel that we too could get the cars, the jets, the houses. If we just followed his daily routine of workouts, strict diet, morning meditation . . . we too could be like Tony.

He firmly believed that we were all capable of greatness, and before long we did too. As the Spice Girls' 'Wannabe' blared from the speakers we scribbled down notes of what we wanted from our lives and, just as Susan Jeffers recommended with affirmations, I wrote my desires in the present tense – as if they were already real:

> I have £100,000 in my bank account! I am writing a great book! I have happiness, freedom, love! I go on flights all the time, travel regularly, love a hot handsome man who is kind and tall – a man who allows me my freedom. I have a lean body, great wardrobe, lots of blow-dries! Sheila, Helen and Mum are happy! And I am happy! I am bursting with energy and productivity! And I have braces to fix my teeth.

I was back to my initial vision of Perfect Me – skinny, rich, good teeth. All F**K It zen was gone.

This was why I read self-help books – this was what I wanted. I didn't want an ordinary life; I wanted an extraordinary life! And so did everyone around me. It felt so good to be with people who all wanted the same things as me. To be better. To be happier. To be their best selves.

'I have a PhD in results, motherfuckers!' Tony shouted and we all cheered back.

Day Three – dubbed Transformation Day – was the big one. Tony explained that there are two reasons we make changes in life: either because we are in so much pain we have no choice or because the potential rewards are so great we can't say no. In order to make changes we needed to focus on the benefits we'd get from the change and also scare ourselves witless with the thought of what would happen if we didn't change.

First we were asked to identify our limiting beliefs, the beliefs that shaped our world and stopped us from getting what we wanted. As sad music played, I wrote down my two most persistent and limiting of beliefs: men don't like me and I'm crap with money.

Tony asked us to close our eyes and imagine what would happen if we held on to these beliefs in five, ten, fifteen years from now? An image came to me instantly: I was standing by a bathroom mirror. My skin looked ashen. My hair was grey and limp. I opened the bathroom cabinet to take pills, antidepressants, and I closed it again. I was wearing a white shapeless nightdress. I was a spinster in my fifties but I looked much older. The bathroom was in a rented flat I could hardly afford. I was broke and alone. I pictured myself putting on make-up and plastering on a smile as I went to visit my friends in their family homes, alive with love and noise and people. I fake-smiled as I sat at their kitchen table and told them that I was fine before asking about them and listening for hours. Then I returned to my flat, alone, irrelevant, invisible.

The vision was so real it was a shock. This was what my life would be if I carried on the way I had until now. I started to cry and so did everyone around me.

A woman to my right was wailing as if she'd just lost her child. A man behind me was sobbing. Edvard Munch's *The Scream* was being reenacted by seven thousand people in a conference hall in London's Docklands. It went on for an eternity as Tony urged us to feel the horror. We did.

Then the music changed. Something lighter came on, something that sounded like fairy dust being sprinkled on the stadium. This was our cue to change our emotions.

We were then asked to identify the opposite of our limiting beliefs and shout them at the top of our voice. 'I am great with money!' I bellowed. 'Men love me!' I yelled less loudly, in case the (good-looking) man two seats down thought I was weird. We were then to visualize what life would be like if we lived according to these new beliefs.

I closed my eyes. I was in the bathroom again, looking at the mirror. But it was a different mirror and a different bathroom. This time I was smiling and humming to myself as I put my make-up on; I was wearing slim black trousers and a cream blouse. My hair was shiny. I glowed. A voice called to me from the living room and I walked into a room with big windows, a lush grey sofa and art on the walls. The voice was coming from a man, a kind-faced, dark-haired, smiling man who was sitting on the sofa.

'Are you ready yet?' he was asking.

'Yes,' I said as I leaned down to kiss him. He pulled me down onto the sofa and I laughed. We were going to see friends together. I pictured us skipping down the street. I imagined being healthy, energetic and productive. Someone alive and vibrant. It was bliss. I had seen the movie of my life – the disaster version and the fairy tale.

I wanted the fairy tale.

We all started high-fiving and hugging each other. We were gripping strongly now, like long-lost brothers and sisters. Men in ironed jeans and chinos embraced each other and held on tight, swaying, reluctant to let go. I squeezed Daisy and when I moved away I saw she had tears in her eyes. I did too. We were alive. Inspired. In love, with ourselves, with each other, with the world!

We ran around, sharing our visions.

'I want to be more so I can do more!' said a woman in purple leggings.

'I want to bring Tony Robbins' message to Putin – I think then we can have world peace!' said a man with gelled black hair and an accent.

'I want to have sex,' said Daisy. 'Lots and lots of sex!'

'Me too!' I said.

Then it was dark again and we stood with our eyes closed as the soundtrack from *2001: A Space Odyssey* reverberated through the arena. I opened my eyes and saw a sea of rapt faces – and for a second it frightened me. This is what it's like to be in a cult.

We walked with bare feet towards the purple glow of a neighbouring Travelodge. Our shoes and socks had been left in the building, along with our old limiting beliefs. We were now marching, with rolled-up jeans, towards a new destiny.

My mind went blank the second I put my feet on the

burning coals – until my last step, when I could feel heat. For half a second, I panicked as I remembered what I was doing but, by then, it was over. My feet were being hosed down by helpers.

I'd done it. I'd walked across a bed of hot coals.

It was so easy it was almost underwhelming. I couldn't make sense of it but I didn't need to. I left Tony on Sunday evening, feeling that I could not only walk on fire; I could walk on water. Possibly even fly.

This was the feeling I'd been waiting for my whole life – the feeling that I could do absolutely anything. Forget all the years of doubt and worry and loneliness. That was all behind me. I had crossed the fire. I was different.

My new life was going to start right now.

No more Old-Neurotic-Mildly-Depressed-Overweight Me.

Time for Perfect Me.

Perfect Me – The 10-Day
Tony Challenge

To reach perfection all I had to do was follow Tony's 10-Day Pure Energy Challenge. If I could 'commit with full force', I would 'experience the power, vitality, energy, and joy of your body being totally alive with health'.

Life would never be the same again! Starting TODAY!

- Get up at 6am! Sit up in bed and do Tony's deep breathing and something called 'priming' which involves thinking of everything I'm grateful for and everything I see in my future. I see fancy cars. Hot men. Bestselling books. A nice flat. And I'm grateful for everything. Grateful for my bed! For my friends! My family! For my laptop!
- Go downstairs. Boil the kettle and drink hot water with lemon. No more coffee for me – it's acid! Too much acidity in the system causes lethargy and illness! My body is now a temple. A dilapidated temple undergoing renovation!
- Make salad for breakfast. Yes, salad. Open bag of lettuce and chop up an avocado. No more marmalade on hot buttered toast – bread is the

devil! All white food is evil. Green, that's the
colour I want. Tony says that we should 'Go
Green!' to alkalize our bodies. No more processed
carbs either! No wheat! No sugar! We are what we
eat! And I want to be a green smoothie! I will no
longer be hungover and spotty, instead my skin will
glow and I'll bounce out of bed with energy!

- Talking of bouncing . . . Tony bounces on a tiny
trampoline called a rebounder every morning to
stimulate the lymphatic system and get rid of
toxins and possibly protect against cancer. I don't
have one. Instead I jump up and down in the
kitchen for ten minutes – OK, maybe one minute
– until I get dizzy. Then I run – OK, walk quickly
– to the top of Parliament Hill, where I jump up
and down some more. I am lymphasizing!

- Keep running – well, walking fast – while pumping
my fist in the air. I wait until I find an empty bit
of the park before shouting: 'I am unstoppable!'
at the top of my voice. This is an incantation.
Affirmations are for wimps, what you need are
incantations, where you really *feel* what you are
saying and you shout it out loud. A woman
walking a Jack Russell appears. It's awkward. I keep
running – OK, walking – muttering the incantation
in my head and pumping my fist in a subtler way,
kind of down around my hip.

- Come home. Tony plunges into an ice bath every
morning, to boost his circulation and immune
system. I barely remember to fill the ice tray in
the freezer – so instead I turn the water of the
shower onto cold. Kick legs under cold water and

shriek. This can't be good for you! I turn on the
heat.

- Go back to kitchen and make a green smoothie by
  stuffing kale, cucumber, coconut water and green
  vitamin powder (£26) in my new NutriBullet (£59).
  Glug down some Udo's Choice Oil (£24), which
  Tony recommends because it is full of essential
  fats. Not all fats are bad! We all need good fats!
- Work from 9am to 1pm. I am a working, focused
  machine. No tiredness. Tiredness is all in the mind.
  I write another article about mascaras. Take regular
  music breaks to get into a 'peak state'. Jump up
  and down by my desk to Rihanna and Beyoncé.
  Feel inspired by their power and beauty. I too can
  be beautiful and powerful! Oh yes, and rich!!
- Find myself worrying that the intro to my piece on
  mascaras is crap but stop myself going down this
  negative path by throwing my shoulders back.
  Tony says the quickest way to change your mood is
  to change your posture. I sit up straight, with
  chest, chin and eyes up. Yes, sir!
- Salad for lunch. More lettuce. More Udo's Oil.
  Want to chop up some cheese and ham but Tony
  doesn't like too much red meat or dairy. Settle for a
  tin of tuna but think he said something about
  mercury in it? Maybe I should go vegetarian? Yes!
  Maybe even vegan?
- Another brisk walk. More muttered incantations
  and subtle fist pumping:

I am powerful and strong! Fist pump.

I do it all easily and effortlessly! Fist pump.
I am powerful and beautiful! Fist pump.

- 2pm. More work. Write about a new pair of tights that claim to be the best-ever tights in the world. Try them on. They rip straight away.
- 4pm. Pee on a stick to check the acidity of my urine. Yes, to change your life you must first change your urine! Tony says my pee should be pH7 but mine is 6. This is bad – I am acid!
- Drink water. Lots and lots of water. Water is an essential and major component of all living matter! My body will soon be as clean as a mountain stream.
- 4.30 – the late afternoon slump but I don't need caffeine, I need to oxygenate, or in other words, breathe! Tony says that instead of taking coffee breaks, we should take ten 'Power Breaths' three times a day. I inhale for eight seconds and try to hold for the recommended thirty-two seconds but splutter out air after ten. Oh well.
- More dancing and bouncing. Download the soundtrack from the event on Spotify.
- 6pm – look at Tony's Facebook group. People are posting motivational quotes: 'Own Today!' 'Make your Move!' 'If your dreams don't scare you – they aren't big enough.' We send each other messages: 'You're freaking awesome!!' These are my people! Positive, motivated people! Making the most of their lives!

Text from Daisy: *'You're outstanding!'*

'You too!!'
'You freaking rock!!!'
'Have you peed on your stick?'

* 7pm. Don't drink wine – it's acid! It kills brain cells!
  Get high on life!

Rachel walks in as I've just finished my third salad of the day
and am doing more jumping up and down in the kitchen to
Guns N' Roses' 'Paradise City'.

'I think I preferred F**k It,' she says and walks upstairs.

9

Broke

'If Tony Robbins is a billionaire who wants to make the world a better place – why does he charge so much?' – Rachel.

The till made a dull beep and the guy behind it looked up at me. 'Your card hasn't gone through,' he muttered. 'Wanna try again?'

Cheeks burning, I pulled it out of the machine and pushed it back in again, typing in my PIN. Another beep.

'It's saying it's declined.' He shrugged.

'I don't know why,' I said.

I looked in my wallet to see if I had enough cash but I didn't.

I took out my Barclaycard and handed it over. Paying the £11.20 for a box of tampons and bottle of red wine on credit card. A new low.

When I got home from Tesco, I poured a glass of the red. Perfect Me had lasted eight days – OK, five. I caved when Rachel poured herself a glass of white and it looked so nice and my mouth watered . . . and anyway, it was a Friday night and . . .

'I might just have one glass,' I said. 'It's the weekend; one isn't going to kill me.'

One glass ended up being one bottle.

'I don't know why you do this to yourself. You set yourself up for a fall with all these extremes,' said Rachel.

'I know, I just hate how much I drink, and how much crap I eat . . . I want to get my life in order . . .'

'But why is it all or nothing?' asked Rachel.

Rachel was like my mother – understated, moderate, quietly successful by just getting stuff done without any drama. She didn't need motivational seminars or YouTube videos. She got more done before she left to go to work than I did the whole day. She didn't download £10 productivity apps, she wrote to-do lists on the backs of envelopes and crossed off every task.

Even though I knew her view made sense, I was determined to stay on the Tony bandwagon. So I spent the rest of July yo-yoing between salad for breakfast and cake for lunch, green juice followed by coffee before finally admitting defeat. By the start of August I was back to crappy telly and wine – wine, that, it transpired, I could no longer afford.

When I got home from the supermarket I did something I had not done since February – I logged on to my bank accounts. I felt a cold shudder when I looked at my current account. £3,200 overdrawn. Shit. Shit. Shit. How had it got that low?

I scrolled through the spending: coffee shop, wine, pub, pub, Waterstones, but then I saw a debit I didn't recognize: £92 – CHARGES. What charges? Someone's been hacking my account!

I called Barclays.

'Hello, I think there's been some suspicious activity on

my account. £92 has been taken out and it's not something I recognize. I think someone may have cloned my card.'

'I'm sorry to hear that, let me bring up your account details . . .' said the man on the line. 'Yes, I see it here, £92 . . .'

'Could you tell me what it was for and if that person has taken anything else?'

'That's the monthly charge for your overdraft facility.'

'What?'

'It's £3 a day for any overdraft over £1,000.'

'What? Since when? Why wasn't I told?'

'We sent out two letters informing you,' he replied. 'Did you not receive them?'

'I don't know . . . I don't read all the letters . . . I'm very busy . . . How can you do this? It's not right to charge £3 a day! How long has this been going on for?'

'The charges were introduced two months ago.'

I hung up and went up to my room, where a pile of unopened post lay on my desk – the letters were there, along with credit card bills and a notice telling me I had been late paying my VAT. I felt clammy panic rise up my body. This was bad. Really bad.

What the hell had I been doing for the last six months? Why hadn't I been working? I used to work hard, I really did. What happened? When I started this project I wanted to become more efficient and successful – but as the year went on I'd said F**k It to everything and believed that *The Secret* would provide.

After spending all of February crying over bank statements and vowing to change, I had gone right back to my old ways. I didn't keep up the whole look-at-your-bank-balance-every-day business, I got distracted creating Vision Boards with pictures of courgettes and yoga mats and writing fake cheques for £100,000. I'd gone into some nutty self-help bubble. *Money comes to me easily and effortlessly.* What a load of rubbish. No inspirational quote was going to fix my debts. And that cheque from the Universe had bounced, clearly.

I paced up and down my room. What a fucking idiot.

I didn't know what to do. My next Barclaycard bill was due in ten days. £120 and I didn't have it.

I felt I was coming out of my skin. I had to get out of my body – out of my head. I could no longer be me.

I went down to the kitchen and poured myself a big whiskey before going to the living room and lying on the sofa. I flicked on the television. The Kardashians were arguing over the new clothes that Kanye had bought Kim. I drank more whiskey and fell asleep. When I woke up Lindsay Lohan was on the screen. She was crying. She was about to be thrown out of the hotel she was living in.

When Rachel came downstairs the next morning, I was still on the sofa, where I had fallen asleep fully dressed. I was crying again. This time it wasn't at the beauty of squirrels or an advert for a building society – it was at my own stupidity.

'Do you want me to lend you some money?' asked Rachel.

'No. Thank you, but no. This is my problem, I have to fix it.'

'Do you want me to sit down and go through things with you – we could do a budget, make a plan.'

Do a budget, make a plan. Two phrases that made me break into a cold sweat. She'd offered before but I'd always made excuses. I was now all out of excuses.

That night we went through my bank statements.

'What was £56 in Waterstones?' asked Rachel.

'I don't know,' I said. 'Books?'

'What kind of books?' she said.

'I don't know – self-help, I guess.'

I found the receipt. It was for a book on de-cluttering, another one on sugar-free eating and one on juicing. I remembered looking through the sugar-free one in the cafe at the top of the bookshop, reading recipes for spiralized courgettes while drinking hot chocolate and eating a slice of carrot cake. I had yet to cook anything from the book and had not even opened the juicing book or the *Life-Changing Magic of Tidying Up* by Marie Kondo. Instead I'd added it to the clutter in my room.

'And what was £55 in Whole Foods?' asked Rachel.

'Vitamins,' I replied.

'You're spending £55 on vitamins?'

'Yes, but I thought that they'd give me more energy and I'd get more stuff done and then I'd get myself sorted,' I said. I realized how deluded it sounded.

'Marianne . . .' she said. I started crying again.

'I know, I know. Please don't say anything.'

But she kept going – through my flights to Italy, my bar bill from F**k It . . .

'What was £500?'

'The Tony Robbins course.'

'It cost £500?'

'Yes.'

'And there were how many people there?'

'Seven thousand.'

'That's millions he was earning for a few days. If Tony Robbins is a billionaire who wants to make the world a better place – why does he charge so much?' asked Rachel.

'If you don't pay for these things you don't appreciate them, you don't take them seriously. And he gives loads of money to charity.'

I didn't tell her that I'd bought the cheap seats and that people paid up to £1,200 to sit closer to him and that a good portion of the event had been spent trying to sell us longer, more expensive courses such as his Business Mastery course and his Date with Destiny week – both of which cost several thousand.

At regular intervals Tony invited people up on stage to give forty-five-minute talks about how their lives had turned around as a result of these products. Again and again, we were told that these people had made investments in themselves that had turned their personal incomes from $10,000 into $1,000,000.

At Tony Robbins the message was clear: not having money was an excuse, spending on this stuff was an investment – an investment that would reap rewards. But when? When were the rewards going to come? I was now seven months into my self-help experiment and I wasn't seeing much in the way of rewards. Every high had been followed by a crashing low. My work life was erratic, my friendships were suffering, my finances . . . well, my inability to deal with money seemed to represent all my flaws: my laziness, my childishness, my self-indulgence . . . and this self-indulgence had grown with my self-help consumption.

I started to see how self-help can be dangerous for someone like me. I loved losing touch with reality – it was my forte. Self-help allowed me to do that with bells on. I was too busy reading books, spouting affirmations and dreaming big to get on with silly stuff like earning enough money to pay the bills.

And remember Kate Northrup? My money guru? Do you know how she got into debt? By doing too many personal development courses. Seriously. She wrote a self-help book about how to get out of the debt created by self-help. I had chosen to gloss over that part of the story when I was reading it. But self-help is a business – a big one. And it's selling the same thing that clothes companies, food companies and booze companies are: happiness.

Can happiness really be bought in the form of a four-day event in the ExCeL centre any more than it can with a nice holiday or a new car?

'This is like that moment in a Nick Hornby book where the guy realizes what an idiot he's been,' said Rachel.

I couldn't remember if Nick Hornby had happy endings.

The phone rang. It was Daisy.

'I'm booking tickets for India in January – do you want to come?' she said.

'I can't, I'm broke.'

'Don't say you're broke.'

'OK, fine, I can't afford it!'

'There's no such thing as can't afford!'

'I've just put tampons on credit card,' I snapped.

'Did you read *The Law of Attraction* yet?' she said, either not hearing the tone or choosing to ignore it.

'No.'

'You have to – it will really help. And then Pam Grout's E^2 or there's that book by Marianne Williamson which is awesome . . . *The Law of Divine Compensation*. Come on, you just have to change your outlook on money and it will come. The world is abundant, remember.'

It didn't feel very abundant right now. I wondered how Daisy was affording all the courses and holidays she was going on. She'd flown to America to do Tony Robbins last year and was off on some juice cleanse in Spain in September. How was she paying for all this global soul searching? She must have saved when she was working. Saved in the way that everyone secretly was – without me realizing.

'Are you still there?' Daisy asked.

'Yes. Sorry, I'm here.'

'Have you ever thought about going to a DA meeting?' Daisy asked.

'What's that?'

'Debtors Anonymous – it's like AA but for people who have problems with money.'

'No! Come on, I'm not that bad.'

'My friend goes and she finds it really helpful. She isn't in debt anymore but she got into a situation with store cards a few years ago and she says it's kept her on track. She goes to a meeting in Knightsbridge. I could put you in touch with her if you like.'

'I don't know, it sounds a bit full-on.'

'But if you have a problem with money this might help.'

'I'll think about it,' I said before saying goodbye and watching television all weekend.

To add insult to injury, three days later, The Greek Skyped.

'I am going to be best man at a friend's wedding at the end of the month. It's on one of the islands . . .' he said.

'Sounds gorgeous,' I said, dreaming of blue skies and even bluer sea.

'So, I was wondering –' he cleared his throat a bit – 'would you like to come over and be my guest? It will be a nice wedding, nice people. I would love you to be there.'

'I want to come back to London,' he continued, 'but it's impossible for me to leave my parents. I thought maybe this could be our second date? Just get enough for the airfare, then everything else will be covered,' he continued.

And so I did the only thing that a girl who is being asked out on a date to a Greek island could do. I said 'no'. Not only could I not afford the flight, I did not feel I deserved it. I was punishing myself.

I was also, irritatingly, still thinking about Geoff. Not that he was thinking about me. Every time I went on Facebook he was posting pictures of himself with random girls.

I could hear The Greek's disappointment. 'OK,' he said. 'I hope you change your mind . . .' Gemma called and I told her about the invitation.

'If you don't get on that plane and get a bit of action, I'm going to get over there and put you on one,' she said. 'I'll lend you the money.'

'I can't let you do that.'

'Yes you can, life's short, you have to enjoy it.'

'I don't deserve to enjoy it – I've made such a mess out of everything, I've been an irresponsible idiot with money and I can't go jetting off again. I can't believe how lazy I've been. I'm disgusted with myself.'

'You're not lazy – you are one of the hardest-working people I know. So you're taking a detour this year but that's OK, you know you can always get work. What does Sarah say about it? I bet she's telling you to go.'

I hadn't told Gemma that I wasn't speaking to Sarah

because Gemma loved Sarah but I knew what Sarah would say. She would have told me to screw the credit cards, go out there and get laid, have fun. She would have stopped me from sinking into self-pity. She would have told me to grab life with both hands . . .

But Sarah was no longer around and I was too proud to call her. I was also too ashamed to take up Gemma's generous offer to pay for a Shirley Valentine fling.

'You're doing what?'

'I'm going to a Debtors Anonymous meeting with a friend of Daisy's.'

'Don't you think that's a bit over the top?' Rachel said.

'No, I have a problem with money and this might help.'

'Just do more work – wouldn't that sort out your problems?'

But I did not want to hear reason. I was deep in the self-pity/self-help spiral where all answers had to be found in some form of therapy or self-analysis. And so I got the Tube to Knightsbridge, one of the richest areas of London, to talk to people as broke as me. Or maybe even broker – at least that's what I was hoping, that their lives would be such a mess that I would feel better in comparison.

Annoyingly it didn't work like that. There seemed to be a shortage of specifics in the stories people told. I was desperate for someone to say they'd run up £100,000 on credit cards just so that I could say, 'Look, I'm not that bad!'

They didn't play ball. Instead I listened to other people talk about life in general and then I stood up and said the famous words: 'Hello, my name is Marianne and I'm nearly £20,000 in debt.'

I felt more exposed than I had sitting naked on that office chair in the town hall.

But as I listened to people talking I knew I was in the wrong place. According to DA my debt was a disease, something I was powerless over. But that felt like a lie to me: I wasn't powerless and I didn't want to pretend that I was.

The next day I called StepChange, a debt charity. I cried on the phone as I explained my situation. A patient woman talked me through my various options, including defaulting on my overdrafts and credit cards and then letting them step in and arrange a payment programme with the banks. It would completely screw up my credit rating but if I was sick and unable to work and could not afford a roof over my head, or to feed any dependants, it was an option, she explained. I felt even more disgusted with myself than I had the night before. I was not sick. I was able to work. I had a brilliant career, for God's sake, with no dependants to look after and no mortgage to pay. My financial mess was completely of my doing – and I could get myself out of it. I thanked her and hung up. I did not deserve her sympathy. I deserved a giant kick up the arse.

And so for the rest of August I decided to put a hold on self-help and put all my energies into real help – i.e. earning money and working. I practised Rejection Therapy and emailed every editor I knew and didn't know. For four weeks I worked non-stop, seven days a week, from 7am to 7pm. *The Secret* didn't help me; I helped myself. I tested the different drying speeds of twenty hairdryers, I wrote an article about a horse shampoo that had become an unlikely hit with humans. I spent two days with a make-up artist who painted my face to look like Jack Nicholson from *The Shining*. Wooden door and all. I wrote about summer Spanx

(which still made me sweat in places I didn't want to sweat).
I covered a BBC documentary about cutting-edge surgery
for animals – including an operation to remove cataracts for
Rosemary the orang-utan, brain surgery for Tiara the tiger,
and a prosthetic tail for Fuji the dolphin. I wrote about sun-
screens. Again. I went to an auction house in south London
to buy luggage that had been put into Lost Luggage at
Heathrow and never reclaimed . . .

Never had I been more grateful for my work. What on
earth had I been complaining about? I was so lucky to be
able to earn money doing fun, interesting things – why did
I want more? I just needed to grow up and stop being such
a spoilt brat. Get practical instead of emotional. Take action
instead of getting lost up my own navel-gazing behind.

By the end of the month I was not back in the black but
the debts were, at least, under control. I didn't know
whether I should go back to self-help. Maybe it was just time
to get real. Face facts.

'I think that's what you were meant to learn from all
this,' said Sheila on the phone. 'That your life was pretty
good the way it was.'

But was it? August bank holiday and I'd been invited to a
barbecue by a friend and former colleague. I didn't want to
go but after falling out with Sarah I was scared to alienate
any more people in my life. I took the bus all the way from
Archway to Clapham. It took two and a half hours but
buses are cheaper than Tubes and I was being a martyr.

'Long time no see,' said another colleague, Tom, who
opened the door and led me to the garden. 'What are you

up to? Are you still writing? I haven't seen your byline lately,' he asked.

'Yeah, I'm doing bits but not as much as I used to.'

'Tell me about it,' he said. 'Even my mother doesn't believe I'm a journalist anymore. Nobody's commissioning anything these days. Journalism's going to the dogs . . .'

Another colleague Leslie joined us with a coal-black burger on a paper plate. 'Journalism is dead,' she declared in between mouthfuls. 'Print media is over. It's all kids writing blogs now . . . I got asked to write something for a new website the other day. I asked what they paid and they said "Nothing! But it's good profile for you." Good profile? I'm a journalist. I write to pay bills . . .' And on they went about the death of our industry.

It was depressing, so I tried to offer a more optimistic note: 'Yeah, but the world's changing, there's no point in moaning about it, we just need to make the best of the world we're in now.'

'And how do we do that?' said Leslie.

'We can do so much now that we couldn't do before: look at all those people making a fortune on YouTube – you can do anything from your bedroom,' I said.

'I didn't spend twenty years on Fleet Street in order to start making videos in my bedroom,' said Leslie.

'And it's people writing for free that is killing our industry,' said Tom.

I excused myself to go to the toilet but instead I hovered in the kitchen hoovering up bright orange tortilla chips before joining another group of people engaged in a chorus of doom and gloom 'Have you seen the price of a studio flat in Clapham these days?' chat.

These people were more solvent and succesful than me. They had children, mortgages, pensions and holiday plans while just weeks ago I'd had to pay for tampons on credit card – but, God, they were miserable. And I didn't want to be that way.

'I'm going to head off,' I said after a couple of hours. Nobody looked disappointed. I walked into the garden to say more goodbyes and was met by a woman in her early sixties with dyed black hair in a messy pile on top of her head.

'I'm Victoria,' she said, shoving her hand out at me. Her nails were long and purple.

She was a feminist writer I knew by name. One of those ferociously bright women who had gone to protests about women's rights, equal pay, Greenham Common . . .

'So are you having a good time?' she asked, eyebrow raised.

'No, not really. I'm just leaving.'

'Dull, isn't it?' she laughed, topping up our wine.

'Are you a journalist too?' she asked.

'Yes, sort of,' I replied.

'What kind of things do you write?' she asked.

'I write a lot about mascara,' I said, joking but feeling embarrassed. She wrote about proper things. Politics. Feminism.

'But I've also been busy with another project this year . . .' I told her about the self-help books. I suppose I thought she might have been impressed and that we could have joined together in being bigger, deeper thinkers than the people around us.

I was wrong.

'Why on earth do you need someone to tell you how to

live your life?' she barked, slugging back warm white wine. 'Can't you figure out how to do it yourself?' I opened my mouth to say something along the lines of there always being a need for philosophy or religion to help us understand how to live a good life – but I didn't get a chance . . .

'Your generation –' she continued, shaking her head and curling her lips – 'it's all me, me, me.'

She took a drag on her cigarette. 'Self-obsessed and narcissistic. In my day we had bigger things to fight for. Issues. Injustices.'

And then, just to finish me off, she spat: 'Self-help books only serve to make neurotic people more neurotic.'

After that I didn't bother with goodbyes. I picked up my bag from the living room, let myself out and started walking.

Stupid cow! What does she know? I might be self-indulgent but she was angry and bitter and drunk! She was just jealous of me! Yes, that's it. She was jealous! I am younger and have the world ahead of me and she doesn't!

I kept walking, past normal Saturday people doing normal things, holding supermarket bags and walking babies in prams. I hoped that if I could keep walking fast enough I could outrun the horrible niggling feeling that was bubbling up in me . . . the feeling I had been running from for months . . . the feeling that she was right, that I *was* a spoilt, self-indulgent narcissist who should be thinking of world peace and women's rights rather than whether my dream house should be in LA or London . . . At the very least I needed to grow up, save up for a flat . . . be responsible. Be like everybody else. Get with the programme.

But then I thought of my old colleagues who'd done all that. They were all ticking boxes, doing what they'd been told to do. Yes, they had the houses, the holidays, the families – but none of them seemed happy to me.

I had never felt like them and I felt even less like them now.

I no longer knew where I belonged. The real world or the self-help one.

And then my two worlds collided.

On Monday morning my editor called. 'There's a survey that says that thirty-nine per cent of British women believe in angels. There's a huge industry springing up around it. Could you do a piece? Look into why it's so popular?'

10

Angels, with Doreen Virtue

'We all have angels guiding us . . . They look after us. They heal us, touch us, comfort us with invisible warm hands . . .'

As a child I totally believed in angels, God, the whole nine yards. In my extended Irish family Mary, Jesus and the guardian angels were part of the wallpaper – almost literally in the case of my grandparents, who displayed pictures of Mary and Jesus in cheap gilt frames with a flickering red light underneath to represent the Holy Spirit.

Catholic kitsch at its finest.

My parents had brought us up with it out of a kind of cultural loyalty. That and a desire to have us in a good school. God, it was understood, was a strong enforcer of good spelling and manners, so from the age of four to eighteen I was in a convent school where I believed in God with such certainty I thought that people were lying when they said they didn't believe. I thought they were trying to be cool, like I was when I pretended to like The Cure. Saying that God didn't exist was like saying there was no sky or trees. It was ridiculous. God was a fact.

Every night I'd say three prayers before I went to bed –

first Our Father, then Hail Mary, topped off with a chat to
my guardian angel.

> *O angel of God, my guardian dear, to whom God's love com-*
> *mits me here, ever this day be at my side to light, to guard, to*
> *rule and guide. Amen.*

My guardian angel was a daily companion who got me
through exams and my ever-present fear that a burglar
would break in while I slept. Every night I'd pray to her,
turn off the lights, and then when I was practising playing
dead (I figured murderers wouldn't kill me if I was already
dead in my bed), I'd imagine her flying over me, her golden
wings flittering, like Tinkerbell. She was pretty. As all angels
should be.

Then, at eighteen, quite suddenly, all the God stuff
stopped. When I left school I left my faith behind, the way
you ditch a childhood teddy bear – without even being
aware I was doing it. I'd sit in church at weddings waiting to
be moved but I felt nothing. Nothing at all. Then, in my late
twenties, my antipathy turned to anger when the child
abuse in the Catholic Church came to light. After that I
found it hard even to set foot in a church. Having spent all
my childhood praying like a good girl, religion became
repellent to me and the idea of guardian angels, nothing
more than a childish fantasy.

And so it completely and utterly baffled me to discover
that so many grown-up people believed in them.

Go into any bookshop and you'll find whole shelves
devoted to helping you communicate with your angels, as
well as angel cards (cards with inspirational messages on
them, supposedly sent by angels) and angel meditation CDs.

So I decided to investigate – happy, at least, that I was

now getting paid to do self-help. And, who knew, maybe I could get back some of the faith that gave me such comfort as a child?

If traditional self-help is the kind of thing you associate with pumped-up American men like Tony Robbins, then 'angel therapy' is the kind of self-help I associate with crystal shops and wind chimes. And the queen of this crystal world is Doreen Virtue, who has written forty books on the subject. Forty.

Doreen discovered angels during a carjacking, which is a pretty exciting way to discover angels, I guess. She says that before she got into her car she heard a male voice in her head telling her not to drive, but she ignored it. Then, as she was parking, two armed men came at her. The voice spoke to her again and told her to scream.

She did. Help came, disaster was averted and Doreen now talked to angels for a living, travelling around the world, giving angel workshops and selling a proliferation of angel-based products.

I went to Waterstones in Piccadilly and found three books by Doreen stacked on a shelf marked Angels. She was next to *Angels in my Hair* by Lorna Byrne, the Irish woman who claims to have seen angels since she was a child, and Diana Cooper, whose tomes include an angel colouring-in book.

I covered my bases by buying three Doreen classics: *Angels 101*, *How to Hear Your Angels* and *Messages from Your Angels*. It was only when I got home that I realized this was me all over – why buy one book on something you don't believe in when you can buy several?

I started reading *How to Hear Your Angels* and learned that we each have at least two guardian angels: one is an extrovert angel who pushes you, the other is more gentle and is there to comfort you 'when your Friday-night date doesn't show up'.

My Friday-night date *never* shows up, Doreen.

Guardian angels are not the spirits of loved ones who died, they are messengers from God. Doreen argues that we don't have to be religious to talk to them – but that confused me. If we don't believe in God, how can we believe that he has messengers – with wings?

And they really do have wings, according to Doreen, who says they look similar to the angels we see on Christmas cards. However, they don't use the wings for 'transportation'. 'I've never seen an angel flapping,' she adds. Who has, Doreen?

I ended up skipping through the first few pages, hoping it would get better – only to find myself reading the CVs of the fifteen Archangels, who are above guardian angels on the angel managerial structure.

It turns out that Archangel Jophiel is the 'Feng Shui' angel, who can help you clear out clutter. Archangel Michael, on the other hand, is a handyman: 'You can ask him to help you fix any mechanical or electrical problems.' But, never let it be said that Mike is not versatile, because you can also ask him to 'assist you in remembering your life purpose and then give you the courage to follow through on it'.

I started annotating the pages of these books with a highly complex literary note system: 'WTF?!!!'

A couple of 'WTF' passages included the one where

Doreen suggests that you ask the angels to give you 'an extremely nice, warm, friendly and competent customer-service representative when calling an airline to book reservations' (you can also use the angels to avoid queues at the check-in, apparently). Or the one where she says she's also seen 'a few horses and even one guinea pig hanging around like guardian angels'.

It was enough to make *The Secret* look rational.

With every page I turned I thought, 'Here's five minutes of my life I'll never get back.' I didn't believe it. Not at all. Actually, it made me livid. But what were millions of other people getting out of this? What were they seeing that I didn't see?

Doreen says that we can ask angels for help with anything at any time. I didn't really know what to ask for so I started with some basic chit-chat.

'Hello, angel!' I said out loud in the kitchen when Rachel had gone to work.

I felt like a tit. There were no feathers, flashing lights or sweet perfume – signs that Doreen says the angels give to show they are there – just the sounds of the ticking kitchen clock and radio left on upstairs.

'Do you have a message for me?' I asked the empty room.

More ticking and music from upstairs. 'Uptown Girl'.

So I tried another approach.

Doreen suggests closing your eyes and asking what your two angels are called, so I sat at the kitchen table and did just that. The names Mary and John came into my head. I tried to picture Mary and John as angelic beings, with feathers and lights and love pouring out of them, but I couldn't. With Mary, I just pictured my mum. Not really a shocker, given that Mary is my mum's name. And with John, I pictured a builder in a vest with a gut and builder's bum. He was like Bob the Builder with stubble. I didn't even want to think about what this guy was doing in my subconscious.

'Do you have a message?' I asked Angel Mary (Mum) in my head.

'Get on with it,' came the reply.

Typical. I tried Bob the Builder.

'Just do it,' he said.

'What should I get on with? What should I be doing?' I asked out loud in the kitchen but there was no reply. Bob and Mary had left the building.

So then I tried writing my angels a letter.

Doreen suggests something called automatic writing – where you write a note to your angels and they write back (well, you're doing the writing, but apparently you're channelling them). She reports that some people see the angel replying in different handwriting, using words that you would never use. Weird.

So I tried it. I ditched John the builder and Mary (Mum) and I imagined a generic, pretty angel. I started writing in the notebook that contained my tragic money love story.

Me: Dear angel, are you there?

Angel: No.

Me: Why not?

Angel: Because you don't want me to be.

Me: Why don't I want you to be?

Angel: You tell me.

Me: Cos I think it's all bullshit, fairy-tale stuff.

Angel: Life is a fairy tale.

Me: Is it?

Angel: Yes.

Me: What am I supposed to say now, then?

Angel: You only believe when you need to believe.

Me: What do you mean?

Angel: When bad things happen, then you'll believe.

Me: So I don't need to believe now?

Angel: No.

Me: OK, bye.

Angel: We'll see you again.

Me: Do you think so?

Angel: Yes.

Me: I'm now worried that a bad thing is going to
      happen . . .

Angel: It's not, not for a long time.

Me: What's going to happen?

Angel: Nothing major, you'll be OK.

I did not remotely believe that this was an angel talking, it
was me having a conversation with myself.

For the next week Doreen's books annoyed me. I read all
three in the hope that one of them would make more sense
to me, but they seemed largely the same book repackaged
in different ways. She may spend her days in the 'angelic
realm' but she's no fool when it comes to business. Sell the
same thing forty different ways and you'll find someone to
buy it. Including me, which was infuriating me.

But everything about angels was irritating me. I felt like
I was running away with the fairies. Literally.

'I think you're having this reaction because you are sad that you've lost faith in the Church,' said Rachel, making salad.

'No, I don't think it's that. I just don't believe what this woman is saying and it makes me mad that so many people are spending money on her books and cards and putting all their faith into something that's not true. It's like being asked to put your faith in a unicorn or seeing a fortune-teller. She actually sells mermaid cards too – with messages from your mermaids. Mermaids, for God's sake!'

'So stop reading the books,' said Helen, who was over for dinner.

'But I don't want to knock something that so many people believe in. I want to keep an open mind.'

'Just make sure you don't open your mind so much your brain falls out,' said Helen.

'Why do you have to be so cynical all the time?' I snapped.

'Marianne. Lighten up. At this rate you're going to find yourself and lose your sense of humour.'

As a last-ditch attempt I bought some 'angel cards' (£12) to look at instead of the books. The idea is that you pick one every day and it gives you guidance for that day. Rachel and I had been doing them for a laugh while watching telly. So far we'd always pulled out generic messages that meant nothing to me. 'Have Faith.' 'Be Confident.' Blah, blah.

Alone in bed on Friday night, I started shuffling the cards. This time I asked the small bits of cardboard whether I'd find love. I picked out three cards. I flipped the first one over.

'God is in charge,' it told me. What a cop-out.

The second one was just as unhelpful: 'Let go of fear.'

But then I turned the third.

'Romance angels are helping you,' said the card, with a picture of Archangel Michael in a forest flirting with two naked cherubs. My heart quickened.

I sat up. What did that mean? Was that just a coincidence? Or were there angels up there? It was a coincidence, surely.

Two days later my phone beeped.

'Is that your angel texting?' asked Rachel.

'Ha, ha.'

It was Geoff: *'In London on Thursday. Dinner?'*

I got my hair done, bought a new top and squeezed myself into jeans that were too small. My valiant effort to say F**k It to the societal pressures to stay skinny was all well and good, but it's hard to feel empowered when your legs look like over-stuffed sausages.

When I walked into the restaurant, he was at the bar, even better looking than I remembered, in a fitted blue shirt, dark jeans and an even deeper tan.

He stood up and went in for a kiss on my cheek and I felt my cheeks flush.

Be cool, Marianne, be cool!

'You look nice,' he said.

'So do you!' I said, too excited. 'How was the trip?'

'Fantastic . . .'

He told me about it all – LA, Vegas, Palm Springs . . . I tossed my hair and leaned in to his every word.

'And –' He paused.

'Yeah?'

'I met someone . . .'

A cold stab in my stomach.

'Oh, wow.'

'Yeah, she's really great.'

'That's great,' I said.

'She's the sister of one of the guys in the band,' he kept talking but I was not listening. 'You'd really like her . . .'

I kept nodding and saying 'great'. This seemed to be the only word I had at my disposal. Great. Great. Great.

There was a whistling sound in my head.

I went to the toilet and willed myself not to cry.

Then I sat back and listened some more to how perfect this new woman was. How talented. And beautiful.

Great. Wow. Great. This all sounds Grreeeeat . . .

When I got home Rachel was waiting for me on the sofa.

'Why am I not good enough for him? Why doesn't any man I like like me back? What's wrong with me?' I said.

'Nothing's wrong with you.'

'Why don't men ever like me?'

'Loads of men like you. You just got invited to a Greek island, for God's sake.'

'I mean guys I fancy. Solvent, grown-up men. Geoff has a job, a house. He's sorted. Why can't I have a man like that?'

'I think you have a knack for putting your attention on the wrong guys. You only like the ones who don't like you – and that's not their problem, it's yours.'

My non-date with Geoff was the end of the angels. We'd spent just nine days together. It was too weird and wacky for me.

In Italy, I had got a glimpse of something bigger than me, something beautiful. When I stood in that sun-filled hall and felt my feet being pulled to the ground, I tapped into powers I did not understand. When I was lying in the pool, I felt loved by the world. I had been moved in the way that you feel moved in front of a piece of beautiful art, and the way I had been moved in the past by the beauty of the Church.

But I was not being moved by anything sacred here. There was no feeling of awe.

I worried about how much money vulnerable people were spending on these cards and books and how much they handed over responsibility for their lives to something that might not exist. Was this any different to the Church selling pardons and telling people they could buy their way into heaven?

Desperate to understand just why so many rational adults felt differently to me, I did some research. I read articles that quoted psychologists who argued that in periods of economic gloom people look for comfort – which is why angel books, cards and tattoos, are now so popular, even in our non-religious times. We can't handle what's happening on earth so we put our faith in something else.

They said that when people had stories about being saved by angels, they may be suffering from hallucinations. Others said that in moments of crisis a feeling of calm descended on us not because there was an angel present, but as a survival mechanism. This is what the brain does to help you find a way through the worst experiences of your life. In other words – the guardian angel is us.

Doreen says that we should ask the angels for guidance, but surely most of us knew, deep down, what was right for us, if we would just take the time to sit still and listen to our own instincts? I figured that when you got messages from angels, it was your own wisdom speaking, not a higher force.

I remembered talking to a life coach for an article, years before. We were talking about this guy I liked and who I saw a lot as a friend but who never made a move.

'I think he likes me too,' I said, 'it just doesn't happen for some reason . . .' and I started listing all the various things that had got in our way at various occasions. The life coach told me to close my eyes and take ten deep breaths. Then with my eyes still closed she asked me: 'Do you think there is a future with this man?'

My answer was clear as day. 'No'.

'So why are you thinking so much about him?' she asked.

'Because I have to think about something.'

And I had done the same with Geoff: he had never said anything to lead me on. He just saw me as a friend, I'd made up the rest in order to do what I always do, which is run like hell from something real. I messaged The Greek. He didn't reply.

I ended September feeling angry – at Doreen, at angels, at Geoff – but mostly at myself. Nine months into self-help and what had got better for me? I'd ignored a man who liked me by becoming obsessed with one who had no interest. I was more stupid with money than I'd ever been. After finally ripping off the sticker with my pretend weight of nine stone nine pounds, I saw that I'd put on nearly a stone since *The Secret* by saying F**k It, let's have the ice cream/pasta/cake for breakfast. And now I'd wasted two weeks trying to talk to angels? Who had I become? I mean, really? What was I doing to myself?

11

Sick

'All this thinking about yourself is not good for you.'
– Mum

I was making myself sick, for a start.

At the beginning of October, I was struck down with a sore throat, shivers and hacking cough. I would have asked my angels for their healing powers, except, well, I didn't believe in them. Instead I went home to Mum and spent a week being fed toast, watching *Gossip Girl* and eating paracetamol.

At first it was fine. It was actually nice to have an excuse not to work or do self-help and just to lie under the ice-cream-coloured duvet I had as a child. It felt good to have Mum bring me tea and ask me if I want marmalade or jam on my bread. But after ten days – about the time Netflix started asking me 'How often do you watch teenage drama? Often/Very Often?' – the novelty wore off.

The doctor told me it was a virus and that I just had to rest and drink lots of fluids. But a week later, when I'd been sick for almost three weeks, I looked for an alternative diagnosis. A self-help diagnosis. You see, in self-help land a bug is never just a bug. There is always something more happening, some sort of deep-rooted emotional or psychological cause.

The Secret says that you cannot get sick unless you are on the frequency of sickness – Was I on the frequency of sickness? Rhonda said something about someone who cured themselves of cancer by watching comedies so I started watching *Parks and Recreation* on my laptop. It was funny. But it did not make my glands any less hamster-y.

Tony Robbins talked about a doctor who cured people with nothing but water and so I drowned myself in fluids. But he also said that anything that happens frequently is happening because it fulfils one of your human needs such as a way of getting love and attention or significance – did I get sick in order to be looked after, to feel special?

John Parkin of *F**k It* used to get sick a lot too – I think he had eczema. I found a podcast in which he said that he only started to get better once he said F**k It and accepted his dodgy skin. So I lay in bed with eyes closed, repeating in my head: 'I accept my sore throat and headache.' I was then furious when all this acceptance did not prompt an instant cure.

Louise Hay, the matriarch of modern self-help and founder of Hay House publishing, even created a list documenting all the emotional causes of illness. She said that people who got regular sore throats were 'holding in angry words' and 'feeling unable to express the self'. This rang true – I never spat things out! I never could tell people what I was thinking. Gemma had spent years encouraging me to stop my people-pleasing ways and to 'speak my truth' but look what happened when I spoke my truth with Sarah. I should have kept my swollen gob shut.

Another site said that constant coughs and colds were a

way of staying like a child. Oh. I did not like that theory but, seeing as I celebrated my thirty-seventh birthday at home with my mother getting fed homemade vegetable soup, I had to admit there might be something in it.

I tried these theories out on Mum, who was having none of it.

'Marianne, you've had ENT problems since you were in primary school. Some people have arthritis, or migraines – it's just a weakness you have. Just rest.'

'Yeah, but arthritis is caused by resentment. And migraines, I think are – actually I don't know what causes them. I think it's something to do with putting too much pressure on yourself.'

'Oh, for God's sake, Marianne. People get sick. End of story.'

'But I always get sick – much more than other people. Rachel doesn't get sick as often as I do, neither does Gemma, or you . . .'

And that was true. I got sick all the time. A late night, I'd get a cold. Busy period at work, I'd wake up with a sore throat. For most of my twenties, when I was working in newspapers, I was a walking, talking case of tonsillitis. Ironically, I was the deputy health editor at the time.

After surgery to remove my rancid tonsils didn't cure me, doctors told me I was on the verge of Chronic Fatigue Syndrome and I panicked. A colleague gave me a copy of a book called *The Joy of Burnout* by Dina Glouberman. It argued that sickness is a way of telling you that something has to change in your life, so I quit my job to go freelance and had, generally, been healthier since.

But was I burning out again now? Was self-help making

me sick? Was my sickness my body's sign that all this thinking about myself was not good for me?

For nine months I'd thought of nothing else but me, myself and I, analysing every second of my life and every facet of my personality. There was hardly a minute in the day when I didn't think, *Why did I say that? Why did I do that? Am I self-sabotaging? Am I scared of being rejected?*

At first, I had thought the self-analysis would be helpful. I had thought that if I kept going I'd get to the bottom of the mess in my head and I'd be fixed – but it wasn't working like that. The more I looked at my flaws, the more I had. I could have spent a whole year addressing my money issues alone – and I hadn't realized that was one of my problems. I hadn't even got into men yet! Let alone my fear of confrontation, and the crazy voice in my head that told me everything I did was a total failure.

And that voice was getting louder every day. Despite the daring deeds and beautiful moments, I felt like a bigger failure than ever because I was failing at self-improvement. Why wasn't I perfect yet? Or at least richer? Or more productive? By now, surely, I should at least have had more money in the bank than I did at the start of the year, I should have taken up jogging or been meditating every day. As it was everything in my life had got worse.

One of the arguments against self-help is that if any self-help book worked we'd buy one and that would be it – we'd be cured! I'd downloaded five in the last week. The more self-help I read the more I wanted to read. I kept thinking that the secret to happiness lay in the next book, the next book, the next book. It no longer occurred to me to figure anything out myself. Instead I kept turning to the men and

women in my head. What would F**k It John say I should do? What would Tony say? Or Susan?

I had the same relationship to self-help that I had to wine: one glass was too many and twelve was never enough.

My friends no longer got a moment on my Facebook feed – it was too full of quotes from the Dalai Lama. I used to hate inspirational quotes, written in italics set against a mountain backdrop – but my brain was now a sea of affirmations and slogans. 'Don't cry because it's over, smile because it happened.' 'The future belongs to those who believe in the beauty of the dream . . .'

At weekends and evenings I'd found myself ignoring my old friends to go with Daisy to lectures on living an 'abundant life', 'listening to your spirit' and 'manifesting miracles'.

As I lay in bed with unwashed hair and unwashed pyjamas, I thought about how disconnected I'd become from my old life. I hadn't heard from Sarah since May and I hadn't seen Gemma in months. I had only met her baby boy once, which was inexcusable.

I hardly even talked to my sisters anymore. I was sulking with Helen after she'd suggested that my attempts to talk to angels were an even more worrying development than naked yoga.

She was right – I *had* lost my sense of humour.

I'd become that person you'd back away from at parties. The one who gives a two-hour answer to the 'How are you?' question – an answer that involves therapy-speak about my childhood and inappropriate details about issues with men.

I kept thinking about what that woman had said at the barbecue in August.

'Self-help books only serve to make neurotic people more neurotic.'

Was that true?

I called Rachel.

'Do you think that any of this is helping?'

'What do you mean?'

'Like, do I seem wiser to you? Or happier? I'm worried that all this thinking about myself is making me a bad, selfish person.'

'Well, it's good you feel that way. It means you're not *totally* self-obsessed.'

Emphasis on the totally.

I went back to sleep and woke up four hours later in wet sheets. It was 4pm and already getting dark. I went into the kitchen, where Mum was making bread.

'How are you feeling?'

'Better. I think my temperature broke.'

'Good, now change your sheets, have a shower and wash your hair – it will make you feel better.'

'OK.'

'And tomorrow I want you to go next door and see Carmel. She's always asking after you when she sees you in the paper and you always say you'll go and say hello and you never do.'

'OK.'

'I mean it. The poor woman can hardly walk but she never complains. Do any of these books tell you to do things for other people – or is it always about yourself? It's not healthy for anyone to think about themselves as much as you have. You wouldn't be able to lie around like this if you had three children to look after and a house to keep clean.'

Her comments stung. I wanted to flounce out of the room and tell her that she was judgemental and critical and

miserable and unenlightened but I couldn't. I knew she was right – it wasn't just a virus making me sick, it was me.

I was quite literally sick of myself.

That night we watched *X Factor*. A crying teenager was sent off. 'This is very cruel,' said Mum. 'We're no better than the Romans.'

The next day I went to see Carmel, who was eighty-five and recovering from a hip operation.

'How are you feeling?' I asked.

'I'll be back on the dance floor soon!'

'Good! You look well,' I said. And she did. Hair still stiff from recently removed rollers, a pretty lilac cardigan which matched the flowers on her skirt.

'I like your cardigan.'

'Thank you.'

I felt ashamed that I was sitting in her immaculate sitting room with unbrushed hair shoved into a messy ponytail and an over-sized sweater that I may have slept in. She was eighty-five and still put lipstick on every day. I couldn't even be bothered to put a brush through my hair.

'That's a lovely picture,' I said, pointing to a black-and-white photo on the mantelpiece of her and her husband on their wedding day. 'You must miss him.'

'Every minute of every day . . .' she said, looking out of the window, her eyes becoming damp. 'But enough of that. Isn't it a beautiful day?' she said. I looked out of the window too, at the leaves turning burgundy and gold, falling from the trees. This was usually my favourite time of year but I hadn't even noticed it until now.

'And how is it going at the newspaper?'

'OK. I'm not working in the office anymore, I work from home, so that's nice.'

'Such freedom you have.'

'I know, I'm lucky.'

'And what fun are you having? Any suitors?'

'No, not really, life is quiet.'

She carried on chatting, telling me about her book club and a charity fundraiser at the church.

Radio 4 was on in the background and the news came on. We started listening to accounts from Syria. It was a shock to hear the news after months of avoiding it.

'I've never known the world to be as unhappy as it is today,' said Carmel, shaking her head. 'You have to count your blessings, that's all we can do. Make the best of every day. Life's short.'

'I know,' I said. 'You're right.'

I went out to Carmel's driveway and swept up the leaves, enjoying the feeling of the cold fresh air making my cheeks pink. Someone was burning leaves nearby and the smell filled the air. It was one of my favourite smells. It meant that Christmas was around the corner, the nights drawing in.

As I brushed the rough bristles against the ground, gathering up piles of gold, orange and red leaves, I felt myself calming down. It felt good to be in the fresh air, in the physical world, using my body instead of getting lost in my head. It felt good to be helping somebody . . .

And then I had an epiphany: I'd been doing all this self-help stuff wrong. I didn't need angels and affirmations: I needed to focus on being a good person rather than a happy one! Think of others rather than myself! That's why Mum and Carmel had a steadiness and contentment that I lacked – they didn't have time to think about themselves, they were too busy looking after other people. They Just Got On With

It! And that's what I'd do. I would go old-school. Become a selfless saint rather than a selfish navel-gazer!

That would show everyone!

12

The 7 Habits of Highly Effective People, by Stephen R. Covey

'Begin with the end in mind.'

The church is empty except for a handful of people kneeling near the front by the organist. The scent of lilies hangs in the air. I walk up towards the gleaming mahogany coffin standing by the altar. My shoes click on the stone tiles and so I put my weight on the balls of my feet, tip-toeing.

I get closer to the coffin. The lid is open. I keep walking and then I am there. Right next to the deceased. I don't want to look. I mean, nobody likes looking at a dead body – especially when it's your own.

But I do look and there I am. Dead. Stone cold and rigidly dead.

My skin looks even more deathly white than usual and a layer of powder sits on my face, creating a chalky effect. My lips have been painted a weird shade of raspberry. Who on earth picked that colour? The clothes are better – black trousers and a cream silk blouse. I am slim in death – so that's something.

I look up and see Mum crying behind the coffin, she is

blotting her nose with a paper tissue. Sheila and Helen are standing next to her, looking bored and irritated.

I take a seat on the front bench and look at the piece of paper on it – there's a badly photocopied photograph of me on the front. It's a school picture. Surely someone could have found a more recent picture than that? I look at the dates on the printout. I am forty-two when I die. Wow. Forty-two. What happened? But deep down I know what happened.

I sit quietly, wearing the same outfit I am wearing in the coffin. A priest appears and starts talking about life and death and God's mysterious way but his heart's not in it. He's going through the motions. And can you blame him? He's never even met me.

'I'd like to invite Marianne's loved ones to say a few words,' he says, with hushed solemnity, bowing obsequiously as he backs away from centre stage.

Sarah appears. Her hair looks great – it's in a bob. 'You look lovely!' I want to say but I don't. Now is not the time. She walks up to the pulpit and takes a deep breath. She looks down at Steve and the little girl sitting next to him in the congregation.

'Is that your daughter?' I want to shout. 'That's so exciting! You have a child!'

She takes a deep breath.

'Marianne had it all but it was never enough,' she says, her chin jutted forward in defiance, determined to say the truth.

'This was her own doing and I'm done feeling guilty about it.'

She looks at the coffin – at me – and then into the

congregation. Steve nods with her. *Steve, don't back her up . . .
I thought we were friends!*

She steps down and sits next to Gemma, who is crying.

Then it's Sheila and Helen's turn. They go up together.
Sheila looks at the congregation. 'She left a mess. As usual,'
she says. A slight laugh in the audience. Look! They are
laughing lovingly about my poor housekeeping! It wasn't all
bad! I was known and loved.

'Thanks for leaving us to look after Mum,' she says, this
time looking at the coffin. Helen stares out towards the
back of the church, her face a mask of disdain. She wouldn't
even look at dead me. They sit down.

Then Mum. She looks so old and frail, stooped over in a
black dress, clutching her tissues. I want to hug her, rub her
back, say I'm sorry. She is shell-shocked, her eyes swollen
from tears.

'Thank you all for coming, it's very kind of you. I don't
know what to say.' She looks broken. 'I just don't understand . . . I don't know how she could have done this to
herself.' Her voice breaks and she crumples in on herself as
her shoulders shake. Helen brings her back down to the
seat. The anger in the church is palpable.

I had done this to myself – that's what Sarah had said. I
have a feeling, a kind of hazy memory of this, like a dream
. . . had I killed myself?

The doorbell was ringing. 'I'll get it!' Rachel called from
downstairs and I followed the sound of her feet running
from the kitchen to the front door. The smell of roast lamb
filled the house.

I was not at my funeral. I was in my bedroom sitting at my desk with a pen in my hand and my trusty notbebook. I was supposed to be writing down the wonderful things I wanted people to say about me at my funeral, as a way of inspiring me to be my best self. It had not worked. I went downstairs to join the others for Sunday lunch.

The 7 Habits of Highly Effective People by Stephen R Covey is the *War and Peace* of self-help. It had been sitting on my bookshelf for years, unread beyond a few pages and, even though it's considered a classic, I've yet to meet anyone who has read it – but maybe that's because I am not keeping the company of the world leaders who were all said to be fans of Covey's wisdom.

Full of references to Aristotle, Thoreau and Benjamin Franklin, the message of the book – which I'd gathered from interviews with the author, rather than reading the actual pages – was that we cannot seek happiness as a goal in itself; instead happiness only comes from being a good person. Covey took a dim view of the modern self-help industry, believing that the reason people are unhappy is because they were looking for short cuts, all surface over substance.

'Happiness is a by-product of service and a life of integrity, and when people don't live true to principles and they are not involved in service, you are going to find depression and despair,' he was quoted as saying, in an article written shortly before his death, in 2012, aged seventy-nine.

Covey, who was a Mormon with nine children and forty-two grandchildren, did not advocate walking around muttering affirmations about abundance. No Vision Boards. Just a slow, day-by-day, commitment to doing the right thing.

After my three weeks of self-pitying sickness and ten months of self-indulgent self-examination, this was what I needed. There would be no more selfish happiness-seeking! Instead I would be a person of strong morals and principles! A person of her word! A person of discipline! A selfless person!

A Highly Effective Person!

There was just one problem. I seemed to have lost the ability to read.

Monday 3rd November and I sat by my desk with a clean notepad and my old copy of the book and quickly remembered why I'd never got further than a few pages.

The talk of 'paradigm shifts' and 'synergizing' was too complicated for my fried mind. The diagrams weren't any better: Triangles, circles, arrows, flow-charts – all with teeny tiny words squeezed in them. I squinted. Turned them upside down. Nothing doing. I did not understand a word of it. It took twenty minutes to get through one paragraph.

I tried to whip myself into action, like an old horse, with an uplifting pep talk that went thus: *Come on, you lazy cow, get on with it. People out there are doing hard things with their lives, this isn't one of them. Why can't you read? What's wrong with you? This is the kind of book that really successful people read – world leaders! Good people! If you want to stop being such a self-centred bitch you need to read this book!*

But the whole tough-love thing wasn't working.

I could practically smell the burnt rubber as my brain tried to take in the words. So by Friday afternoon, I gave up on the book and found a cheat sheet online. Even that was tough going. Over the weekend I read and re-read the sheet, trying to understand what it was saying. In the end, I came to my own interpretation of Covey's Seven Habits:

- Habit 1: 'Be proactive'
  We may not be able to control what happens to us but we can control our reaction to it. Stop blaming others, stop being a victim, take responsibility for yourself, your actions, your words and your thoughts.
- Habit 2: 'Begin with the end in mind'
  How do you want people to talk about you at the end of your life? Keep that in mind every single day.
- Habit 3: 'Put first things first'
  We all get distracted by emails and work dramas, but remember to focus on what is important to us rather than what seems urgent.
- Habit 4: 'Think win-win'
  Real success should not occur at the expense of others.
- Habit 5: 'Seek to understand/then be understood'
  Go into conversations prepared to listen – really listen – to the other person.
- Habit 6: 'Synergize'
  Once you've really listened and worked to create win-win situations with others, amazing things happen.
- Habit 7: 'Sharpen the saw'
  We are the saw in this scenario. In order to keep being the best you can be you need to be a 'sharp saw' not a tired, blunt one. We stay 'sharp' by

> keeping physically and mentally fit, taking time out
> to rest and looking after our spiritual and
> emotional well-being.

But even the cheat sheet made my head hurt. 'Proactivity'. 'Sharpening the saw'. My saw was not sharp; it was blunt and no longer fit for purpose. But I was not allowed to complain anymore.

In the book Covey tells the story of Holocaust survivor Victor Frankl, who lost his family but kept his sanity in camp, saying, 'Everything can be taken from a man but one thing: the last of the human freedoms – to choose one's attitude in any given set of circumstances . . .'

And so, while every bit of my head was begging me to stop the self-help, I attempted to be a Good 'Proactive' Person. I stopped drinking, I stopped moaning, I exercised and I set myself the task of performing one act of kindness a day; I made Rachel dinner, I helped a woman on the Tube with her big suitcase . . . but the world was laughing at my efforts.

On Monday 10th November I accidentally downloaded some malware onto my computer which deleted about fifty per cent of my files. On Tuesday I got an email from my accountant reminding me that my tax return was due at the end of the month. I spent two days going through old bank statements and hating myself. Again.

Then on the bus home from the supermarket, my phone got nicked. And, no, I did not have insurance. Actually that wasn't true. I *did* have phone insurance with my bank account only it was invalid because I'd never bothered to register my phone in order to activate the policy.

I wanted to scream and shout, but none of this stuff was

supposed to touch me. I should be Highly Effective and see the bigger picture! If Victor Frankl could handle a concentration camp I should sure as hell have been able to cope with a stolen phone!

The dangerous expectation that can be created by self-help books is that if you're not walking around like a cross between Mary Poppins, Buddha and Jesus every day you're doing it wrong. You must try harder.

Sometimes it felt like these books wanted to hammer out the very nature of the human condition – a condition that has many emotions, including bad ones. Nobody is perfect. But I'd been trying to be.

The higher I was setting my standards the more I was feeling like a failure.

As the month went on I started to come apart. At night I was having nightmares which involved me killing members of my family and being chased around my childhood home, which somehow morphed into a multi-storey car park.

My mind had always been a bit messy but now it was beginning to spin out of control. I was having lots of conversations but all of them were in my head. I became sure that all my friends and my family hated me. I imagined people talking about me. I was trying to push ahead with work but I seemed to have lost my ability to write too. I spent five days struggling with an article that should have taken a day and got an email back from my editor, who described it as 'unreadable'.

In thirteen years of writing I'd never had such a comment. On the upside I had the name of my autobiography but on the downside, it was proof that the self-help stuff wasn't sending me in the right direction career-wise.

I was like that whirling wheel that spins on your screen when your computer is about to crash. I was trying to keep going but shutdown was imminent.

And then I planned my funeral.

Covey says that most of us spend our lives climbing up ladders that are leaning against the wrong wall. We need to get clear about what we really want in life, what's important to us, what our purpose is, and then every day we should live according to that vision. And the best way to get clear about what that vision is, according to Covey, is to imagine your own funeral and imagine what you'd like others to say about you.

And so, while Rachel cooked Sunday lunch, I sat down at my desk and opened my notepad.

My Funeral, I wrote. And underlined it.

Right. My funeral.

What did I want people to say at my funeral? What did I want to have achieved by the time I'd died? I had no clue. I didn't know what I wanted for dinner most days – how on earth could I know what I was supposed to do with the rest of my life?

Who would be there talking about me? Would I have children? A husband? Or would I have friends who I'd met while travelling the world? Would I be single when I died? Was that OK? Am I happy that way? And would I be rich? Or would I have led a simple life and given everything I had to charity?

I mean – what made a good life? I didn't know and I felt

like a failure for not knowing. The feelings of anger and frustration that had been simmering since August were barely contained now. Why didn't I know what I wanted to do with my life? What was wrong with me? Why was I so fucking useless? *Concentrate, Marianne. You stupid cow.* I closed my eyes and forced myself to picture it. My funeral. And then the vision came to me with shocking clarity. I killed myself at forty-two. I had fallen down that black hole I'd always been so scared of . . .

The doorbell rang. I went downstairs feeling shaken. Rachel's friends were standing in the kitchen opening bottles of wine. I said hello to everyone but my mind was still playing out me being dead. Everybody hating me.

'You OK?' asked Rachel.

'Yeah, why?' I snapped.

'You seem stressed.'

'No, I'm fine.'

How could I tell her that I was stressed out from attending my funeral after committing suicide five years from now? And so I poured a glass of red, drank it quickly and poured a second. By the time I was on my third I was beginning to feel the familiar warm fug that made being in my head slightly more bearable.

In between chatter about kids and jobs, Rachel's friends asked about the self-help and I told them about the funeral exercise – without telling them the details.

'Didn't Joan Rivers say she wanted to be found dead under George Clooney?' asked Rachel. They all laughed and I pretended to laugh along too.

Ha, bloody, ha.

I topped up my wine and zoned out as chat moved to holiday plans and stories from some debauched party they'd been to. Usually this kind of afternoon would have been my idea of heaven but now I felt so removed from it all. Why wasn't anyone taking life seriously? Why couldn't we talk about big things? Like what made a good life? Or what was the purpose of it all?

Why were we all wasting time talking rubbish? It was all so pointless.

'Are you sure you're OK?' Rachel asked, while we were clearing up.

'Yeah, I'm just tired,' I said.

I went upstairs and saw two missed calls from Mum.

I rang her back.

'I just wanted to remind you it's your aunt's birthday tomorrow.'

'OK, thanks.'

'So send her a message.'

'Yeah, I will . . . Mum . . .?'

'Yes.'

'What would you like people to say about you at your funeral?'

'What do you mean?'

'I mean when you die, what kind of eulogy would you like?'

'I don't want a eulogy. When you're dead, you're dead. All this standing up and saying how wonderful so and so was, it's just a lie. Nobody can stand up and say she was a right old bitch, can they?'

'But, OK, what would you have liked to have achieved in your life?'

'That you girls are happy.'

'No, but what about you personally?'

'Marianne, I don't know. You know I don't think about things as much as you do . . .'

'Come on, there must be something you'd want to be remembered for?'

'I suppose I'd like it if people said, She did no harm.'

I could not decide if that was the humblest or most ambitious of goals.

By the end of November, the pressure to decide what my perfect life would be coincided perfectly with a piece I'd been asked to write for a magazine about always being single. Scientists believed that they'd found a 'Single Gene' which meant that some of us were born with a disposition to live alone. I wrote about how I was always single and maybe had this gene. The magazine wanted more details. I was getting enquiries from my editor: 'Have you ever been in love? Do you want children? What do you see in your future?' All massive, personal questions to be answered on deadline for the whole world to read about.

On a Tuesday afternoon in Bread and Bean while 'Do They Know It's Christmas?' was playing on the speakers I felt I had to decide every aspect of my life.

I wasn't taking a swim in Lake Me, I was drowning in it. Self-examination had turned to self-loathing. When I started imagining my fictional suicide, I knew it was time to stop.

The fact that I'd given up at Habit 2 of the 7 Habits of Highly Effective People said it all.

13

Depressed

'You're touching the void – and you've got to step back because you won't be any good to anyone if you go under.' – Bald London Cabbie

'You need to go to the doctor. You can't carry on the way you're going.'

'What do you mean?'

'Up and down like this – it's not right. One minute everything is great and the universe loves you – and the next minute everything's terrible . . .'

'It's not that bad.'

'You've spent the last hour crying in the pub on a Saturday night.'

We were in the Queen's Head in Islington. There was a buzz in the air. All around us normal people talked about normal things. I had met Helen in an attempt to pretend I was one of them. Normal that is. It hadn't worked.

First I asked her about her funeral – a conversation she did not want to have.

Then she'd made a comment about putting off going to the dentist.

'But *why* are you putting it off?' I asked, leaning in to her.

'Can we not turn this into a therapy session?' she snapped.

Tears sprang into my eyes.

'What's wrong with you?' she demanded.

'Nothing.'

I sat in silence.

'Marianne, what is wrong with you?'

'You don't like me anymore,' I blurted out. That's when I really started crying. Like a four-year-old.

'Marianne, don't be stupid,' she replied, shaking her head.

'You don't want to see me anymore,' I said.

'That's not true.'

'You think I'm an idiot.'

'I'm not spending my days thinking about you,' she said.

'You think I'm stupid for doing this self-help stuff.'

'I don't think you're stupid, but do you think it's helping?' she said.

'I don't know.'

'I think you need to get different kind of help,' she continued.

I was confused: 'What kind of help?'

'Medical help.'

'What do you mean?'

'Antidepressants.'

I thought Helen was the one overreacting. I didn't want to push my emotions down with pills and booze. Well, maybe a bit of booze was OK . . . but . . .

'I don't need medication. I just –' I didn't know what to say. I just what? Felt like every minute of the day I was on a knife-edge, clinging on to sanity? Or that some days it felt like I was being dragged further out to sea, losing all feeling

of solid ground under my feet, moving away from all the
things that used to define me – my friends, my work, my
routine, going to the pub, shopping . . .

'Just what?' said Helen.

I didn't tell her about the knife-edge or the sea. Just as
I didn't tell her about the nightmares where I'm killing
people or the fact that before my fictional funeral I'd killed
myself.

'I'm just tired,' I said. Tired. How many times had I said
that word when I didn't know what else to say? When I
didn't know how to say I'm lost, I'm scared, I'm lonely, I feel
like I'm losing it . . .?

'Why don't you take a few days off. Hang out with
Sarah. Be normal for a while.'

'I haven't spoken to her in months.'

'What? Didn't you sort that out?'

'No.'

'Marianne.' Helen, like the rest of the world, loved
Sarah.

'Stop it, I know.'

'Well, why don't you go away for a while? Go to Ireland
and see Gemma? She always makes you feel better.'

And she did.

Gemma and I had met while working in newspapers in
Dublin in our twenties. We bonded over midnight deadlines
and vats of red wine. We were opposites in every way – she
is petite and olive skinned and tans in two seconds. I'm tall
and pale and hide from the sun. She is fearless and says
everything that's on her mind, I am perpetually anxious and
keep everything bottled up. But from the second we met it
just worked.

Normally we'd travel back and forth to see each other

every couple of months but since I'd started self-help she'd had her first child and I'd been too busy and broke to go over. For months she'd been telling me that I didn't sound right and that I was pushing myself too far. I'd denied it and told her everything was fine. I couldn't make her listen to my self-induced madness when she had a newborn to look after.

'I can't to to Ireland, I have to get on to a new book. I'm already behind,' I said to Helen.

'You can't do another book now. I don't think you should do any more books, full stop. You are messing with your head too much. You need to stop now before you do some proper damage.'

Maybe she was right.

Just a few months earlier I was doing Rejection Therapy in this same pub: pouring my own pint, playing with the band and having sex chat with the new mums. I'd felt the fear, faced my finances and relished (almost) rejection. My self-help mission was a triumph! It was opening doors to me – making me do things I'd never done in my entire life. I'd felt alive! Excited! Full of possibility. What had happened?

I looked around the pub – at all these people drinking, laughing at stupid stories and talking about nothing at all. I didn't know if they were lost or I was.

I leaned over the railings on the deck to look at the deep black sea churning beneath. Wind whipped hair across my face. The cold was not so much bracing as murderous. I staggered back inside as the ferry rose and fell, rose and fell. I stumbled down the steps to the toilet but the smell of vomit was so strong, I walked straight out before I was sick too. The corridors were filled with people stretched out under blankets and sleeping bags. Bodies were curled up in doorways, on tables, on windowsills. I found a spot on the floor, closed my eyes and tried to sleep. The motion of the sea soon did its job, sending me to sleep until a tannoy announced we were in Dublin Port.

I'd followed Helen's advice and decided to go to Ireland. Money was an ever-present worry so I went by ferry (just £45 return) but I cancelled out any savings by checking into a cheap guest house. I figured I just needed a couple of days on my own before I saw Gemma. A couple of days on my own, without self-help, would get me back to 'normal'. It didn't.

For three days I lay on the synthetic yellow bedspread, feeling like I was falling, falling, falling.

I lay staring at the ceiling as the voice in my head told me for hours on end about what a mess I'd made of everything . . . I was failing at self-help. I was failing at everything. People hated me. Everybody hated me.

The only relief was the tinny sounds of the television, which I kept on low all the time. *The Big Bang Theory*. *Friends*. *Frasier*. The canned laughter sometimes felt comforting and sometimes felt like a menace. Were they laughing at me? At one point at 4am, when I couldn't sleep and was holding on to sanity by watching infomercials for an abs cruncher, I had the thought: This is what it's like to go mad . . . This is actually what it's like.

Gemma had been texting every day and each day I said I'd call her the next day but I hadn't picked up the phone. Then she arrived with baby James in the pram. She looked so beautiful, her hair shining in the winter sun. I felt ashamed that she could get herself dressed and out of the house on a few hours of broken sleep, while I was an unwashed mess.

'Come on, get dressed. We're going out.'

'I don't want to.'

'You have to. You need to get air.'

And so we walked slowly along the canal, through Baggot Street and up to Portobello. Then I went back to the guest house. I had said next to nothing. I had actually lost the power of speech. A couple of times I'd opened my mouth but no words would come out. So she kept talking and her words became a life raft. I clung on to her conversation and its connection to the normal, healthy, balanced world, as if my sanity depended on it.

The next day she came again and we walked some more. The same happened the next day. And then I started talking, slowly.

I told her about the voice in my head, the nightmares and the morning dread.

'Some days I feel like my brain is on fire, like it's burning. All I can think about all day is what a mess I've made of everything.'

I expected her to tell me that everybody feels like that sometimes and that I just needed a bit of time out.

She didn't.

'How long have you been like this?'

'I don't know – a while.'

I could see that these feelings had started creeping in again in late August, during all the money stuff. The middle-of-the-night panics ramped up and so did the constant television watching – I couldn't handle being alone with my head. The self-loathing.

Then in September, with angels, there was a kind of

manic attempt to keep the show on the road but the anger
was building in me – anger at stupid angels and their stupid
make-believe wings, anger at Geoff and his stupid American
girlfriend, anger at life – and anger at me . . . and then I got
sick and stopped answering the phone.

'Why didn't you say anything sooner?' she asked. 'I knew
you weren't right but you kept saying you were fine.'

'I didn't want to bother you. You have a baby to look
after, you shouldn't have to listen to me.'

'I always want to listen to you,' said Gemma. 'I worry
about you.'

'I didn't realize how bad I was getting.'

'You've been here before.'

'I know.'

I have always been prone to getting down. It starts so grad-
ually I don't notice it. I start waking up in the middle of the
night with a feeling of non-specific panic and waking up in
the morning with a feeling of dread and anxiety. Bit by bit
this grows until it feels like the day – and the world – con-
tains nothing but cliffs for me to fall off.

I get tired. I retreat. I don't want to go out. I plug myself
with more and more caffeine in order to get my work done,
but eventually my brain slows down so much that getting
from the start of a sentence to the end feels like a marathon.
I get sick. I feel like I have a cold I can't shake. I start to
become obsessed with sleep. I feel that if I could just sleep
some more, I'd be OK. If could just eat more broccoli, I'd
be OK.

But it doesn't matter how much I sleep or how much
broccoli I eat, I don't feel better.

At first I'm like a piano with all the top notes removed
– nothing gives me joy, nothing makes me laugh.

Then even the low notes are removed. I am nothing but
an empty box.

'I hate that I get like this. Other people cope with really
bad situations and they don't get like this. People live in war
zones and lose their parents or have cancer . . . they have a
right to be depressed, I don't have a right to be depressed. I
just need to pull myself out of it. Helen thinks I should go
back on the meds,' I said to Gemma.

'What do you think?'

'I don't know.'

I'd been on antidepressants twice before – in my late
twenties and early thirties. The first time the doctor suggested them I was horrified.

It was during my twenties, when I was working around
the clock in my high-flying job with chronic tonsillitis.
Every time I went to see him to get more antibiotics I would
cry and he would pass me the Kleenex from the pink flow-
ered box on his cluttered desk. He kept telling me I was
depressed. I kept saying, no thank you very much, I am not
depressed.

I thought it was normal to feel like the bottom of your
world was falling out every day – I thought that was just
how people felt. You just had to try harder, keep going, hope
that one day it would get better. Also, being diagnosed as
depressed was code for being a failure. For not being able to
nail this life business.

Then he asked me a series of questions.

'How often can you relate to the following – not at all,
sometimes, nearly every day,' he read out loud. 'Little interest or pleasure in doing things.'

'Nearly every day.'

'Feeling down or hopeless.'

'Nearly every day.'

'Trouble falling or staying asleep, or too much sleeping.'

'Nearly every day.'

'Feeling bad about yourself, or that you are a failure or have let yourself or your family down . . .'

'Nearly every day.'

Then the big one. 'Do you sometimes think you would be better off dead or of hurting yourself in some way?'

The doctor looked up at me. His hooded eyes showed a mixture of boredom and deep compassion. White hairs sprouted out of his nose and his pores were the size of craters.

'I sometimes think that the only way to stop feeling like this would be to be dead,' I said. I was shocked by my own words.

I was not suicidal. I had no plans to kill myself, no active desire to be dead at all, it was just that it seemed to me that the only way to stop the groundhog day of misery was . . . well . . . to not be alive.

The words hung in the airless, magnolia-painted room and for a second I was carried away with the magnitude of my own misery.

I looked at the doctor, tears streaming down my cheeks, waiting for sympathy and concern. Instead I got a response that punctured my melodrama perfectly.

'Oh, I wouldn't worry about that,' he replied. 'I would say that that was a perfectly normal response to life.' He handed me a prescription for Seroxat.

Within four weeks I noticed a difference. I remember sitting at my desk at home and looking out of the window at a tree. And it looked beautiful. It was the first time in months I'd found anything pretty. An unfamiliar feeling of lightness settled around me and I tried to put my finger on what it was – then it hit me: Oh look, you're happy! This is what it's like to feel happy!

It had been so long.

I stayed on the medication for a year and the difference was night and day.

Then I decided I didn't need it. I didn't want to have to medicate myself just to get through life, and I was OK for a few years, until I had another dip in my early thirties. I went back on the meds and then stopped again.

I wanted to be able to figure life out on my own. I felt sure I could handle it myself, if I could just drink less. Do more exercise. Think more positively. But I'd been trying to do that, and look where it had got me.

'I'll give it till January. If I'm still bad then I'll go to the doctor,' I said to Gemma, who was the only friend who knew that I'd gone on antidepressants.

'OK, until then let's try to have fun – no books.'

'But I am already behind – I said I'd do twelve books in twelve months, and I've only done nine.'

'Who cares?'

'I do! I have to finish. I'll feel even more of a failure if I don't get to the end.'

'In what land are you a failure? In the newsagent's today you had articles in two magazines and one newspaper. In what planet does that make you a failure?'

She was right. If someone had told me a few years ago that I would be in three publications in one day, I'd have jumped up and down with joy. Now it felt like a reflection of what an embarrassment I'd become.

'Yeah, but they were shit articles and one of them was about how I can't find a boyfriend.'

'But it's not even about work – you're a good person. I love you. Everyone loves you. I wish you could see that. Why are you even doing any of this? You are driving yourself crazy and for what? You don't need to improve yourself. You are a good person the way you are. When are you going to realize that?' she said.

'I don't feel like a good person,' I said, and my voice cracked. Tears poured down my face.

'Marianne, these things you are saying to yourself about being a failure and a bad person, they are not true – you have to know that. I just want you to get to the end of all this and realize that you were fine to begin with. You don't need to be anything more than what you are right now.'

I kept crying. I wished I felt like that.

'I'm worried about you,' she said. 'Our brains are like elastic bands – you can pull them a lot and they'll ping back into shape, but if you stretch too much, one day something's going to snap. I don't want you to snap.'

'Me neither.'

I stayed in Ireland for three weeks. When I wasn't sleeping, Gemma, James and I would go for blustery walks, followed by television by the fire.

As each day passed, I felt a bit better.

On 20th December, I got the ferry back to Wales and took a train to Euston. It was gone 8pm on a Friday night and my bag felt heavy.

I could either wait for the 91 bus or get a cab. I got in line for a taxi. An American couple were in front of me, with wheelie bags the size of coffins. They looked nervous. They got in their cab. I waited. A people-carrier pulled up. I hated people-carriers.

'Where to?' asked the small, bald driver.

'Archway, please,' I replied, looking out of the window at the lights and the crowds of people. Groups of office workers in Christmas sweaters, girls in high heels and goose-bumped legs. This was usually my favourite time of year. Strings of lights, whiskey and 'Fairytale of New York'. Now I felt nothing.

'It's a busy night,' said the driver.

'Yeah,' I replied.

'Are you off out later, then?' he asked.

'No.'

'I'll keep going till about 3,' he said.

I felt rude to be so monosyllabic when he was in the mood to chat. 'Nights must be hard,' I said.

'Not really. No traffic, people are less stressed and you can earn more. I only need to do three nights a week to keep me going.'

'That's good,' I said.

'Not a fan of work, me.' He laughed. 'A lazy bugger.'

'Me too,' I replied. He looked at me in the rear-view mirror and smiled.

'I thought you looked relaxed,' he said.

'Really? I don't feel relaxed, I feel like I'm going crazy,' I said, and as soon as it came out of my mouth I wondered why I'd confessed that to a total stranger.

He kept staring at me in the mirror. 'Why's that then?' he asked.

'Oh, it's a long story,' I replied.

'What do you do for a living, if you don't mind me asking?'

'I'm a journalist – or I used to be. I'm not getting much work done these days.'

'Why's that then?' His eyes were staring at me.

I felt embarrassed. What would a sixty-something cabbie think of the craziness induced by a year of manic self-improvement.

He kept looking at me.

'Have you heard of self-help books? Those books that tell you how to be more confident, stop worrying and over-come your fears?'

'Yes,' he replied.

'Well, I've been reading a different book each month and doing everything it tells me to do to see if they make you happy.'

His eyes darted between the road and the mirror. I awaited a blank, non-comprehending silence.

'So you've been digging deep, then,' he said.

I was stunned. 'Yes, I have.'

'It's like the layers of an onion . . . you're peeling off each layer . . .' he continued.

'Yes, exactly,' I replied. Staggered.

'It's not easy, is it?'

'No. I feel like I'm falling apart,' and as I said it I could feel the familiar heat of tears running down my face. Jesus Christ, could I not get through a single day without crying in public?

'What does that feel like, when you're falling apart?' he asked, seemingly unbothered by the tears.

The darkness of the cab felt like a confessional as we drove down the Caledonian Road.

'I can't do anything that I used to do,' I blurted. 'I can't seem to get work done and I used to work all the time. I don't want to go out like I used to. I have lost touch with my friends. I think the world hates me and that I am a bad person. I'm having nightmares, dreaming that I'm killing my parents. I am crying all the time.'

There was a pause as he took on board what I'd said.

'Well, it's big stuff you're doing. Big brain stuff –' he said.

'It's just bloody self-help books! I didn't know that this was what was going to happen.'

'You'd never have started it if you'd known,' he said. 'What you're doing is kamikaze, love. You've been poking around in your head and that's dangerous stuff. And I can say that because I've been there.'

'You've lived your life by self-help books?'

He chuckled. 'Worse than that; I did a PhD on Thomas Hardy. Miserable bloke. So I gave it up and moved to a cottage in Italy. Middle of nowhere. No running water or electricity. I stayed there for nine months and all I did was walk for seven, eight, nine hours every day. I'd just walk and think. I'd think about everything. I stopped eating. I had euphoric highs and crashing lows . . . Sometimes it felt like heaven but then sometimes it was hell. I had to come back or I'd have lost my marbles . . . I was touching the void.' He paused. 'That's what you're doing right now, you're touching the void – and you've got to step back because you won't be any good to anyone if you go under.'

That's exactly what it had felt like over the last few weeks – I'd been touching the void.

He kept talking. 'I was around in the Sixties when all the hippies used to say: "Just let go, man . . ." but if any of them really knew what it felt like to let go they'd know it feels bloody awful. Letting go is terrifying.'

Tears continued to stream down my cheeks.

'It really is,' I said.

Letting go of the old me: the me addicted to work, to people liking her, to fitting in . . . didn't feel good, it felt more horrible than I could explain. I'd started the year thinking that I wanted to change, but changing was terrifying. If I wasn't the old me, then who was I? How did I know that I was going to come back together again? What if I was just going to stay a broken mess like this forever?

'I feel like I'm having a breakdown,' I said. 'Like I'm losing my mind.'

'Well, you are in a way,' he said. 'But that's OK. I think it was Gide that wrote: "To discover new lands you must first lose sight of the shore." That's where you are now. You've lost sight of the shore but it's OK. You just need to float a bit now. Take a rest. Look after yourself, do some normal things. And if you want to cry, cry. I used to cry all the time; I'd wear dark glasses so that people in the cab wouldn't see. Sit in the park and cry . . .'

'OK.'

'Have you thought about speaking to anyone? A therapist?'

'No,' I said.

'You might want to. They'll just make it about your family – they always do – but remember this isn't about them, this is about you: This is your bid for freedom.'

I got a shiver. Ever since angel month, I'd been wondering why the hell I was doing any of this. When I'd started, I'd just wanted to make my life a bit better – the way you feel better when you lose half a stone or get fit, or when you meet someone you like. But he was right. Without realizing it, I was looking for freedom: freedom from the feeling that there was something wrong with me, freedom from the never-ending feeling that nothing I did was ever good enough, freedom from being constantly scared of every-thing and everyone . . . freedom to just be me. Or just be.

A man wearing a Santa hat knocked on the window. The noise frightened me. I realized that we'd stopped driving. We were outside Rachel's. I had no idea how long we'd been there.

'Better get back to it.' He smiled.

'Of course, sorry to keep you.'

'Don't be daft.'

He got out of the cab and opened my door. He went to the boot and pulled out my bag. We stood on the pavement for a second, looking at each other.

'I'll see you again,' he said.

I nodded and he got back into the taxi and picked up the gang of twenty-somethings who were screaming 'IT'S CHHHRRRRISTMASS!'

I hadn't even got his name. He didn't know mine. This man who had seen into my soul.

I walked up the steps to my front door. It was so cold I could see my breath come out in clouds. Christmas tree lights sparkled through the neighbour's window.

Had that really just happened? That conversation?

Before I could turn the key, the door opened and Rachel was standing in the hall, grinning.

'Were you snogging the taxi driver? You've been parked outside for more than an hour!'

14

The Power of Now,
by Eckhart Tolle

*'Many people live with a tormentor in their head
that continuously attacks and punishes them and
drains them of vital energy. It is the cause of untold
misery and unhappiness as well as disease.'*

Christmas passed uneventfully. I ate, drank, slept and
watched a lot of television. Rachel got me a book featuring
pictures of the Nativity as acted out by dressed-up guinea
pigs. It made me laugh. The fact that I was laughing again
was a good sign. Our family managed to get through it
without killing each other and two weeks of *National Lampoon's Vacation* and purple Quality Streets were a soothing
balm on my brain. Normal life.

On New Year's Eve, I left Mum's and headed to Rachel's.
She'd gone to Scotland to see friends so I stayed in on my
own, which was fine with me.

I'd always hated New Year: the pressure to have the best
night ever just because it's 31st December. Instead of going
out, I ate spaghetti bolognese and watched fireworks out of
the window. Daisy was in Kerala on a yoga retreat. Sheila

was in Mexico and Helen was at a house party. Gemma was with her family. I wondered what Sarah was doing.

I fell asleep on the sofa and woke up when Jools Holland and his gang were singing 'Auld Lang Syne'.

Thursday 1st January. The start of a new year.

By now I was supposed to have gone through twelve self-help books. There should have been highs and lows, tears and revelations, romance and rejection, all coming together to form some sort of profoundly moving (but neat and tidy) epiphany.

The new and improved me would have felt shinier and more enlightened. Oh, and skinnier and richer, obviously. Ideally with a cashmere-sweater-wearing hottie in the wings. I mean, let's face it – isn't that what self-improvement usually comes down to? Money, sex and looks. But I had not become the Perfect Me I'd set out to be. Instead, I had ended the year more of a basket case than ever.

At 12.30am my phone beeped. It was The Greek. *'Happy New Year!* ☺*'*

I messaged him straight back. *'You too!'*

He replied: *'I'm sorry I have been quiet. My father has been in hospital. I think of you often.* ☺*'*

I thought of him in Athens, caring for sick, elderly parents while the Greek economy was also going down the pan. He had real problems.

Dots appeared on the screen. He was still typing.

'Have you finished your challenge?'

'I don't know!' I replied.

'Want to talk?' he messaged.

He Skyped and in the small hours of 1st January I told him everything that had happened since I'd met him that day in the coffee shop.

'I don't know whether to keep going with the whole thing or just leave it. I don't think it's been very good for me – it's been extreme,' I said.

'Maybe it needs to be extreme for it to change you. When you read the books before, your life did not change, did it?'

'No.'

'Now it has changed.'

'Yeah, but it doesn't feel like good change.'

'Maybe you had to be broken down in order to be built into something new,' he said.

'But when does the something new come? Right now I'm just broken.'

'You sound OK to me.'

'Sorry, I am. I am being dramatic. I feel much better. I rested a lot the last month. How are you?'

He talked about his father's illness and the stress his mother was under. He was sleeping just a few hours a night, in between caring for them both. I didn't know how he was doing it.

'I am their son. They did everything for me and now it's my turn,' he said with no hint of resentment or self-pity.

'What I'm doing must seem so self-indulgent compared to your life,' I said.

'I think what you're doing is great. But remember that you already have a good life and you should enjoy it.'

The next morning, I woke up at 7am on the sofa. Helen had texted at 4am, '*HAPPY NEW YEAR!!!*' And Sheila had sent a photo of a cocktail and a sunset.

I got up and looked out of the window at grey skies. The street was deserted. Everyone sleeping it off. I put the kettle on and made a coffee. So. Another year. What next? Quit the self-help or keep going? The consensus seemed to be that I needed to stop. Any rational person would say that I needed to stop.

But I didn't want to. I didn't know why but I didn't. I wanted to see this through – I felt sure something good would come of it if I did. But I needed help.

I followed the taxi driver's advice and went to see a therapist. It started off pretty promisingly.

'I'm not surprised you've come unstuck,' she said. 'You've been conducting experiments on yourself. You have been your own guinea pig and you've had no supervision.'

'I'd never thought of it like that,' I replied.

'Do you know what your unconscious is?' she asked, leaning forward on her beige leather La-Z-Boy.

'Not really.'

'The unconscious mind is a reservoir of feelings, thoughts and memories that live below our conscious awareness. What you've been doing for the last year is poking at your unconscious, bringing up things you didn't even know were there. And now they're coming to the surface, which is why you're crying and getting angry and having nightmares.'

Then it was exactly as the taxi driver had predicted.

'So in the dreams,' she said, 'it's your job to save your family?'

'Yes.'

'And you're not doing it?'

'Yes, I mean no – I'm not able to save them.'

'And do you often think it's your job to save everyone?'

'No. I don't know. I don't think so.'

'Is that a role you take in your family?'

'Are you going to make this all about my family?' I asked. She smiled. 'Let's see.'

'Do you think I'm having a breakdown?' I asked, trying to change the subject.

'You are having a time when you question everything. It can happen when there's a big change in life and the old rules you used to live by no longer make any sense.'

'That's how I feel now.'

'And what were you hoping to get out of all this when you started?'

'I wanted to be happy.'

'And what does happy mean?'

'I don't know – just happy.'

'None of us can be happy all the time – but what we can be is content. To have some level of peace.'

'OK, I'd like that then.'

'So why hasn't that happened, do you think? You've read all these books, absorbed all this wisdom. Why do you think they haven't helped you?'

'I don't know. Do you think self-help works?'

'I think the problem with self-help books is that you are reading them with the same mind that has made you unhappy. You need an outside perspective to challenge you and show you a different view,' she said.

That made sense actually.

'So do you think I should stop doing the books?' I asked.

'Do *you* think you should stop following them?'

Bloody hell – did therapists really do this? The whole turning the question back on you stuff? I thought that was just a joke.

'No. I want to finish what I set out to do but I worry that

this whole thing is just self-indulgent. Why can't I just get on with life like everyone else?'

'I don't think that what you're doing is self-indulgent. You're on a journey of self-discovery and that is worthwhile, in my opinion. It's an investment. An investment in yourself – but you shouldn't do it on your own.'

Well, you would say that, I thought, and then our time was up. She asked me if I wanted to see her again. I said I'd get back to her. On my way out she asked: 'Have you read a book called *The Power of Now?*'

'No, I have it at home but I couldn't get past the first couple of pages.'

'You might like it now.'

And so it was, in January, I found The Book; the book that told me that the best of times will come from the worst.

When I first tried to read *The Power of Now* by Eckhart Tolle, a couple of years before, I'd thought it was impenetrable New Age gibberish. I couldn't understand how it had become a number-one bestseller, loved by everyone from Oprah (of course) to Paris Hilton, who took it to jail with her when she was arrested for drink-driving. In fact, I couldn't understand it, full stop.

Despite being determined to prove that I had a greater – or at least an equal – reading ability to Miss Hilton, I gave up at around page twenty.

Sentences such as 'It is a misperception of your essential reality that is beyond birth and death, and is due to the limitations of your mind, which, having lost touch with Being, creates the body as evidence of its illusory belief in separation and to justify its state of fear' were too much for me.

Then there was talk of things called 'pain bodies', which are 'semi-autonomous psychic entities'. Excuse me, what?

This time, however, it was different. This time every weirdly worded sentence read like the truth. Actually, I might capitalize that, just for effect: 'The Truth'.

For the next three days I read it constantly.

Not since A-level English class when Mrs Batch introduced us to a colour-coded note system to deconstruct *Wuthering Heights*, had I made so many scribbles in a book. Every other page had an ecstatic 'YES!!!' in the margin, whole chunks of text were underlined with stars and exclamation marks by the best bits. I could see why Oprah described Eckhart Tolle as a prophet for our times and I began to suspect that there was more to Paris Hilton than met the eye.

German-born author Eckhart Tolle was a twenty-nine-year-old graduate student living in a bedsit in North London when he had his 'spiritual awakening' in 1979. On the night it happened, he was planning to kill himself. After years of constant depression and anxiety, he'd had enough. 'I cannot live with myself any longer,' he thought.

But in that moment Tolle had an epiphany: 'If I cannot live with myself, there must be two of me: the "I" and the "self" that "I" cannot live with.' He then concluded that only one of these selves was real and, as soon as he realized this, all his negative thoughts stopped.

The next day he woke up and everything was different – he was in a state of 'uninterrupted deep peace and bliss'.

That morning, he writes, 'I walked around the city in utter amazement at the miracle of life on earth, as if I had just been born.'

Tolle had transcended thoughts – the voice in his head.

Tolle explains that most of us spend our lives with a constant 'voice in our heads', the inner critic who judges and interprets reality, and determines our mood. He explains that when we see people talking to themselves on the street, we assume they are mad – but that's what's going on in all of our heads all the time, we just don't say it out loud.

We all have a voice that 'comments, speculates, judges, compares, complains, likes, dislikes and so on,' says Tolle.

Quite often the voice isn't even focusing on what's happening now, it's rehashing some old situation or worrying about an imagined one in the future.

'It is not uncommon for the voice to be a person's own worst enemy. Many people live with a tormentor in their head that continuously attacks and punishes them and drains them of vital energy. It is the cause of untold misery and unhappiness as well as disease,' writes Tolle. When I read that, I sat bolt upright in my bed.

This small German man was reporting from the inside of my head.

Tolle explains that this voice stops us from ever enjoying the only thing that's real: the Now. Only by living in the Now can we find peace and joy.

Reading every page felt like a religious experience.

This was it! *The* book.

If I could figure out how to shut up the vicious voice in my head, then everything would be better. But how?

*

The first step is to be aware of what the voice in our head says. Tolle tells us not to judge the thoughts or get annoyed with yourself for having them, nor should you get carried away with them – just step back and observe them.

He says that the more we observe our thoughts – rather than get caught up in them – the more they will lose their power. They'll still pop up occasionally but they won't take hold like they used to. You'll be able to dismiss them the way you would a dottering old uncle.

And so I did what I was told. I started to observe my thoughts; to listen to the records playing in my head. It made for grim listening.

First there was the 'fat record'. This started from the second I opened my eyes and felt the weight of my chunky thighs as I swung them out of bed. That record went something like this: *You're disgusting. Why do you eat so much? You have no discipline, you ate too much yesterday.* This would then lead to a mental inventory of all I had eaten yesterday and a vow not to eat carbs today.

Then as I went down for breakfast, I'd start the lazy record: *Why didn't you get up sooner? Why did you turn off your alarm? Why did you drink so much last night? You've got so much to do today, you didn't get anything done yesterday. Why are you so shit?* Then I'd go through in my head all my productive friends and how much more sorted they were than me . . .

Then, as I tried to do some work, this record would play: *This is shit – why is your brain so foggy? Pull yourself together, drink more coffee, this is waffle. Why are you making such a mess out of an article about tights? For God's sake, any moron could do this. Other writers could have done this in half the time, they'd have written three pieces by now and, look, you're still halfway through this crap one . . .*

Then as day turned to night and I'd try to drown out the voice with booze, I'd turn on the 'I drink too much' record: *Why are you drinking? You said you wouldn't drink today. You have no discipline, you'll feel crap tomorrow . . .*

And if I was with friends: *People think you're boring. Shut up, nobody is interested in you, just listen and be nice, people think you're stupid and self-obsessed.*

Or men: *No guys ever fancy you, you have dodgy teeth and a fat arse, and you're ginger. He thinks that you fancy him and he's thinking, no way,* etc., etc.

Then, of course, there was the 'money record', which could be put on at any point of the day and night – actually usually this one came on when I was trying to fall asleep: *You're a fucking idiot, you've messed everything up, you're a disgusting spoilt human being. People your age have pensions and a house. What do you have? You don't even have savings. You'll never afford your own place . . .*

So, there you go: the torturous soundtrack to my day. It was so normal to me I hadn't even realized it was there.

This was the reason I got sick all the time. I was poisoning my body with my thoughts. I thought that I was using this tough line to spur myself on, but it had the opposite effect. My bullying voice took the joy out of everything and drained me of energy. It also paralysed me – I was too busy drowning in past mistakes and imagined future disasters to actually get on with the task at hand. I was too busy hating myself to appreciate the nice life that I had playing out around me. I was in a mental prison of my own making.

*

Tolle says that we don't need to sit cross-legged on the floor in order to be in the Now. He says that taking time during the day to look out of the window for a minute or two is enough to bring us back to the moment. Going for a walk and looking at the sky, trees and birds also helps. As does becoming absorbed in the physical sensations of whatever you are doing – from washing the dishes to walking up stairs. As a general rule, he says, we cannot be in our bodies and in our heads at the same time. So, when your thoughts are racing, he advises that you feel the energy of your body. He suggests you close your eyes and feel the energy in your hands, your feet, your abdomen, your chest. It will calm you down instantly.

And this is what I did. I kept looking out of the window, taking deep breaths and feeling my extremities while writing an article about a new diet. The ice diet. Yup, you eat ice and it helps you lose weight. On account of the fact there's no calories in ice. I could not make this stuff up.

After a week of breathing, talking to trees, feeling my feet, the volume of my negative thoughts had not really gone down. In fact, I discovered something interesting: I was quite attached to them.

I realized this while eating pasta at Helen's. The flat was warm and cosy and the food delicious. It should have been an easy evening. But in my head I was really going to town with this cheerful self-talk: *You shouldn't be drinking, you're a lazy waste of space. But don't say that, Helen will think it's stupid . . . and why are you eating more pasta? Your jeans are already hurting you. And you shouldn't be eating carbs. Every meal you've eaten today is carbs.*

I did the 'be here now' stuff – took deep breaths and felt

my feet – but I kept playing the old records. The truth was that I was getting a perverse pleasure out of my 'poor me' doom-and-gloom narrative.

'The mind, conditioned as it is by the past, always seeks to re-create what it knows and is familiar with. Even if it is painful, at least it is familiar,' says Tolle. 'Observe the peculiar pleasure you get from being unhappy.'

My God, he's right. I *did* get a thrill out of being unhappy. But why?

Tolle says it's down to our 'ego' – which he defines as the false identity we create for ourselves based on our thoughts and the stories we tell ourselves. We all think that someone with a big ego is someone who thinks they are better than other people, but actually it can be the other way around too.

'Every ego wants to be special,' Tolle once explained to Oprah. 'If it can't be special by being superior to others, it's also quite happy with being especially miserable. Someone will say, "I have a headache," and another says, "I've had a headache for weeks." People actually compete to see who is more miserable! The ego doing that is just as big as the one that thinks it's superior to someone else.'

He adds that many of us build our identities around our problems and so we are loath to give them up because it would feel like losing who we are.

Tony Robbins had said exactly the same thing – that our biggest addiction is to our problems. He also said that as much as we may think we don't want problems, we do really because they are fulfilling a need in us. It was only now that I understood how true that was.

And so as I listened to a pretty girl singing a Coldplay song on *The Voice*, I had a minor epiphany.

I LOVED MY PROBLEMS. I MEAN, I REALLY REALLY LOVED MY PROBLEMS. EVEN THOUGH ACTUALLY, TECHNICALLY SPEAKING, I DIDN'T REALLY HAVE ANY PROBLEMS AT ALL, APART FROM THOSE MADE UP IN MY HEAD.

Tolle says that at any moment, if we are worrying, we should ask ourselves, 'Is there a problem right now?' and ninety-nine per cent of the time there isn't.

But I kept inventing some. I would rather stay in my negative thoughts, no matter how unhappy they made me, because they were who I thought I was. They were the story I'd been telling myself for as long as I could remember.

Tolle says that stepping away from your ego (your stories) literally feels like death, so your ego (in the form of your crazy, manic thoughts) will do all it can to keep you in the same old loop. 'Once you have identified with some form of negativity, you do not want to let it go, and on a deeply unconscious level, you do not want positive change. It would threaten your identity as a depressed, angry and hard-done-by person. You will then deny or sabotage the positive in your life,' writes Tolle.

And, as if my negative thoughts weren't bad enough, we all have an attachment to our negative feelings too. Enter the mysterious 'pain body' which, according to Tolle, is old pain that we carry around with us. From the day you wet your pants at school and felt ashamed, to the pain of your first heartbreak and that anger with your father . . . all that emotion, if not felt, expressed and let go of at the time, stays with you and informs how you respond to day-to-day life, even fifty years after the event.

We unconsciously look for situations that confirm that our 'pain body' is right. So, for example, insecure people will find constant affirmations that nobody likes them and will even seek relationships with people who are not interested in them, just to confirm the feelings of their pain body.

That was it. I was always looking for situations to find hard. Things to struggle with. I was always looking for people to reject me – even though, as I found out in Rejection Therapy month, most of the time it was me doing the rejecting.

'You would rather be in pain,' Tolle writes, 'than take a leap into the unknown and risk losing the familiar unhappy self.'

Exactly! I always put myself back into the role of the poor fat ginger girl that nobody would ask to dance at school. Because then I could feel sorry for myself and play the victim, instead of getting out there, getting my hands dirty and taking the punches like everyone else.

While trawling his website for more Eckhart content – I could not get enough – I found an even pithier summary: 'The pain body is this: an addiction to unhappiness.'

This was me! I was addicted to my unhappiness.

I loved being miserable! I got a kick out of being unhappy! Out of the poor-me stuff!

On the night bus home, I struggled to understand this new reality. All the stuff in my head was just total made-up nonsense. It wasn't real at all.

I woke up still stunned by this realization. Who would I be if I lost all my stories about being fat and ugly, and bad with money, and always getting sick? Those stories were my identity. Would I still be me? Or would I be . . . well, nothing?

The idea of losing my problems didn't feel good – it actually felt terrifying. Like taking a step off a cliff.

As I did my daily walk around the park, pondering these deep existential questions, it dawned on me that maybe this is why self-help books often don't help in the long term. We think we want to change but we don't really. We keep going back to our old ways, our old selves, our old stories because it's too scary not to.

Because to *really* change means to lose ourselves completely.

This is where my head started to spin out. At the end of the third week of January, I found myself wandering through Hyde Park, trying to make sense of something that made no sense to me.

If we are not our thoughts and not our feelings – what exactly are we?

According to Tolle, our ego wants us to feel separate from the people around us, while the truth is that we are all part of the same consciousness, the same life force. We are One with the flowers and the trees, One with the animals and with each other – we are One with all of life. We are all the same mass of energy or consciousness that has just taken on different forms. He describes it as being like a wave thinking that it is separate from the sea. It's not. It's part of the ocean and it temporarily takes on its own form but will always go back to the ocean. This is what life and death are like for us, he says. Our bodies will come and go but our 'Being' will always be there and we are all part of the same 'Being'.

He writes: 'underneath the level of physical appearances and separate form, you are one with all that is.'

I read and re-read these sentences, trying to nail them

down, but they were slippery. Was Being another word for God? Was that right? Was there a God? Was there a divine force? Is that what he was saying? I didn't get it. And of course we are separate. I am me and you are you and . . . Oh, my head hurt . . .

I looked up to find that I'd walked through Hyde Park and up Edgware Road and was now on Baker Street. It was after work and the pavement was full of smartly dressed office workers dashing for the Tube.

I went into a Costa and ordered a hot chocolate. A woman next to me was picking at a blueberry muffin while a young couple were smiling and flirting with each other. They were on a sober date – an idea almost as baffling as consciousness.

I opened my laptop and found myself typing 'Is there a God?' into Google. For two hours I flicked through sites I did not understand on New Age stuff about Consciousness and Energy and Connection . . . I didn't get it but I wanted to get it.

I had never thought about the big things before; I was always too busy obsessing over my petty neuroses to do that. I'd spent my life locked in this stupid tiny prison of my thoughts and I was missing the experience of being alive!

As I walked down the Marylebone Road, cars stuck in Friday night traffic, my head was spinning. Why were we all here? If we're all connected – why aren't we nicer to each other? Why can't life be a kind of heaven?

I called Mum. She was a teacher, she knew things.

'*The Power of Now* says that we are more than our thoughts and feelings – but if that's true, then what exactly *are* we?' I asked her. 'I mean, are we just Energy? or Love? or Consciousness? Do you think there is a God? Not like a

Catholic Mean God but a kind of higher power that con-
nects us all?'

After a long pause, Mum's response to the major philosophical question underpinning all our existence was
succinct. 'I don't know, Marianne, but I have to go. *Graham
Norton* is about to begin.'

Even though I didn't fully understand what Tolle was
saying, his words had done something to me. By the end of
January, I felt a kind of calm that was entirely new to me.

At night, instead of lying awake for hours worrying
about everything and nothing I would go through each part
of my body, feeling the energy in my feet, my legs, my hips
. . . and I'd usually fall asleep somewhere around my shoulders.

Days still started with a jog of anxiety but I'd talk myself
around with the words 'Be here now, be here now . . .'

I'd go downstairs and mindfully make my coffee and
actually taste my toast instead of wolfing it down. Then I'd
go for a quick march in the park nearby. My usual approach
was to listen to some crappy Euro dance track while I
squeezed my bum and walked as fast as I could up the hill,
trying to kickstart some sort of motivation for the day. But
on Friday 30th January I took a different approach.

As I did my morning walk around Hampstead Heath,
my thoughts ran through to what I had to do that day:
another article on hair frizz to finish and a piece on mindfulness to write for an Irish newspaper. Usually this would
have sent me off in a tailspin of adrenalin, I'd walk faster
and faster and berate myself for not waking up sooner. I

would, ridiculously, have got stressed writing about how to de-stress with mindfulness.

That day, I did not feel overwhelmed by my to-do list.

Instead I felt peaceful. I tried something radical: I took out my earphones and walked in silence.

I slowed down my pace and listened to the gentle thump of my feet on the ground and the swooshing sound of my jacket sleeves rubbing against my side. I became aware of the cold air brushing against my cheeks. My senses were heightened by turning off the music.

I thought I could hear seagulls and I wondered if that was right – could I be hearing seagulls in London? There was a barking dog too and then the distant roar of an aeroplane.

I stopped still.

I looked at the bare brown trees dotted around the park. They were elegant, quiet and strong. I'd like to be those trees, I thought. I bet nothing bothers them.

I could feel my heart beating.

Two women marched past me in their Lycra. 'He didn't even send a text,' said one. 'That's disgraceful,' spat her friend. They marched on in indignation and low-level fury.

I thought about how silly we are, getting outraged over nothing.

A muddy blond Labrador ran past me with a stick in his mouth, panting with delight and shaking with excitement. Dogs are so happy, aren't they? They don't need anything but a field and a stick and they are bursting with joy. They don't get offended or slighted or worried about their precious egos. They just know that right now their paws are slapping around in a muddy field and there's a chewed-up tennis ball flying through the air and that's the best thing ever!

Why can't we be like that?

I came home feeling serene. I did all my work in five hours – with no drama at all.

At about 3pm, I stopped for a late lunch. The mid-afternoon light was coming through the windows and the quiet of the house had a gentle hum to it. There was a slight vibration from the tumble dryer finishing its cycle upstairs. I could almost sense the electricity and water pipes doing their thing.

I took a breath.

I looked at how pretty the food was on my plate and put a piece of broccoli in my mouth. It burst with life on my tongue. How had I not noticed how bursty-with-life broccoli was before? I mean, I'd always liked broccoli but this tasted like magic broccoli.

I looked out of the window again. There was a squirrel sitting on the grass in the garden. I thought of how they drive Rachel mad – always digging up things and chewing – but it looked almost regal sitting there with its luxurious tail. How could you be angry at that?

I took another breath.

I looked at the wood of the table and stared at the caramel grain. I looked at the deep orange tulips standing to attention in a vase. They looked so alive to me – like little people right there on the table. In that moment, I could see the aliveness of everything. The magic of everything.

Why on earth had I been making it so hard? All I needed was here. I felt a warm rush of love flood my body, a feeling so strong it was almost painful. It was so overwhelming that tears pricked my eyes.

I thought about my mum and felt such a love for her I could have burst. I thought of my sisters and friends . . . I thought about people I hadn't thought of for years, even people who had hurt me or annoyed me; I could see that they had all had their purpose. I thought of the people whom I had hurt and I hoped they felt the same way about me.

It suddenly seemed almost overwhelmingly perfect that we had blood coursing around our veins and a heart that beats and a sky that went all pink and purple and gold in the evening. We had people who loved us and plants and life and death and light that shone through windows.

I could hear the kids chatting next door and the sound of a plane in the sky . . . It might be going to New York where my sister lived . . . I was related to someone who lived in New York! How cool was that? People knew people everywhere and they got on planes to see them, travelling through the sky . . .

The pipes were making a throbbing sound and I felt sleepy and warm and ready for a nap. I walked into the living room and sat on the sofa and put a tartan rug on my lap. The sofa was squishy. I closed my eyes and felt myself going under . . . ah, snoozes, one of the best things in the world. And there are so many best things . . . coffee, smiles, hugs . . .

I woke up in darkness. The house was still empty. The bliss was still there, in my body, in my head, in the room . . . then for a second my thoughts kicked off again: *Why did you fall asleep? You have stuff to do . . . You're so lazy. Rachel doesn't sleep in the day . . .* But this time I laughed at how predictable all this was.

This is just your brain doing what it does, I told myself. This is just a record.

Then it stopped. And then I felt a bit lost.

Letting go of that voice felt strange – and scary.

It was 7.20. Rachel wasn't home yet. I sat in silence. Now what?

If living in the moment is the answer to happiness – did that mean that was me sorted, then? I didn't need any self-help or self-improvement?

Should I just go and find a park bench and settle in? Not worry about my debts, and let go of my ambitions and dreams?

Which brought me back to this whole project: Why was I doing it? What was I striving for?

Eckhart Tolle would say that I had everything I needed right then. I was alive, I was breathing. I was safe. And yet I still wanted more.

Was that wrong? Did that mean I was not in the Now?

Because even though part of me wanted a nice future, every time I thought about my aims and goals, they stressed me out. The wanting stressed me out. I would start to panic and tell myself to try harder, do more, make things happen. Wanting is the opposite of being in the Now.

Tolle describes stress as 'being "here" but wanting to be "there"'. He says that it's natural for all of us to plan things for the future but that we must never prioritize the future over today. You can set goals and work towards them but you must give the most attention to the step you are taking now, not the end destination.

If you don't do that, 'your life is no longer an adventure, just an obsessive need to arrive, to attain, to "make it". You no longer see or smell the flowers by the wayside, nor are you aware of the beauty or the miracle of life that unfolds around you.'

My life had been a never-ending attempt to 'make it' and 'arrive'. I'd thought I'd be OK when I got more successful, when I was slimmer, or when I got money. I'd thought I'd feel better if I had a boyfriend – or became more improved.

But none of it had worked because happiness lies not in striving but in sinking into each moment and taking it all in. Enjoying the work, not the result. Enjoying the sound of Rachel laughing. Enjoying the taste of hot buttered toast. The feeling of falling into a thick velvet sleep on the sofa on a Friday afternoon.

Being in the Now doesn't mean that you drop out and do nothing. You can take as much action as you like, as long as you do it with your feet firmly grounded in the Now. Tolle argues that actually our best work and inspiration come from a place of calm and peace, not striving and stressing. I thought of Italy and how easily I had grabbed the Werther's Original when I stopped trying. It was the same idea.

But few of us live life like this. We're all too busy running after the next thing, the next thing, the next thing. It's how society tells us we should be. It's insane.

'Humans are a dangerously insane and very sick species,' says Tolle. 'That's not a judgement, it's a fact.' He suggests picking up a history book and studying what's happened in the last century. World wars, genocides, destruction of forests and wildlife – this is not the behaviour of a healthy society, he argues. We are literally killing each other and destroying the planet we rely on for life. We are also killing ourselves.

Tolle was suicidal when he had his epiphany. He believes that it's only when we hit rock bottom that we realize there has to be a different way to live life.

Which was what the last few months had done for me.

I thought of Gemma's elastic band and how close I had come to snapping. It was no longer an option to keep living the way I had been: always beating myself up, pushing myself and punishing myself.

As Tolle writes: 'When you are trapped in a nightmare, you will probably be more strongly motivated to awaken than someone who is just caught in the ups and downs of an ordinary dream.'

I had woken up.

By the end of January, having spent a month washing dishes, gazing at trees, feeling my feet, there was nowhere else I'd rather be, nobody else I'd rather be.

On Saturday 31 January I was having coffee in Bread and Bean. That Depeche Mode song came on the radio . . . 'All I ever wanted,/All I ever needed/Is here in my arms' and I sang along quietly while looking out of the window. Snow was falling like a secret being whispered. The world looked soft. An overweight bald man wearing hot-pink trainers walked down the street. I had a warm feeling inside. A feeling of calm and joy so profound that, yet again, tears pricked my eyes and I saw that life was good, I was fine. These moments are precious but if we pay attention we realize they're happening all the time.

15

Get the Guy,
by Matthew Hussey

'You become so obsessed with meeting THE guy, you don't meet ANY guys.'

'All this smelling the roses stuff is fine but where's the action? Where's the shagging?' asked Rachel's friend Paul, who was three pints down and in fighting form. We were in the St John pub in Archway and the place was packed with people keen to celebrate the end of dry January. It was my first night out in weeks.

I'd been waxing lyrical about living in the moment and just accepting everything as it was. I felt I exuded a calm and serenity that all around me would sense (and envy), but so far nobody was picking up on the fact they were drinking with a redheaded Buddha.

'I thought you were going to do a dating book,' agreed Rachel.

'I was,' I replied, 'but I don't know whether to bother with more books. *The Power of Now* was kind of it for me. I wanted to be happy and now I'm happy, so job done.'

'But dating might be fun after all the soul searching,' said Rachel.

'I don't find dating fun,' I said. 'And anyway, all the books say that you don't need to find someone else to make you happy – you can only do that yourself. And I have.'

'Is the bloke who wrote *The Power of Now* single?'

'No, he's with someone.'

'What about F**k It John?'

'He's married.'

'So they must think that love is good. Don't you want to meet someone?' asked Rachel.

I never knew how to answer that question.

'Why don't you get the next round and flirt with the barman?' suggested Paul. 'When he gives you change, stroke his hand and look into his eyes.'

'Oh, for God's sake. I'm not going to do that.'

As I waited at the bar I got annoyed. After everything I'd done in the last year, all anyone wanted to know was when was I going to find a man.

Why did everything have to come down to that? Wasn't it enough to have found peace and contentment? To feel the bliss in broccoli and to have turned the voices in my head into a low hum rather than an all-out slanging match? To have maybe, possibly – don't tell anyone – had a 'spiritual awakening'?

'What can I get you?'

I looked up at the barman's big brown eyes and felt a hot jolt of excitement. Oh!

'Two red wines and a pint of IPA, please,' I said.

I felt myself go red and looked away.

And just like that I was back. Back in the real world. Back in the dating game – if, indeed, I had ever been in it.

———

Put the word 'dating' into Amazon and you get 13,111 results. Books with titles such as *Act Like a Lady, Think Like a Man*; *He's Just Not that Into You* and *Getting to I Do*. Each promised to unlock the secret to how to snag Mr Right and each made me cringe.

After an hour or two of looking, I ordered *Get the Guy*, a book by an English dating expert Matthew Hussey. It had lots of five-star reviews with readers saying it was down to earth and helpful, without being gimmicky or game play-er-y. Even Eva Longoria is said to be a fan, though I find it hard to believe that she has problems pulling on a Friday night.

According to the blurb on the back of his book, 'Matthew Hussey is the world's leading authority on attraction. He's studied over 10,000 men, and analysed over 5,000 dates, all to bring you the truth about how men really think and how you can attract the best of them.'

This tome promises to teach you: 'How and where to meet the best men; Eight words that instantly build attraction and chemistry with any guy; Bulletproof techniques to get the guy you like to notice you.'

Conveniently for me, one of the best places to meet men, according to Hussey, is coffee shops. 'You could ask him to move away so you could grab something off the shelf,' suggests Hussey, 'or you could ask if he would hold your umbrella while you fish out your purse or ask him where he stands on the flat white versus cappuccino debate . . .'

From the sublime to the ridiculous. One minute I'm wondering, 'Is there a God?' the next I was being taught how to flirt in the coffee queue . . . which got me thinking about The Greek. We'd been speaking every week since the

New Year and it felt wrong to go back into the dating world without telling him.

By chance I was near Soho for work, so I called him from the coffee shop we had met in.

'I wish I was there with you,' he said when I told him.

'Nah, you're not missing anything. It's grey and wet here,' I said.

'So what's happening?'

'Well, I've got a new book to start . . .'

'What is it?'

'It's a dating book.'

There was a silence.

'Ah, OK,' he said, followed by another pause. 'Well, OK. It's good that you have some fun.'

'What about you? Are you seeing anyone?' I asked.

It was the first time we'd talked about this.

'No,' he said. 'There is a girl in my local bar that I am flirting with but I don't know . . . I don't have much to offer a woman at the moment.'

He said he had to go.

Hussey says that most of us leave our love lives to fate. We focus on every other area of our life – our friends, our family, our careers – then the years pass and one day we wake up and realize that we're thirty-seven and Mr Perfect hasn't dropped in our laps. Then we panic.

We become so obsessed with meeting *the* guy we meet *no* guys.

Hussey says that to meet more men you need to, well, meet more men. Literally as many of them as you can.

'Every interaction with another human being is a possible gateway to some new world or experience, which could, in turn, introduce you to the love of your life,' writes Hussey. He advises we start conversations everywhere – in parks, bookshops, at the gym. Ask people's names. Compliment them. Smile. Ask men about their books and gadgets – all men like to talk about their gadgets, according to Hussey. You don't have to fancy them, it's just practice in smiling, chatting and flirting.

It's a numbers game. In fact, Hussey reckons that if you were in a party of a hundred men (some party!), you would have chemistry with about twenty of them. Out of that twenty, after talking to them there might be ten you would like enough to go on a date with. Of these ten, five might warrant a second date – and of those, you'd be doing well if you like one enough to see again.

Hussey asks: How many new guys do you meet in an average week? If it's only one (or zero) how long is it going to take for you to find someone you like? Answer: A long time.

So my challenge for the first week of operation Get the Guy was to smile, compliment and chat to anyone. And that's what I did – I became a one-woman charm machine. I talked to the binmen about the weather. I talked to the man in the launderette about his holiday. I told the waiter at our local Italian – who described the chocolate cake as 'three floors high' and assured us that 'I am here for your desires' – that he had a great way with English. I told the guy at the corner shop that I liked his sweater. I told Mike's new colleague at Bread and Bean that I liked his beard. I told Mike that I liked his tattoos. He looked confused that I was commenting on them after a year of seeing him pretty much every other day. But he said thank you and he liked my sweater.

'Thank you. My friend says I have to stop wearing these big sweaters but I like them.'

'I think you should wear what you like,' said Mike.

'It wouldn't put you off that a girl wore a big sweater?'

He paused. 'Nah, it's nice when someone is comfortable with themselves.'

Yay! Compliments all around.

On Day Two of dating, on 4th February, I asked a man on the Tube about the book he was reading called *Stuffocation*.

'What's your book about?' I asked.

'Er, it's about how we don't need so much stuff in our lives.'

'Is it good?' I asked

'I'm only on the first page,' he said, 'so I don't know.'

I looked down in his lap; he really was on the first page.

I continued: 'Do you think it's going to make you want to go home and chuck out all your possessions?'

'No.'

Oh well.

When I got off the train, I popped into the supermarket to get some food. It was 6pm and it was full of men. Matthew says that anywhere is fair game when it comes to meeting guys, but could I really chat up men in the Tesco in Archway? Or did that cross a desperation line I didn't want to cross?

The first man I saw was wearing a leather jacket and standing by the freezers. I shuffled closer and saw he was looking at ice creams. Was I going to do this? I stood, frozen, by the freezers, trying to think of what to say.

Hussey hadn't given instructions . . . *F**k it! Marianne, just open your mouth!*

'Er, have you had that flavour before?' I asked.

He looked surprised but he smiled at me and said, 'No.'

'What is it?' I asked him.

'Peanut butter and raspberry jam,' he replied. Then I must have made a face because he laughed and said, 'Yeah, I know. A bit too hectic maybe.' I liked his use of the word 'hectic' but before I could engage him in a fascinating conversation about vocabulary, he put the ice cream back in the freezer and walked away.

I felt rejected. It was embarrassing. I looked around to see if anyone else had noticed the encounter. It didn't look like they had, but I picked up a tub of the hectic ice cream, just in case. That way it looked like I really was just interested in the ice cream.

My adrenalin was pumping, though, and I wanted to make use of it. A small, arty-looking man with a bright blue scarf was deciding between a bland-looking Niçoise and an equally bland-looking feta salad. He picked the feta.

Do it, Marianne. Go on . . .

'Have you tried that one before?' I asked.

'No,' he said, but this time I got a big smile. 'I hope it will be nice,' he said, 'it's my dinner.'

He sounded Italian and it seemed he would be happy to chat but I didn't know how to move this salad conversation forward. 'Enjoy!' I said in a silly, fake voice before going home and eating the ice cream for dinner. On my own. It wasn't all bad, though – peanut butter and jam ice cream is surprisingly nice. Not hectic at all.

I realized halfway down the tub that in fact I was pretty good at talking to men now. My months of Rejection

Therapy and fear-fighting had made me much less embarrassed. My only problem was with men I actually fancied, as I discovered the next afternoon on Hampstead Heath when a tall, black-haired man in a tweed blazer appeared with a Labrador. He was walking in my direction and was scruffy but smart, good-looking but not pretty-boy good-looking. A cross between Heathcliff and Ryan Gosling. I could see in one split second that he was kind and clever, good with his hands and probably very successful in something arty but practical . . .

As he came closer my thoughts raced.

Just look at him and smile, say hello!

He got closer.

Come on, do it.

He got closer still.

Smile, Marianne. Just smile. Or look at him – that's enough . . .

But I didn't smile or look. Instead I diverted to a side path to avoid him. I was so scared I practically threw myself into a bush.

Seriously – what was wrong with me?

After all I'd done I could not simply smile at a handsome man.

Why did it always come down to this? Why? When was this going to change?

What was the worst that could happen? I'd smile and he wouldn't smile back? Come on, so what?

I walked back home furious with myself. What progress had I made after a whole year if I was still this useless with something everyone else could do? I was nearly forty, for God's sake! There were thirteen-year-olds with more game than me.

I passed the St John pub and out of habit I looked through the window to see if I knew anyone in there. There was nobody except the twinkly barman who had served me when I was out with Rachel and Paul. I kept walking and berating myself . . . then it hit me. I had messed up with Heathcliff, but I could talk to the barman. I had to.

And then I remembered something Matthew says in his book – staff are paid to be nice, so you're not going to get rejected. So I did it. I turned around and walked back to the pub, pushed open the heavy door and headed to the bar, where I pulled myself up onto a stool. An older man at the end of the bar nodded at me. I nodded back. I felt self-conscious. I never sat in pubs on my own.

And there he was. Standing by me. Smiling. Twinkling.

I smiled back, then panicked.

Don't be obvious, Marianne! He'll think you do fancy him and that you're a desperate loser who can't get a boyfriend and has to hang out in bars on her own.

'Hello,' he said.

'Hello,' I replied. Heart pounding.

'What can I get you?' he asked.

'Um. A small glass of red wine, please.'

'What kind?'

My mind froze. You'd think after all the years of practice I would know what kind of wine I liked by now but I didn't.

'Er . . .'

'Shiraz, Merlot . . . Pinot Noir?'

'Merlot, please.'

As he went to pour the glass I pulled out my phone. You know, to pretend that I had friends and a life. That I was in demand. Nobody had texted. I started scribbling in my notes . . . *I am alone in a bar . . .*

He passed over the glass and I uttered words that no woman should utter to a man, ever: 'That looks very small.'

'You did ask for a small one, didn't you?' he said.

'Oh yes, I did. Sorry.'

I never ask for small glasses and only did it this time because I didn't want him to think I was an alcoholic.

For the next twenty minutes or so he served other customers while I sipped my (small) wine and texted Rachel asking her to rescue me. What now? Matthew said I had to ask his name or find out something about him.

Mr Twinkly poured the man at the end of the bar another pint and then walked up to me.

'Do you want another one?' he asked me, smiling. He had such a nice smile. I smiled back.

I didn't want him to think that I was the kind of girl that hung out in bars on her own trying – but failing – to pick up the barman, so I started lying.

'I'm meant to be meeting a friend but she's just texted to say she's stuck at work . . . I don't know whether to wait more or go home.'

'Have another drink, it's cold out,' he said and smiled again. Was he saying that because he liked me – or because he was a barman and that was, well, his job?

'OK, sure, one more.'

'Small?'

'Oh sod it, make it a large . . .' I smiled back. Was this flirting?

Then I did it: 'I'm Marianne, by the way, what's your name?'

He smiled. 'Antonio.'

'Where's your accent from?' I said, heart pounding. Cheeks on fire.

'Brazil.'

'How long have you been here?'

'Ten months.'

'And how do you like it?'

'It's OK but it's hard. I work, I get the Tube, I sleep . . .' he said. This was hopeful. At no point did he say, I work, I get the Tube, I make love to my beautiful girlfriend and then I sleep . . .

'I think that I am not a city guy. I come from countryside. A small village.'

'Why did you come to London if you don't like cities?'

He shrugged. I won't lie, the conversation was a bit of a downer.

That's why Matthew Hussey says that we have to start conversations with the guys we like – if we don't, we build them up into this perfect thing, when actually a five-minute chat might make it clear that you're not at all suited to each other. But even though my guy was a bit miserable, I still liked him. At least he was honest.

It also sounded like he was lonely. As he went to serve someone else I practised the sentences in my head: 'Well, if you ever fancy seeing fun bits of London, then let me know . . .' or, 'If you ever get a day off, I'd be happy to show you around.' I'd say it when he moved back down to me –

I felt a tap on my shoulder, it was Rachel. I'd forgotten I'd texted her.

She looked at the barman, who was walking over.

'Shall I go?'

'No, no, no!' I said, terrified he'd overhear. After that I lost my nerve. The pub got busier and he went off to serve other people. We had our drinks and left. I hadn't told him I liked his smile or asked him about his iPhone. I felt embarrassed and rejected. This was how I always felt around men I liked – embarrassed and rejected. No matter what they actually did, that was how I felt.

That night I was too unsettled to sleep. Man stuff – it always opened up all sorts of feelings of hope, insecurity, fear . . . Did he think I was a loser for sitting there on my own? Was it really obvious I liked him? What did he think of me? I started putting on the old records – thinking about how fat I was, itemizing everything I'd eaten that day . . . Then I worried about my teeth and the fact that my hair was a mess . . . Why can't I have straight glossy hair instead of hair like a ginger Brillo pad?

Stop it, Marianne. Feel your feet. Be Here Now.

I closed my eyes and focused on my body, bit by bit, working my way up from my toes to . . . hips . . . and . . .

'Which one is he?' Paul bellowed when we walked into the bar. 'The skinny one or the one with the shirt?'

I'd made the mistake of telling Paul about the barman and now I was regretting it. He made me go back to the pub, promising he would not get involved and now he was being an idiot and I wanted to die.

'Shut up or I'm leaving,' I spat, before punching him hard on the arm and walking to a table as far away from the bar as I could find.

'I swear he didn't hear me,' said Paul when he came back with drinks. 'So is it the one with the shirt?'

'Yes.'

I calmed down. I looked up at the bar again just as Mr Twinkly was looking over.

Our eyes met. I felt sick.

Matthew Hussey says that eye contact is vital for flirting. He says we all think we're good at eye contact but we're not – for men to pick up the clue we have to go really OTT. He says you should look over at the guy you like and hold the gaze for a second more than is comfortable. Then look away. Then, look back at him again, with a playful smile that makes it clear to him that you are interested.

I found eye contact like this terrifying. Playful smiling too – what even is that? What's the difference between a normal smile and a playful smile? The Greek told me that if a girl smiled at him three times he'd go over. So the smiling thing was big. And I could smile at everyone under the sun – just not at men I fancied. I looked back up and smiled at him. He smiled back. I felt a shot of electricity go through me.

I pretended to listen to Rachel and Paul chat, while my heart pounded and I downed my drink.

'OK, I'm doing it.'

Rachel smiled and clapped.

'Shh. Don't make a thing of it,' I said, standing up and feeling as shaky on my legs as I had been during the stand-up. I walked to the bar. He smiled. I smiled.

'How are you?' I asked.

'Good, how are you?' he said.

'Can I have a bottle of Merlot and a pint of IPA please?'

'How many glasses for the wine?'

'We don't need any, thanks.'

'You'll just drink it straight from the bottle?' he asked.

'Yes, or if you have a straw, I'll take that,' I said.

Look, almost witty banter!

He got the drinks and came back to me.

This was when Matthew would have liked me to tell him that I liked his smile or eyes . . . to ask him about the flat white or cappuccino debate but instead this was what came out of my mouth: 'My friends have been teasing me because I've got a crush on you.'

There was a pause. He looked at me. I looked at him.

The words hung in the air. Around me the chatter of people catching up on a Friday night, unaware of the high-stakes emotional poker that was taking place just a few feet away. I kept looking at him. He kept looking at me.

'Oh,' he said.

Then he pushed the card machine towards me and said: 'That will be £25 please.'

Oh.

My hands trembled as I typed in my PIN, picked up the drinks and walked back to the table. I worried I would drop the bottle, my hands were shaking so much. I felt humili-ated, angry. But then very quickly there was another unexpected feeling . . . an unfamiliar feeling . . . what was it? Yes, that was it: I was euphoric. I had done something I would never have done before! I had bombed – but so what? Why the hell do we make such a big deal of these things? I didn't know this guy. He didn't know me. All that mattered was that I'd faced my fears – again – and had given it a go. Hussey agrees. He writes: 'Sometimes the guy you are inter-ested in will give you the cold shoulder or be into someone else . . . it doesn't matter. All that matters is that you tried. That's the success story here.'

'Maybe he didn't understand the word "crush",' said Rachel when I told them what happened.

'Maybe.'

'Or maybe he has a girlfriend,' she said.

'You did it – that's what counts,' said Paul, raising his glass. 'Now let's go across the road and find the next one.'

In the Hideaway a DJ was playing Marvin Gaye's 'Sexual Healing'. More drinks were ordered. Then more. And more.

By now I was smiling at anyone and everyone, including an old toothless guy who spent his days outside the bookie's and a twenty-something with an open shirt.

Then I smiled at a man with wild curly hair who was standing by the bar. He smiled back. We held each other's eye contact for a few seconds. I looked away and looked back. He was still looking at me.

Hussey says that women think that men don't approach us because they don't like us – but that's not the case. Most are so scared of looking stupid in front of their friends, they don't make a move, even if they think you're the hottest woman in the room. So it's our job to try to make it easier by positioning our group close to his.

Hussey doesn't recommend drinking a bottle of wine before you make this approach but I found it helped.

'Oh sorry,' I said, as I bumped into Mr Curly while I ordered more drinks at the bar.

'I'll forgive you,' he replied. His eyes were so blue.

I smiled playfully. Or maybe drunkenly.

'I saw you earlier,' he said.

'I saw you too.'

'You really hold eye contact,' he said.

He had a big nose and smelled of an aftershave I recognized but couldn't remember the name of.

'Can I get you a drink?' he asked.

'Thank you. I'll have what you're having.'

'Malibu and pineapple juice.'

'Really?'

We talked. He worked in IT. He played the ukulele. He

was getting a divorce. She was taking him to the cleaners. She had taken the cat too. I could only hear half of what he was saying over the music. He got more drinks. I could barely see straight. We danced to Britney Spears. I was hot in my sweater. I didn't know where the others had gone but now it was just the two of us. We were dancing to . . . Rihanna's 'Only Girl (in the World)' . . . I flung my hands up in the air and closed my eyes. This was what life was about! Dancing! Drinking! Having fun. What was there to be scared of? Guys liked me. Of course they did.

Then we were walking home in the dark. 'I just didn't expect to be someone who got divorced,' he was saying. 'I hate living on my own.'

Then he was talking about the cat again.

Next thing I remember, we were outside Rachel's, kissing on the steps. It was a horrible bumpy-toothed kiss. Messy and grope-y and weird. He tasted of pineapple and cigarettes.

'This is nice,' he said.

I nodded.

He watched me as I walked up the steps and fumbled with the keys. 'I'll call you,' he said. I knew even in my drunken haze that we had not swapped numbers.

The next morning, I woke up fully clothed and feeling like death.

'Well, at least you had a kiss,' said Rachel, while we were watching *Field of Dreams* with Kevin Costner and eating a giant Snickers bar.

'That's true.'

'How are you feeling about the barman?'

'Can we please never speak of that again?'

———

Him: 'Hi, Marianne!'

Me: 'Hi, Jon!'

Him: 'I love your hair.'

Me: 'Thanks!'

Him: 'When it comes to getting a dirty job done, I'll take a redheaded woman . . .'

Me: '???'

Him: 'It's Bruce Springsteen.'

Me: 'Take it he's talking about cleaning the oven?'

Him: 'I wouldn't mind seeing you bent over my oven. Or is that too rude?'

Actually, yes, it was. I didn't reply.

An hour later another message: *'You can wear rubber gloves.'*

I didn't reply to that one either.

Another hour later, a final plea: *'We could forget the gloves?'*

Hot on the heels of the Bruce Springsteen fan came another suitor who only had one profile picture and he was wearing sunglasses in it. I should have known that this was not a good sign.

Him: 'Hiya. How are you?'

Me: 'I'm good, how are you?'

Him: 'Well. Nice pics of you. Found love yet?'

Me: 'Thanks. No love yet. What about you?'

Him: 'I'm not looking for love. I'm looking for an affair.'

Me: 'So you're married?'

Him: 'Yes. Does that freak you out?'

Me: 'No, doesn't freak me out but it's not a road I want to go down.'

Him: 'Is there anything I can do to change your mind?'

Me: 'No, I'm afraid not.'

Ten minutes later: *'Can you hook me up with any of your friends?'*

Matthew Hussey is not a fan of online dating. He says it's fine as a way of broadening the net, but we should not rely on it exclusively because it's too easy to stay on your sofa chatting online as a way of avoiding interacting with people in the real world. Which is exactly why I down-loaded Tinder.

Who needed to be rejected by barmen or bump teeth with broken-hearted divorcees when you could flirt without even leaving the house?

I'd never been on Tinder before and it was a revelation – this was where all the single men of London were! Posting photographs of themselves with tops, without tops. Smiling faces and moody black-and-white faces. In the pub, by a sports car, up a mountain, cuddling dogs. On their own or surrounded by glam girls – the picture that says, Look, women love me! I'm a catch!

I erred on the side of generosity: anyone with a nice smile and their top on was given the benefit of the doubt. As a result I got a lot of matches and every few hours there was a new message: *'Hi Marianne! How's your day going?'*

I found it weird to tell a total stranger about how my day was going – did they really want to know that after days of putting it off I was finally going to wash my hair? Or that I was just about to head to the shops to get milk? I didn't think so, so I settled on the boringly vague, *'Great, thanks! How are you?'*

By the end of my second day on Tinder, I had four dates lined up.

Cue mental breakdown. All *Power of Now* zen vanished in the face of dating.

My full-time job was now hating my teeth, my bum and my hair. The voice in my head went into overdrive worrying that my dates wouldn't like me or would tell me I looked nothing like my pictures – which, of course, I didn't. I had put up my very best photographs. I know that this is part of the game but, seriously, I could have been done under trade descriptions.

I called Mum, which was a mistake. 'Don't drink too much. You know it makes your face pink and puffy,' was her advice.

But I did drink too much. Drinking was what I did when I got nervous.

First the civil servant. He lived in Surrey but said he would come in to meet me on the Southbank. We met in the bar of the BFI on Tuesday 10th February. I had spent three hours getting ready, trying on jeans and tops. Dresses and boots. Skirts and sweaters. By the time I'd left home (wearing jeans and a silk top and boots) I'd also calmed my nerves with two big glasses of wine. It was 6pm on a Tuesday and I was half a bottle of wine down. And after all those nerves and anticipation, I knew the second I saw him that I did not want to put my lips anywhere near him. We chatted easily but had zero chemistry.

This is another reason Hussey says online dating doesn't work – in the real world we find people attractive because of tiny things such as the way they walk, the way they talk or their hand gestures. Online you can't pick up on these clues, which means that you spend a week having a nervous breakdown over a man that you know within ten seconds of meeting is not for you.

On the Tube home I felt excited, though. My first Tinder date. Done. It wasn't so hard or scary.

Wednesday night was coffee with a photographer who had just come back from Iraq. He sounded interesting. He thought so too. I spent two hours being run over by his voice.

Thursday night with a guy who described himself as '6-ft Scouser with a taste for the absurd'. His profile pics were of him wearing a comedy moustache and wig, and pics of him in what looked like a flamenco outfit at a festival . . .

None of this was my kind of thing. I was too uptight for fancy dress. And I find absurd stuff stupid and childish. But then there was a nice normal smiley picture and I could see he lived locally so I just swiped anyway. We had a bit of texting that made me laugh. He told me he was good at making burgers and didn't like lazy people. I told him I was a terrible cook and was very lazy. He said he admired my honesty. I told him I liked burgers.

He said he didn't like endless texting; did I want to meet?

We met in the Crown and Goose in Camden at 6pm and within twenty minutes of quite boring conversation, he went in for the kill.

'So are we going back to yours, then?' he asked.

'What?'

'Are we going back to yours after?'

'No.'

'Why not?'

'Because I don't want to.'

'OK.'

He didn't seem that bothered. If anything he was relieved to have got the question out of the way.

Unsurprisingly, Hussey is not a big fan of jumping into bed with someone in the first ten minutes. He says that while all men want sex, they also don't like it when they feel you'd have sex with anyone. They want to feel special.

'Does that ever work for you?' I asked.

'What?'

'Just asking like that.'

'Yeah.'

'So what happens?'

'I meet a girl and I say, "Are we going back to yours?" and she says, "Yes," and we have sex.'

'And then what?'

'What do you mean?'

'What do you do after you have sex?'

'Then we have sex again.'

'And then what?'

'We find other people to have sex with.'

I felt like Mother Teresa on a date with Hugh Hefner.

'What are you waiting for, a thunderbolt?' he asked.

'Maybe.' I said.

'You wouldn't settle for a bit of mild rain instead?'

I found this funny. He was funny when he wasn't being sleazy. I laughed and then he went in for a kiss. I let him.

It was a wet beardy kiss but quite nice. I could smell his musty jacket. 'Are you really sure I can't come back to yours?' he asked.

'I've never been more certain of anything in my life,' I replied.

I went home alone feeling deflated. He made the whole dating thing seem so joyless. Meet someone, jump into bed, meet someone else . . . rinse and repeat. I knew it was a numbers game but I didn't have the mental and physical stamina to play. It was only Thursday and I was exhausted.

Three dates in one week and I hadn't met anyone I liked. I'd been holding out for a fourth date with a charity worker whom I was meant to be meeting for a drink in the Charlotte Street Hotel on Saturday night – which also happened to be Valentine's Night. He texted me on Saturday morning to tell me he was not feeling well. I told him to get better and we could rearrange. Later he unmatched me. I was hurt and confused but also relieved.

I spent Valentine's Day on the sofa with Rachel watching an Ashton Kutcher movie. He was on honeymoon with Brittany Murphy and it was a disaster. I fell asleep before I got to the part where they discovered they loved each other really.

Week three and my final Tinder date was meant to be with Alistair, a Scottish guy who worked for the NHS. His profile said that he 'liked to make sweeping assumptions about people based on their profile pics'. He guessed that I was Irish, liked swing dancing and vintage clothes. I guessed that he was Scottish.

We had messaged for a few days and he made me giggle. It was easy.

He asked if I wanted to meet up. I said yes. We agreed on Thursday 19th. He told me that he'd get in touch later in the week to arrange things.

Wednesday night, I still hadn't heard from him. It was annoying. Pride meant I didn't want to be the one to message him first but I wanted to know if it was still happening so I could make other plans if it wasn't.

So I messaged him: *'Hello Alistair, how are you? Just wondering if we're still on for tomorrow night?'*

The reply came back five minutes later: '*I've been super busy with work doing early starts and working late, so won't be that early.*'

No 'Hello, how are you?' No apology for not getting in touch. Not even a 'Yes, I'm still up for it.'

Then another message came up: '*Could probably meet about 8/8.30.*'

Oh, do me a favour, why don't you?

My first reaction was to just delete him and silently fume, but then I took a breath and decided to take the high road.

I replied: '*Let's leave it, you've obviously got a lot on.*'

He answered: '*Yeah, it's a busy week.*'

He then gave me a long list of what was going on at his work and how tired and stressed he was . . . I got angry again. I could not care less about his office politics. I didn't even know the guy.

I knew this was Tinder but surely some sort of effort is supposed to be made at this point in proceedings. Where was the charm? The wooing?

When he'd finished sharing his to-do list, he added: '*I would still like to meet though, unless you've changed your mind.*'

And actually I *had* changed my mind.

I replied: '*I totally understand work taking over but I'm a bit old-fashioned on the manners front. It would have been nice to hear from you, even if it was to postpone. To be honest I'm probably juggling too many dates at the moment, so let's leave it altogether. Best of luck with everything and thanks for the funny texts. I really enjoyed them.*'

I was very pleased with my line about having too many dates. Actually I was pleased with it all. I'd never before stood up for myself in this way – with men, with friends, with anyone. It felt really empowering to say, politely, Actually this isn't good enough.

It felt groundbreaking.

Hussey says that by making this stand I had made myself a High Value Woman. This didn't mean High Maintenance or Hard to Get – it means someone who is self-confident and self-assured, someone who knows what she wants and isn't afraid to articulate that.

He writes: 'A woman who is certain about herself has a deep feeling of self-worth . . . If she is not getting what she wants or needs from a relationship, the self-confident woman will feel comfortable articulating her needs, or walking away. This is true in the earliest stages of meeting guys as well – if the man she is talking to is boring the hell out of her, or a boaster, a woman of certainty will politely extricate herself, instead of wasting her time.'

I thought of how many boring conversations I'd sat through, feigning interest, in order to be polite. Hussey says when we articulate our standards, men will raise their game to match them.

He was right.

Alistair's tone changed completely after that. He sent back several messages apologizing for not messaging sooner and asking me to please not delete him, that he'd love to take me out some time . . . but it was too little too late. I unmatched him.

I was sure Alistair was a nice guy – he'd just got complacent and lazy. I was just as bad. Over my two weeks on Tinder I'd dropped text conversations, without saying goodbye, just because I'd lost interest. I was sending messages while I watched telly, eating, chatting to Rachel. It was hardly real communication. It all started to feel like a game; it was easy to forget I was dealing with real people.

As I approached the last week of February, I was mentally and physically knackered. I'd had more interaction with men in the previous three weeks than I had done in my entire adult life and it had spun me out. Dating made me second guess everything – was I being too fussy? Not fussy enough?

But on the other hand it felt good to demystify the whole dating game. To see that guys were just like me – out there doing their best to find someone. And I was pleasantly surprised to discover that it was quite easy to meet guys – but meeting *the* guy was something else. Was that going to ever happen for me? And, more importantly, did I even want that? I had one more week to find out. But no more Tinder, it was time to get back to accosting strangers on the street. Or in the board room.

16

Get a Husband?

'I never thought you'd get married and have children.'
– Mum

There was a burst of shocked laughter. One man coughed as he half choked on his coffee. Another turned away in embarrassment. An older woman with a grey bob let out a squeal.

'Well, I have to say that this is a first!' said a suited man with a shiny bald head, shuffling in his seat. He looked around the conference table where twenty-odd business men and women sat, in stunned silence, with folders, note-pads and biros in front of them.

A voice from the back of the room interjected: 'I'd take you out but I don't think my wife would like it.'

I looked around and smiled at the speaker.

'Mine neither, but if I was single . . .' said another.

'If I was twenty years younger I'd take you out on the town!' laughed a man who looked like Father Christmas in a three-piece suit.

'Well, nothing ventured, nothing gained!' I said, my cheeks burning, and sat down.

Another first. Standing up in a room full of strangers and

asking if anyone wanted to take me on a date. I didn't know whether this counted as a high or a low on my road to self-development . . . Who was I kidding? It was the latter. Clearly.

When Paul suggested that I go to a networking breakfast with him because there were lots of men there, I agreed because Matthew Hussey says you need to say 'yes' to invitations.

It was only when we were on the Tube at 6.30am that Paul broke the news that every new person had to stand up and speak a bit about themselves. 'You can either say that you're a freelance writer who is available for copywriting,' he said, 'or you could stand up and say you are looking for a date.'

So that's what I did. After listening to one guy talk about his print services and another sell his online marketing skills, I stood up in a room of twenty suits, wearing a sticker with my name scribbled in blue felt-tip, and asked for a date. At 7.30 in the morning.

A year earlier I would have sooner died – but now, well, it was just a Thursday morning. I felt embarrassed but not as much as I would have expected. And as soon as I sat down, the room filled with chatter. 'Good for you!' said a female voice from the back of the room. 'I am also available for dinner! All interested parties could form an orderly line!'

Everyone laughed. A room full of stuffy business people instantly became lovely, human people.

As normal business resumed, a man wearing a navy blazer and large signet ring passed me a note on a piece of paper that read: 'I'll take you out . . .'.

'OK!' I wrote on it and passed it back.

'Coffee after this?' he wrote and passed it back to me.

'OK!' I wrote again.

We were halfway down our lattes when he popped the question.

'Do you want to get married?'

Was he proposing or just asking for some general information? I couldn't tell but either way, this was a big question to be asked in a Starbucks at 9.30am, from a man whose last name I didn't even know.

'Er, actually, I'm not sure,' I replied. 'I don't know if I want to get married and have children. I don't think that's the path I'm going to go down.'

He looked surprised. The fact that I'd stood up and asked for a date in a business meeting probably gave him the sense that I was in a hurry to settle down. It was a fair conclusion.

'Maybe you haven't found the right man.'

'Yes, maybe,' I conceded.

We had a nice chat about his travels and his business and the fact that his parents had died.

'I'm ready to settle down and start a family. I've built up my business, done well. I have no interest in one-night stands. I'm done with all that. I want something real.'

I admired his honesty and envied his certainty.

'I'm away on business next week. When I come back we should have dinner. I'll be in touch.'

'Um, OK, sure, maybe . . .'

And off he went.

As I got the Tube home after yet another weird experience, I felt no closer than I had been at the start of the project to knowing what I wanted. Did I want to get married and settle down? Did I want kids? Was the fact that it hadn't happened a sign that it wasn't my path? Or was my independence just a symptom of my fear? Do you need to be with someone else to live a good, full life, or can you lead a good, full life on your own? Would all these questions go away if I met the right guy? Or was I so closed off I wouldn't know the right guy if he smiled at me in a coffee shop?

We live in a world where happiness is equated with marriage and kids – and where, more often than not, being single is greeted with a sympathetic smile and some comment along the lines of, 'You'll meet someone . . .' or 'Never mind, you still have time . . .' and that really annoyed me. The implication being that if you don't, your life will have been a failure.

But was the lady protesting too much?

When I got off at Archway I phoned Mum.

'Where are you?' I asked.

'I'm at home, ironing.'

'OK.'

'What are you doing?'

'I've just been on another date.'

'Oh! And how did it go?'

'I didn't fancy him.'

'Did he like you?'

'It seemed like it.'

'Oh!'

'Mum, there's no need to sound so surprised.'

'I didn't realize you were a femme fatale!' she seemed to find this idea very funny.

Then I asked her a question that I had never asked her before: 'Don't you think it's strange that all my friends are getting married and I'm not?'

She paused and there was a silence on the line. I could hear the radio in the background.

'Well, you've always been very independent,' she said.

'You can be independent and still have relationships.'

'I never thought you'd get married and have children,' she said.

This was big news to be getting outside the kebab shop on Junction Road.

'Don't you remember me telling you that when you were a teenager?'

'No.'

'You and your sisters were asking me what I thought would happen to each of you when you grew up and I told you that I did not think you'd settle down. And you got really upset and your father got very annoyed with me.'

'I don't remember that at all. Why did you think that?'

'I could never see you living a domestic life; I always thought you'd feel trapped.'

My first feeling was one of relief – relief that my mum was saying that I didn't have to go down that path. The thought of marriage and kids and a house and forever really did make me feel trapped – so trapped I wanted to scratch my skin off . . .

But then I felt a kick in my stomach. Suddenly I was back in our childhood kitchen, drinking tea when she said it. I remembered feeling a stab of hurt that even Mum didn't think anyone would want to marry me.

'She knows me really well, obviously,' I said to my therapist – yes, I went back – the next day, 'so maybe she's right and I am meant to live on my own.'

'It's hard to know if her saying that was what made you go on and live how you have.'

'That's true but it was a relief when she said it yesterday. All my life I've felt like a failure because I wasn't getting married or having boyfriends like other people – but maybe

I wasn't doing that because that's just not what's meant for me. I like my freedom and I really like to be on my own. When I think of what I want in the future I think of travelling and fun. I want to have great sex and romances but the idea of settling down makes me feel trapped. And Mum's right – I hate cooking and domesticity.'

'But that's a very old-fashioned view of relationships,' said my therapist. 'People make relationships work in all sorts of ways.'

'Do you think that I can be happy if I don't get married?'

'Of course,' she said. 'I think you'll have a good life whatever you do.'

'But do you think that I'd be happier if I met someone?'

'If it was the right someone then yes. But you need to really love them, love their smell, love their skin. Don't settle.'

'How do I know if it's the right person? Maybe I'm just being too fussy?'

'I don't know, but I think all you can do is try to be open . . .'

The thing about being open is it's tiring. Every day being hopeful but not wanting to get your hopes up. Looking at every man on the street thinking – should I ask his name? Ask him where he stands on the flat white versus cappuccino debate?

But then, just when I was about to give up, it happened. And by 'it' I mean He.

He was standing at the traffic lights in Old Street. He was tall, dark and beardy. He was wearing a tweed jacket just like the guy I'd fancied in Hampstead Heath. Actually, I

couldn't be sure it wasn't the same guy. He was just as handsome. Salt-and-pepper hair . . .

Oh, God. Don't bolt, Marianne. Do something.

According to Hussey, even in the twenty-first century, 'I
could really use your help with something' are a woman's
most attractive words. These words appeal to a man's
primal instincts to provide and protect. It went against every
feminist instinct in my body – but I did it; I played the
damsel in distress.

'Excuse me,' I said, looking up at him. He had headphones in and didn't hear me.

I lightly touched his sleeve. He jumped with shock. He
took out his headphones. I could hear classical music
coming from them.

'I'm sorry,' I said. 'I was just wondering if you could help
me? I am trying to get to the Hoxton Hotel . . . do you know
which way I should head?'

He paused for a second and looked at me. His brown
eyes softened.

'Er, yeah, you just keep straight on this road and then
turn left by the lights.'

'OK, thanks very much.' I smiled at him. He smiled back.

'I'm going that way, actually,' he replied.

We walked alongside each other in awkward silence. The
drizzle that had been coming down all day got heavier. He
had an umbrella.

'Do you want to share this?' he asked. Hussey says you
must always say 'yes' if a man offers you his jacket, or an
umbrella. It makes him feel useful. I stood under it with him
and we walked in more awkward silence. We were very
close for two strangers.

I panicked and started babbling, asking him where he was going and what he did.

I found out pretty quickly that he was meeting his brother and that he worked for a charity. A charity! Finally, my sexy saint!

'So you're a good person?' I said.

'I don't know about that but I try,' he said, looking at the ground.

A good-looking but humble charity worker! And I was standing under an umbrella with him! Thank you, Matthew Hussey! Thank you, world.

'I'm going straight on here but the Hoxton is just down there,' he said, pointing to the left.

'OK, thanks very much.'

'No problem.'

'It was nice to meet you.'

'Yeah, you too.'

We stood for a second under the umbrella. I remembered standing by the turnstiles at the Tube in January with the artist with the hipster beard. This time I did not run away. I stood still and kept looking at Mr Umbrella. He kept looking back. I laughed. He laughed too.

'Er, I'm not in the habit of picking up girls on the street but, er, would you like to meet for a drink sometime?'

'Yes, that would be great,' I replied in a way that, you know, suggested this was perfectly normal. Handsome men asked me out on the street every single day.

'Oh! Oh, OK, good.'

'Good!'

'Well, I suppose I should take your number.'

I gave him my number and tried not to grin. *Play it cool, Marianne, cool.*

'OK, bye,' he said.

'Bye.' I waved and walked down the street.

'I'm Harry By The Way!'

'Hello Harry By The Way!' I shouted back at him. He smiled and I practically skipped to the bar.

He texted later that evening, asking if I was free the following night. For the intervening twenty-four hours, I over thought everything. I couldn't concentrate on work. I couldn't eat. I worried that I was not pretty enough for him. Hussey says this is rubbish – if a guy has already seen you and has asked you out, he already likes the way you look. Then I thought about all the ways he might be the perfect guy and I might mess it up. In my head I was already picturing me meeting his friends, who would all be successful and clever, and then I was wondering where we'd live . . . he lived south of the river, which wasn't ideal, but I could try Brixton if I had to . . . I pictured his house, which I'm sure would be filled with books and big windows. I pictured us having dinner parties and lazy Sunday breakfasts . . .

I was projecting like crazy.

This is another big No-No, says Hussey, who explains that women are too quick to meet someone and find a way of making him into 'Mr Right' in their heads. By doing that we're allowing ourselves to fall for someone before he's even proved himself, and our keenness makes us look like we are of 'low value'. He says we have to remember, even when we like someone, that they still have to prove themselves to us.

We went for Ethiopian food. It was my suggestion.

There was a place in Tufnell Park and I'd always been curious about it. He was already there when I arrived. It was nice to see him. I felt shy and awkward saying hello. He went in for a kiss on the cheek and then I moved away while he was going in for the second cheek kiss. 'I never know whether to do one or two,' he said.

'Sorry,' I said.

Then we went to the table and I felt self-conscious about everything – about walking in front of him, about him looking at me walking . . . I went to sit down just as he was moving around the table to pull my chair out for me.

'You've ruined my moment,' he joked. 'I'd been practising my chair move all day.'

I stood up again and said, 'You can do it now.'

'No, it's too late,' he said, smiling.

We ordered drinks and started talking. We ordered a big pancake thing with lots of different food on it. I got self-conscious eating around him. The more we talked, the more I liked him. He was smart, funny. He seemed like a good person. He had his own flat. A good job. He was a real-life grown-up man. Too grown up for the likes of me. He asked me about past relationships and I felt my face flush as I said that there had been nothing serious. He offered to walk me home and he put his arm around me and I felt paralysed. My body was rigid.

'I had a nice time,' he said.

I didn't say anything.

'Did you have a nice time?' He smiled.

'Er, yes . . .' I was frozen, like an idiot. *Stop being a moron, Marianne . . . Act normal!*

Matthew Hussey says that a big part of dating is 'being

comfortable with allowing an atmosphere of sexual tension'. I AM NOT.

He writes: 'Women who aren't comfortable with this will often deflect a man's affections and immediately change the subject when he tries to communicate *his* sexual desires. Sometimes she'll deflate the tension by closing down when the conversation veers into more intimate territory. This is fine if you are not interested in pursuing something more with him. If you are interested, it can stop momentum cold.'

This is what I do. I stop momentum cold.

Hussey says that there are lots of successful women who can talk to anyone – but are terrified of being playful, flirty and feminine. So there. That was me.

Flirting makes me cringe so much my teeth blush.

Harry walked me home and as we stood at the door, he started to lean in for a kiss and I panicked. I pecked him on the cheek, bolted up the steps and said: 'OK, night!' I said it like I was saying goodbye to my grandmother. When I turned around at the top of the steps, he had already started walking away.

My heart sank.

The next day I texted him to say thanks for a lovely date. He didn't reply all day. At 8pm a short message saying it was great to meet me too. No request for a second date. I had to rescue this! *'Would you like to do it again?'* I texted.

Two hours later, the reply: *'I'm away a lot for work over the next few weeks so the timing isn't right.'*

I'd blown it.

For years I'd thought I didn't have boyfriends because I wasn't pretty enough, skinny enough, blonde enough. I now realized this was bullshit. I didn't have boyfriends because I was terrified.

I could meet guys, it turned out – much more easily than I had thought. And I could chat to them happily. The only problem was when I met a guy I might actually like. Then I ran scared. And all the dating tips in the world probably weren't going to help me. If you've been single for as long as I had, there is always deeper stuff going on . . .

17

Daring Greatly,
by Brené Brown

'Connection is why we are here.'

*'Courage starts with showing up and letting our-
selves be seen.'*

'I've never been in love and nobody has ever been in love
with me.' The words hung in the air. The room silent.
Twenty-five pairs of eyes looked at me from a circle of plastic chairs.

'I've never had a proper relationship. Never lived with
anyone. Never got close.'

The eyes kept staring. Silent. Impassive.

'I don't know what's wrong with me . . .' My voice and
legs were shaking.

'I–I–I don't think that anyone decent could ever love me.'

And there it was: the truth. The truth I didn't know was
there. The truth that was under everything.

I did not feel that anybody in their right mind would
want me. I thought there was something wrong with me. I
could not be loved the way other people could.

Now I was crying so hard I couldn't catch my breath.

Snot mixed with tears and I felt like my legs were going to give way.

I had never felt so exposed and vulnerable in my life.

Before I'd started my self-help adventure, a friend had told me about this crazy therapy week her sister had gone on. There was a lot of secrecy around the whole thing but from what she could tell it seemed to involve telling her deepest darkest secrets to a bunch of strangers and bashing cushions with a baseball bat. There was also talk of letting go of 'baggage' and getting in touch with your 'inner child'.

The whole thing sounded hideous.

'I mean, how desperate would you have to be to put yourself through something like that?' I said to my friend at the time, while I filed the name in the back of my mind, half suspecting that one day I would be that desperate.

And so it was that I found myself on something called the Hoffman Process, falling apart in front of twenty-five people in a country house in Sussex.

When I finished my incoherent ramblings, I went back to my seat and someone else stood up to share their story but I wasn't listening. Instead I was replaying the words I'd spoken. I had said more to these total strangers than I had ever said to my friends – had ever even admitted to myself . . .

My legs wobbled as I stood up for the break time. I kept my head down as I walked to the kitchen and joined the queue of people making tea. I couldn't look at anyone. There was a shell-shocked hush in the air. Everyone stunned by what was happening. I felt nauseous. I left the queue without making any tea and went outside.

It was cold. Grey. A robin hopped along the frozen grass. I felt like I'd fallen off the edge of the world. Was that really what I thought? That nobody would love me?

The crunch of gravel behind me and a woman with cropped blonde hair and a pencil skirt was standing next to me, cigarette in hand. I looked up and smiled weakly. Normally now I'd turn on the charm, I'd ask lots of questions, listen, smile and be as likeable as I possibly could be. But what was the point now? The whole room had seen me naked.

'That was very brave,' she said.

Was that code for 'embarrassing, stupid, pathetic'? Was she judging me, in her perfect pencil skirt and short chic hair?

'I could relate to everything you said,' she continued, but she was just trying to be nice. She'd talked about being under pressure at work. I bet she was some senior person in some massive company with a big house and a husband and family and a life. We were nothing alike.

She kept talking.

'I was a coward. I didn't say the truth. My husband left me and I spend my weekends locked in a one-bedroom flat chain smoking and watching hours of crap on television. I eat chocolate until I feel sick. Then I make myself sick. I tried to kill myself last year.'

Oh.

We stood in silence for a few minutes, watching the robin. She dragged on her cigarette.

'I'm sorry to hear that,' I said.

She nodded.

There was nothing more to say.

The bell rang to bring us back into the room.

She put out her cigarette and we walked towards the house. By the door a tall, tanned man was also finishing a cigarette. He was wearing a soft grey sweater and had the kind of poreless glowing skin that only the very rich have. I could not look at him; I was too ashamed that he'd seen me in such a snotty state. But I had nowhere to hide. It was done. The cat was out of the bag. I was a mess. I looked up at him and gave him a weak smile.

Then something incredible happened. This man with expensive skin leaned over to me and put his arm around my shoulders and just stood there.

We said nothing. Three strangers standing in silence. Alone. Together. More tears streamed down my face. He handed me a handkerchief.

'Shall we go back in?' he said.

And we did. Together.

For eight days we sat in circles, talked about our feelings, our lives, and our families. We ranged in age from nineteen to sixty-five and came from all walks of life.

As warned, we bashed pillows with plastic baseball bats while screaming at the top of our lungs to get rid of our anger. We stood in muddy fields, pretending to be burying loved ones in order to say the things we needed to say. We even buried ourselves – or rather the worst parts of ourselves – which meant that together with the funeral exercise I'd tried in 7 *Habits*, I had now gone to two of my own funerals.

With every new exercise, I'd think, 'This is my idea of hell . . .' then we'd be given the next one, which would surpass it – 'No, THIS is my idea of hell . . .' and on it went.

Some parts were so ridiculous, I suspected we were

being filmed for some sort of Ruby Wax documentary –
'Look what these nutty, first-world people have to do to
be happy!' she'd say as the camera panned to us stroking
a velvet cushion that was meant to represent our inner
child.

The week was even more hideous than I'd been expecting.

But it was also one of the best things I'd done in my life.

I shared my worst bits with people and they didn't run
away – quite the opposite. They were unfailingly kind. For
the first time in my life, I did not feel alone. It felt like a
miracle.

But the greatest miracle of all was that despite the fact
that we all had different stories, it soon became clear that
underneath everything we were all the same. We all felt
flawed. Not good enough. Not loveable.

Without realizing it, the problem I had shared on the
first day – the problem I was so ashamed of, the guilty secret
I had been keeping even from myself – happened to be the
most common source of pain for all human beings. A problem which had been alluded to in all the self-help books I'd
read but which I had not picked up on until now.

'We're all afraid we're not enough,' Tony Robbins says.
'At the core, there's a place where people feel they're not
smart enough, young enough, old enough, rich enough,
funny enough, something enough. And it's the worst feeling
because, underneath that, our fear is then, "I won't be
loved."'

Eckhart Tolle agrees. He says: 'that feeling that something is wrong with you, is not a personal problem of yours.
It is a universal, human condition. You may be surprised to
know that there are millions . . . billions of people on the

planet who have the same thought pattern. It is part of the human ego.'

After coming home from Hoffman I discovered a woman who has become famous for articulating this feeling. A few years ago, Brené Brown did a TED talk to a few hundred people in her home town of Houston, Texas.

In a world obsessed with positive thinking and productivity, her subject was not upbeat, it was quite the opposite. It was about shame – something she defines as that 'intensely painful feeling or experience of believing that we are flawed and therefore unworthy of love and belonging'.

The talk went on to become a viral hit, watched by tens of millions of people around the world. It turned into a book called *Daring Greatly* in which she explains that people often think shame is reserved for people who have survived trauma but that's not true. Shame is something we all experience. In fact, Brown says that we are in the middle of a shame epidemic – where nobody thinks they are good enough, thin enough, smart enough, rich enough, successful enough, well dressed enough.

A few people had mentioned Brené Brown's TED talk to me before, including, surprisingly, the Tinder guy who wanted to go back to mine on the first date. But I'd never investigated further until getting home from the Hoffman Process, when I watched the talk over and over again and read *Daring Greatly* cover to cover. Three times. It seemed to capture the essence of what it is to be human. It also seemed to capture patterns of behaviour that had governed my life but which I'd been totally unaware of. It captured just why a week spilling my guts to strangers had changed me in a way that the self-help books couldn't.

Brené says that when we feel shame we do several things. First, we try to be perfect. We think that if we can just get thinner, smarter, more successful, then we'll feel OK and people will love us and we won't get hurt.

When that doesn't work – and it never does – we try another approach: we numb our feelings of shame. We watch television. We drink. We eat too much. We take drugs. Brown thinks that numbing is why obesity, addiction and depression are so rife.

Then when the numbing and the perfectionism doesn't work, we go down the third route: we cut ourselves off, shut down our feelings, decide to go it alone.

Brené was basically describing my life – both before and after self-help. After all, what had this whole project been except a misguided attempt at perfection? And what had I done when that attempt failed? I'd got drunk, watched television and stopped talking to my friends.

I had not gone down the route that Brené says is the only one that works: connecting with others. Showing our real selves to people who will love and accept us – warts and all.

Being vulnerable.

Brené writes: 'If we share our story with someone who responds with empathy and understanding, shame can't survive.'

To this end, Brené is not a fan of the term 'self-help'.

'I don't know what it means,' she said in an interview. 'I don't think we're meant to do it alone. Healing comes from sharing your story with someone worthy of hearing it.'

She was right. I saw I'd been doing the self-help stuff all wrong. I *couldn't* do it alone. After spending my whole life telling myself that I was strong and did not need others – it turned out that I did.

It was petrifying to show my real self to other people at Hoffman – but it was exactly what I needed. In my snotty and tearful state, I felt accepted and loved and seen in a way I had never done in my life. And even though I didn't realize it, that is all human beings ever really want. Not new jeans, new job, new house, new boyfriend, new car – but the feeling that we love and belong.

Brené writes in an earlier book, *The Gifts of Imperfection*: 'A deep sense of love and belonging is an irreducible need of all women, men and children. We are biologically, cognitively, physically, and spiritually wired to love, to be loved, and to belong. When those needs are not met, we don't function as we were meant to. We break. We fall apart. We numb. We ache. We hurt others. We get sick.'

I had spent a lifetime breaking, numbing, hurting and getting sick. A lifetime of going it alone. It was time to stop, with the help of Brené Brown – and my friends.

Brené writes a lot about friends. 'I carry a small sheet of paper in my wallet that has written on it the names of people whose opinions of me matter. To be on that list, you have to love me for my strengths and struggles . . . You have to love and respect that I'm totally uncool.'

She calls these her 'move the body' friends – people she could call in the middle of the night and they would come and do whatever she asked, no questions asked.

I missed Sarah. More than anything I wanted to be back in a sticky-floored pub drinking too much and giggling with her. She loved me as I was. She made me laugh at my flaws.

She made me feel like a million dollars even when I was spotty and hungover.

She knew me. Really, really knew me. And I knew her too. I knew that she was much more sensitive than she ever let on. That she believed in God and was kind to everyone. I knew that she thought that one of the worst things anyone could do was leave people out. She was always the one making friends with the girl in the coatroom or the awkward colleague standing alone at a party. She'd melt them with her love and humour and soon they'd be dancing and she'd make them feel like the funniest and most fascinating person in the room.

It hit me that I'd done the very worst thing to Sarah. I'd left her out. I'd left her out of my new life. I'd thought I had to improve myself on my own – but the truth was the opposite. You can only grow with other people.

I had to call her but I was terrified. I'd left it so long. What would I say?

'Hello, I'm sorry'? Then what? What if she just hung up on me? Or was silent? Or told me what a cow I was?

For two days I picked up my phone then found a reason not to call her. A job that needed doing. A trip to the Post Office. Or an urgent need to call Mum. Finally, on Saturday afternoon, alone on my bed, I picked up the phone and pressed her number. A number I had pressed a million times before. My hands shaking. I didn't know what I was going to say.

It rang. And rang. Then it went to answerphone. I could hear her voice. Bright. Cheery. I panicked and hung up without leaving a message.

I pictured her looking at my name on the phone and pressing silent. I pictured her at home with Steve on the sofa. I wanted more than anything to be there with her, getting an Indian and watching a film before falling asleep on the sofa after too much wine and Dairy Milk. I suddenly missed her so much it hurt. How had I been such an idiot? So cold?

I texted: *'I've been a self-obsessed idiot. I'm so sorry. I miss you. Mx'*

For the rest of the night I couldn't sit still. I was so scared of what the answer would be I switched my phone off. Then turned it back on again. Then off. Then on. No response. The next morning, I woke up at 7am and checked my phone. Still nothing.

'Give her time,' said Rachel over breakfast. 'Come on, let's get out. Go for a walk.'

And so we walked on the Heath and walked up to the ponds we'd jumped into fifteen months earlier. A couple of middle-aged matriarchs were doing breaststroke. The energy and optimism I had felt after that swim, on my first day of my self-help mission, felt a million miles away from where I was now.

'Shall we go in?' asked Rachel.

'We didn't bring our swimsuits.'

'They always have spare ones in the changing rooms.'

I knew that I probably should do it, just to keep pushing myself, to get out of my comfort zone. Again. But I didn't want to.

'No, I don't want to get cold. Let's get lunch.'

We had Sunday lunch at St John. Seeing normal gangs of friends and families doing the most normal of things, eating together, drinking wine, reading papers – it was bliss. A few months ago, when I was busy planning my funeral, I'd have looked at these people and thought they were running and hiding, but now it looked like happiness. This was the stuff of life. Friends eating together and chatting.

Halfway through my lamb my phone beeped. I reached into my bag.

It was Sarah. I felt gripped with panic.

'What does she say?' asked Rachel.

'I don't know.'

'Open it.'

'I'm scared.'

'Come on.'

I clicked it open. There was a picture of a woman in a massive Aran-knit onesie with a hood.

Underneath the message: *'Saw this weeks ago and wanted to send it to you and then I remembered that we were dastardly enemies . . . Let's not be. I prefer it when we're friends.'*

I shrieked and jumped up and down in my seat.

I passed Rachel the phone.

She looked confused.

'We went to Ireland together one winter and it was so cold I went to bed with my puffa jacket on and three sweaters underneath. Ever since then she's sent me pictures of thermal vests and long johns.'

Sarah knew me.

She knew that I was always cold. She knew that I lived for big sweaters. She knew that I was also messy and that I would sleep twenty hours of every day if I could. She knew that I loved Christmas with a passionate love that was only rivalled by a passionate hate of coloured fairy lights.

'Oh, God, you're not crying again . . . ?' Rachel smiled.

And I was.

I was so happy.

I replied: *'I totally want that onesie!'*

Sarah: *'I'll knit you one.'*

Me: *'You knit now?'*

Sarah: *'Yes. A lot has changed in the last few months.'*

Me: *'How are you? I'm having lunch with Rachel if you want to join?'*

Sarah: *'With Steve's mum today. We're in Westfield. I hate Westfield. Another time?'*

Me: *'Dinner tomorrow?'*

We met at Pizza Express at 6pm the next evening.

I got there first and waited, more nervous than any first date. The place was empty bar a couple of mothers cutting up pizzas for their after-school kids. When she walked in I caught my breath. She looked so pretty. I'd missed her so much.

'You look lovely,' I said, as she got to the table. 'Is that a new shirt?'

'I've had it a while . . .' I had stood up and she was still standing. We looked at each other. I didn't know whether to go in for a kiss and a hug. She wasn't moving towards me. She was just standing.

'You really do look great,' I said.

'You don't think I've put on weight?'

'No.'

She raised her shirt. A hard, round tummy.

'Oh my God!'

'I'm five months gone.'

'Oh my God, you're having a baby.'

'Yes!'

'Oh my God!'

'I know.'

'I missed it . . .' I said. I looked at Sarah. I looked at the floor.

'How are you feeling?' I asked, not even knowing if I had the right to ask that question anymore.

'I'm good, fine . . . tired and waking up twenty times a night to go to the loo but I don't want to complain in case you think I'm being negative.'

She raised her eyebrows.

'I'm so sorry. I was being such an idiot. A total cow. I'm so so so sorry.'

'It's OK.'

'No really, I'm sorry. I don't know what to say except that I went under. I stopped being a normal person. I don't know what I was thinking.'

There was an awkward silence. She still hadn't sat down.

'Are you OK there, do you want a different table?' I asked.

She laughed – 'No this is fine –' and sat down by the window.

'Are you sure?'

'Yes, Marianne. It's fine.'

There was an agonizing silence. She wasn't going to let me off the hook. Neither should she have.

'Was I awful?' I asked.

'Yes,' she replied, then felt bad. 'Don't give me those big eyes,' she said.

'I'm not giving you any eyes, I'm just sorry.' But my eyes were filling up with tears.

She paused. I could see she was trying to find a way to say what she had to say diplomatically.

'We were just going very different ways – and I can understand that. What you were doing was a big challenge but I hated feeling like I was losing you. I didn't know what to do. You didn't seem to like me very much.'

'I'm sorry.'

'You were distant and cold. It was like you were looking down on me.'

I cringed. She was right – I *was* looking down at people. After F**k It I had thought I had this life business sussed. I was smug. Arrogant. Taunting everyone with my enlightenment. I had thought I was one of an elite few who had everything figured out and that everybody else was living in blind denial and ignorance.

I pinched my leg to stop myself from crying. This wasn't about me. I was not allowed to get upset here.

'If it's any consolation, after we fell out I had a massive crash and have spent good chunks of the year in bed crying.'

'Yes, that makes me feel better.' She laughed. 'Not really. What happened?'

'I disappeared up my own arse, became a self-obsessed nightmare and basically imploded from thinking about myself too much.'

'Sounds fun.'

'I think I was on a mission to be this perfect person and then I got really stressed when it wasn't happening.'

'Perfect doesn't exist.'

'I know.'

'And anyway, even if it did exist who'd want to be perfect? Remember Jane from the office? With her perfect hair and perfect outfits and perfect salads . . .'

We both made a face.

'Who wants to be a Stepford Person? How boring is that? I don't really get why you want to change yourself so much. I mean, do all the books and meditating if you want to, but you don't have to become a totally different person. A lot of people like you the way you are.'

'Even though I'm a self-obsessed cow?'

'You aren't usually. You're usually warm and kind and funny. I'd like that person back again, please.'

There was a moment of silence.

'I missed talking to you,' she said. 'You just cut me out.'

'I know, I did.'

'I thought we were better friends than that.'

Another agonizing silence. The kind of silence you could fall into and never find your way out. This was vulnerability. And it was gross. But necessary.

'We can't even get drunk together now, to make it all OK,' said Sarah. I smiled. Another pause.

'Bloody hell . . . a baby. I can't believe it. How do you feel about it? How is Steve?'

'He's nervous. He keeps dreaming about leaving the baby on buses.'

'He'll be a great dad.'

'Yeah.'

'I'm so sorry I missed all this.'

'You can make up for it now by helping me with something important.'

'Of course, anything.'

She reached down into her bag and pulled out her phone.

'What do you think of this? Is this nice or too primary school teacher circa 1978?'

She was showing me a picture of a floral maxi dress.

I laughed. 'It's a bit Mrs Hindley in Geography.'

'What about this one?'

It was a low-cut clingy striped jersey dress.

'Yeah, baby – do it. Be proud of the bump!'

I felt a warm rush of love and relief – this was where happiness lay – not in affirmations or green juices but in conversations with friends about floral frocks.

'Is it a girl?'

She looked surprised. 'We're not telling anyone – but yes. How did you know?'

'I had this vision of you at my funeral and you had a daughter.'

'What?'

'It was when I was having my meltdown. I had to do this exercise where I imagined what people would say at my funeral and you were there with Steve and your daughter.'

'What? What book tells you to do that?'

'*The 7 Habits of Highly Effective People*. It's supposed to help you focus your mind on what you want from your life.'

'Did it work?'

'No. I basically imagined being at my funeral and everyone hating me.'

'Sounds like a right laugh.'

'People were so annoyed at me they wouldn't even get drunk and tell great stories about me. You told me that I'd had it all and I'd thrown it away.'

'I apologize on behalf of fictional me at your fictional funeral.'

'Nah, you were saying the truth.'

'Come on then. How did the others go? Did you do a dating book?'

'Yes! I stood up in front of a business breakfast and asked if anyone would take me out for a date.'

'You didn't!'

'I did! I got taken out for a coffee by a guy who pretty

much proposed halfway through our lattes. He told me that he'd decided he was ready to get married and offered me the job.'

'So what did you say?'

'Yes, of course. We ran off to Vegas.'

'I missed a Vegas wedding!'

'You did . . .'

'So there wasn't anyone you liked?'

'Not really. There was one guy but I messed it up. I ran away from him when he tried to kiss me and he didn't want to meet up again.'

'If he was that easily put off he wasn't your guy.'

Sarah always knew exactly what to say.

'Anyone else?'

I told her about The Greek.

'He sounds nice.'

'He is, but we're in different countries and . . . I don't know . . . I'm not sure I felt anything romantic for him.'

'You must have felt something for him if you went up to him.'

'Yeah, I guess, but then I didn't really feel the spark.'

She raised her eyebrows. 'How have you even had time to find out? I didn't fancy Steve until at least our third or fourth date.'

'I just don't think it was there.'

She shook her head. 'Are you sure you're not just running away? When I met Steve I was scared shitless. Falling in love with him felt like throwing myself off a cliff. I made up all these reasons why he wasn't right for me . . . he was too short, too skinny, his voice was too high . . .'

'It's not that high.'

'You know what I mean. But I was just scared. I could see

that he was real and he liked me and I was trying to find a way out. But he kept calling. He wouldn't let me run away.'

'The Greek keeps calling me.'

'Really?'

'Yeah, for a while I didn't pick up because I didn't want to give him the wrong idea but then that felt rude and so now we just chat.'

'What about?'

'I don't know – just stuff. His dad, my self-help. I guess it's all the psychology he's studied but he seems to get what I've done and he's just easy to talk to.'

'Easy to talk to is good. How often do you speak to each other?'

'Most weeks.'

'And do you find yourself thinking about him?'

'Yes, I guess so.'

'And how does he feel about you?'

'I don't know.'

'You haven't ever asked him?'

'No. But anyway, I don't think he's the love of my life. We had a kiss and I didn't really feel anything.'

'Were you ready to feel anything?' she asked.

'I don't know . . . I suppose not . . .'

'Were you ready for love?' her voice was urgent now and her face serious.

I was stunned. We did not usually talk like this.

'I dunno.'

'Do you even know what love is?' she asked, and as soon as she did tears poured out of my eyes like a tap had been turned on.

'I don't know . . .'

She took my hand and squeezed it. 'I just think you need

to give things more of a chance. Love doesn't have to be forever. It can just be meeting someone and having a connection and learning from each other. It can be for a day, a week, a year – it doesn't matter. The important thing is that you give something a chance. Just let it be what it's going to be. It doesn't have to be anything more than it is.'

'When did you get so wise?'

'I think it's the hormones, I'm all mother Earth now.' She smiled. 'Or giving up the booze has given me back some brain cells.'

I found a tissue in my bag and blew my nose. She was right. I was scared to death of love, but the one thing that all the self-help books say is that love is why we are on the planet. Not necessarily married-buy-a-house love but love in all its forms. Human connection.

When we'd paid the bill we walked back towards the station.

'This is a first – going home sober,' I said.

'I know.'

'I love you and I'm sorry for being such a bitch.'

'I love you too.' We had a hug. It was dark and we were under a street light. It was as romantic as any date. Love is love. Whether it's between friends or lovers or family. I had spent my life trying to pretend that I didn't need people but it was a lie. On the Tube home I found that I was crying yet again. But this time it was with joy.

When I got home I messaged The Greek. It was 11pm UK time, so 1am in Athens.

'Are you up?'

'Yes. ☺'

'Why are you up so late?'

'Can't sleep. Wanna chat?'

He Skyped me. Usually I switched off the video when I talked to him, because I worried I looked like the Pillsbury Doughboy on the Skype screen, but this time I let my face pop up.

'Oh, I can see you! Let me put my video on too.'

And his face appeared too. Pale, smiling, twinkling eyes.

'It's so nice to see you,' he said. 'You look great.'

'I don't, I'm knackered . . . You look good.' And he did – my heart flipped when I saw him and I found it hard to look him in the eye.

'Thank you.'

'So what's happening?'

'I just made up with a friend I'd fallen out with.'

'That's great.'

'Yeah, it really is. How's your dad?'

'Oh, the same – not good . . . but tell me something else. What's happening in London? What book are you reading this month?'

I sent him the link to Brené Brown's TED talk. We watched it together. Him in Athens, as his sick father slept next door, me in a dark bedroom in London. This man I'd walked up to in a coffee shop nearly a year ago.

'I like her,' he said.

'Me too.'

'This is how I try to live my life anyway,' he said.

And he did. From the first time we met he had been nothing but open and honest. He'd kept in touch with me even when I tried to shake him off. He didn't hide that he liked me or pretend that his life was perfect. He'd shown me

his real self all along. I had been the one who had been
playing games.

My heart was beating and I was sitting on the carpeted
floor by the door – where the wi-fi reception was best.

'It's funny, isn't it, that we've stayed in touch all this
time,' I said.

'Yes, it is.'

'I was just wondering . . . er, what do you think of me?'

He paused. I could feel the black night sky between us.
The oceans. He kept looking at me. He smiled. 'When I met
you I could not believe it . . . the day before I was talking to
my friend about my ideal woman and then you came up to
me, this beautiful woman, and you were everything on my
list. And that was just your appearance. Then we started
talking and it got even better. I could not believe my luck,'
he said.

I had to really fight the urge to say, 'It must have been a
short list,' but I did still ruin the moment by asking how
many times he'd used that line before.

'Never. When you meet my friend you can ask her,' he
said.

'You really thought that?'

'Yes.'

Another pause.

'And what did you think of me?' he asked, looking
straight at me.

'Um . . .' I looked at the carpet and started picking at a
bit of fluff.

More silence.

'That you were nice and clever and easy to talk to,' I said,
talking to my bookshelf.

I looked back at him once I'd said it. He was smiling.

'And what do you think of me now?'

I looked away again. 'Er . . . that you're nice and clever and easy to talk to.'

He smiled.

'Stop looking at me like that,' I said.

'Like what?' he asked.

'I dunno. Sorry, I'm not very good at this stuff.'

'That's OK.'

'I don't know. We're friends, I guess,' I said, looking at him.

'OK.' He had this really sweet way of saying OK, like anything you said to him would be OK.

'I mean, I don't know. I like you and I think about you.'

Silence. This was it. Again. Vulnerability. Being so scared and open that it felt like I was going to vomit out of my heart.

'I'm getting embarrassed,' I said.

'Don't be embarrassed.' He laughed. 'I think about you too. How did your dating go? Did you meet anyone?'

'Not really. What about you – are you seeing anybody? What's happening with the girl at the bar?'

'Nothing. She was nice but it was just a flirtation.'

'Oh. Good.' I was surprised by how happy I was at the news that the man I'd had one date with ten months earlier was not going out with the girl in the bar, whom I'd pictured as young and skinny with tattoos.

There was another silence and it felt as if the silence between two people can be more intimate and honest than anything we say with words. My heart hurt. I felt I could not catch my breath. I wanted it to stop. It was too much.

And so I used words again.

'Where do you stand on the flat white versus cappuccino debate?'

'Flat white,' he replied. Like this was the most normal question on earth.

'Me too.'

Daisy was back from three months in India. She appeared at the door wearing a long white shirt and beads around her neck, which irritated me, but when she leaned in and gave me a kiss, she seemed calm. No jumping up and down or namastes.

'I brought you something,' she said, handing me over a duty-free bag. I opened it – it was a bottle of whiskey.

'You don't even drink,' I said.

'Yeah, but you do.'

'Thank you! Actually I'm trying to cut down – but I'll keep this for medicinal purposes.'

'Did you have a lovely time?' I said over tea. Her camomile, me builder's.

'It was challenging but exactly what I needed.'

'So were you doing twenty hours of yoga a day?'

'No, actually. I wanted to but Dr Ali told me I had to stop completely. Do nothing.'

'Who is Dr Ali?'

'The Ayurvedic doctor I was seeing.'

'Oh!' I couldn't picture Daisy doing nothing – she had more energy than a Duracell bunny.

'On the second week, during one of the massages I felt something go in my hips and then I spent the rest of the week in bed crying.'

'Did he injure you?'

'No, he said I was holding grief in my body and this was letting it out.'

'Oh.'

'He said I never really grieved for my mother and that I had to stop running and just feel it.'

'Right. I'm sorry, I knew your mum died, but you never really talked about it –'

'It's OK, it happened a couple of years ago. Cancer. I quit work to look after her.'

'I'm sorry. You must miss her.'

'Yeah. I do.'

'Did it help? Just stopping?'

'Yes.'

I waited for her to fill the silence with some more therapy-speak or talk of energy and 'clearing'. But she didn't.

We drank our tea and sat in silence. Daisy fiddled with the vase on the table. Twisting it around, touching the petals of the roses in it.

'Have you got any more trips planned?' I asked.

'I was thinking it was time to get back to work. I inherited some money when Mum died and I've got through most of it so I think it's time. It might be a good thing.'

Suddenly it all made sense. Daisy's manic spending and manic searching, hopping from one course to the next, one yoga retreat to the next. She was grieving and lonely and looking for answers. I made another cup of tea.

At the end of March, it was my sister's birthday. Mum baked a cake. I went to her flat in Ascot to collect it and got the train back to Helen's place in East London, via two trains and a bus. Mum didn't have a Tupperware container big enough so it was on a plate and there was some strange net thing put over it, the kind of thing that you put over food on a summer's day. Something to stop the flies.

This made travelling challenging – I kept thinking someone was going to bump into the cake and send it flying but they didn't. Rush hour that evening was like no other rush hour I've ever experienced. People smiled at me, moved out of my way, even chatted; 'That looks nice,' they'd say, looking at the cake. Their face would soften. The hard, tired, determined, 'I hate life' look that most of us adopted on Tubes melted away.

It was like everyone became human again.

On the last leg of the journey I was waiting at a bus stop by Highbury, next to two guys drinking Special Brew. They looked homeless and when I sat next to them I had the familiar feeling of guilt about how lucky I am and sadness for how other people's lives can turn out. Then I felt guilty for being so patronizing; maybe they're happy in their lives.

'Is that for us?' asked one of the guys.

'I'm afraid not, it's for my sister. It's her birthday,' I said.

'Did you make it?' said another.

'No, I burn toast – Mum made it, I'm just taking it to the party,' I said.

'So where is your mum then?' said one.

'Oh, we don't invite her to the parties, we just get her to make the cakes,' I joked.

'That's charming, isn't it?' one said.

'I know, we're right brats,' I said.

'Does she always make you cakes, then?'

'Yes, I'm thirty-seven and she still makes me cakes.'

'That's nice.' They both beamed at the cake.

For a second or two there was silence as we all stared at the cake under the funny net cage. I looked at the sugar roses that Mum had put on top of the cake. I'd thought they were twee but now they looked like pure love.

I looked at my two new friends. They too were staring. There was a faraway look on their faces.

I didn't know if their thoughts had gone to the birthday parties they'd had or the birthday parties they'd never had. The cakes that were made for them – decorated with Smarties and candles – or the cakes that only existed in their dreams.

I guessed the latter.

In that moment they both looked ten years old, sitting there with their cans of lager and a battered tube of Sour Cream and Onion Pringles.

It felt like the vast difference between our lives was represented by that cake. Having a mother who made birthday cakes seemed like the greatest thing any person could ask for.

For half a second, I wondered if I should invite them to the party but I didn't. Instead we talked a bit more about who was going to be there and how many sisters I had and the fact that it was getting brighter. I asked them what they were doing for the night and they said, 'This and that.'

My bus came and I said goodbye and they waved me off.

I felt ashamed of myself. I had spent more than a year obsessing over what was wrong with my life – or rather what I imagined was wrong with it – but the reality was that I had a mum who made cakes, sisters I loved, friends who made me laugh, a body that worked, a brain that was more or less functioning, a roof over my head. I had it all.

Brené Brown writes: 'Joy comes to us in moments –

ordinary moments. We risk missing out on joy when we get too busy chasing down the extraordinary.'

I had been trying to chase down the extraordinary when actually I already had everything I would ever need.

18

You Can Heal Your Life,
by Louise Hay

'Remember, you have been criticizing yourself for years and it hasn't worked. Try approving of yourself and see what happens.'

My unwashed hair is in its usual spot – a messy bun on the top of my head. My face is bright pink and my mascara has made a bid for freedom, travelling down my cheeks. I have a spot on my chin. I smile into the mirror and repeat out loud:

I love and approve of myself. I love and approve of myself. I love and approve of myself.

I take off my leggings, top and sports bra. My boobs fall in a sweaty droop. I put my hands on my guts and give them a shake. It is the midriff of someone who has had a long-term relationship with cheese on toast and wine. Oh well, sod it. I look again and smile.

I love and approve of myself. I love and approve of myself. I love and approve of myself.

Long pale hairs stand to attention on my thighs. I half start a train of thought about how slovenly I am in the hair-removal department but can't quite be bothered to beat myself up about it. I smile again.

I love and approve of myself. I love and approve of myself. I love and approve of myself.

I turn around to examine the cellulite on my bum, then turn to the side to check out the stretch marks on my hips. I stroke them and feel the raised ripples. I smile again. At myself. At life. At this constant self-examination in which we're always found wanting. What a waste of time!

I love and approve of myself.

My final month. My twelfth book. The finish line.

I decided to end my self-help adventure with a book called *You Can Heal Your Life* by Louise Hay. It's a self-help classic which has sold 35 million copies since it was published in 1985. It's about loving yourself. Hay says that instead of beating ourselves up we must look in the mirror every day and say, 'I love and approve of myself.'

She believes that all our problems – from money to poor relationships – come from two things: holding on to resentment from the past and the fact that we don't love ourselves. Hay also, controversially, believes that all physical illness has an emotional cause and that her own ovarian cancer was caused by the shame she felt about sexual abuse she suffered as a child.

In order to 'heal our lives', Hay says we must forgive everyone who has done us wrong, especially our parents.

A few years ago I would have been dismissive about the effect our childhood had on us. Unless you'd suffered abuse or lost a parent at a young age, I figured most of us had nothing to complain about – but I now see our childhood is pretty much the basis of everything. For good and bad.

So yes, my taxi driver was right. My clever, astute therapist was making it about my family. Not because I had a
terrible childhood – far from it – but because even with the
best of intentions from all concerned, tiny moments can
have a huge impact and it's invaluable to start identifying
these moments that have been invisibly driving us for years.
And I realized I could not do this digging on my own. Since
my first appointment in January my therapist had become a
steadfast partner and support, helping me reach parts of
myself I didn't know existed.

And so – with forgiveness a work in progress – it was
time for self-love.

I grew up in a house where to be told you 'really love
yourself' was an insult. It basically meant you were a
stuck-up cow. Too big for your boots. But Hay thinks that
self-love has nothing to do with being arrogant or full of
yourself. Self-love is about caring for yourself, being com-
passionate with yourself, accepting all your little quirks.

She says: 'When people start to love themselves more
each day, it's amazing how their lives get better. They feel
better. They get the jobs they want. They have the money
they need. Their relationships either improve, or the negative ones dissolve and new ones begin.'

But loving yourself is not easy.

Hay describes how many of her clients refuse to say
'I love and approve of myself' in front of the mirror. Some
can't even look at themselves without crying. They say
they can't love themselves because they are too ugly, too
fat, too unsuccessful, too damaged. They say they'll love
themselves when they lose the weight, get the job, find the
husband.

I can relate to that. I once wrote an article about what I

saw in the mirror and it wasn't good: dodgy teeth, fat hips, chubby chops, spotty skin, wrinkles . . . I used to look in the mirror every morning and itemize my flaws, using them as reasons I would never be loved and never be good enough.

By the middle of April, at the end of my self-help journey, that had changed.

'Daisy just told me I had a bright aura!' said Sarah, bouncing up and down in the dress that clung perfectly to her pert bump.

'I've always said that about you,' I said, also jumping.

'She's nuts.' Sarah smiled, bright red plastic roses on her head. 'But I like her!'

'Good, me too!' I shouted over the pounding base.

We grinned and bounced some more. The floor vibrated as hundreds of ravers flung their hands in the air. Dancing like it was their last day on earth.

Rachel appeared with a hula hoop.

'Where did you get that from?' I asked.

'Some bloke just gave it to me.'

She put it around her waist and started twirling. She was wearing a shimmering turquoise Lycra all-in-one that made her look like a space-age mermaid. Her old-fashioned just don't eat seconds diet seemed to be working for her. Goddamit.

'Where's Daisy?' she shouted, mid-twirl.

I pointed to the stage, where Daisy was dancing next to a man dressed as a carrot. Her eyes were closed and her arms flung into the air. She had a unicorn horn on her head. At 7am on a Wednesday.

The morning rave was Daisy's idea, obviously. She'd

been going to these hip, hippie happenings for months, partying with the kind of people who like to get up at dawn to drink coconut water rather than beers.

It was a whole new world: toddlers with ear-protectors ran around behind their dancing mums, twenty-somethings with cropped tops strutting their stuff on stage, while men dressed as zebras, and, stranger still, in office shirts, danced, danced, danced their hearts out. And we joined in. From 7.30 to 10am we danced and sweated like glorious partying pigs.

'You look so happy!' shouted Sarah.

I smiled. 'So do you!'

'Maybe you didn't need self-help, maybe you just needed to dance more!'

'Maybe,' I shouted.

Being with other people, moving and smiling was a tonic; so much better for my soul than sitting on my own reading and analysing. In fact, throughout the year I'd almost totally ignored the magical powers of exercise, which many people believe to be as effective as antidepressants in lifting mood.

A man with long hair and a bare chest glistening with sweat and rows of coloured beads, smiled at me. I smiled back.

'Great smile!' he said.

'Thank you!' I said as we jumped up and down in unison for a few minutes.

'That's the third one,' said Sarah.

'What?' I shouted back.

'The third guy who has come up to you.'

'It's friendly, everyone is saying hello . . .'

'Nah, they're coming up to you – you're glowing.'

'You mean I'm sweating!'

'Yeah, but it's not just that . . . Your light's on.'

And it was. I could feel it.

When Rachel and I got home, I ran up to the shower and stripped off and stood in front of the mirror. As I looked at myself, I could see that my eyes were gleaming and my skin shone. I kept smiling at myself, taking in the wonky teeth, chubby cheeks and wobbly thighs that used to make me so unhappy. But now, instead of seeing flaws, I saw something else.

I saw a woman who had done crazy, brilliant things in the past sixteen months. Someone kind and strong and brave and powerful. Someone who was alive and vibrant.

Standing in front of that bathroom mirror, I saw a force of nature.

I was not so changed that I didn't feel like a total idiot talking out loud to this person in the mirror, but as I carried out Louise's instructions, I realized that I did believe what I was saying: I did love and approve of myself, no matter what my hair was doing, no matter how big the spot on my chin or how little time I spent waxing.

In fact, at 11am on 13th April, I felt bloody brilliant.

I was so proud of myself. Really, so so proud.

But now I was done.

I was done with trying to eradicate all my bad bits, done with going to war with myself for all my perceived failings. I was done with trying to be Highly Effective or to spend every second in a state of blissful zen. I was tired of the affirmations and faking happiness when I just wanted to swear and be grumpy. I was done with drinking green smoothies and feeling marginally guilty every time I ate cheese on toast. Because, the thing was, I really, really liked cheese on toast. Sometimes it was the best part of my day.

At Christmas, when my attempts to reach perfection had nearly broken me, I had found myself crying, as I do every year, while watching *Bridget Jones*. It was that scene where Darcy tells Bridget that he likes her, just as she is.

Bridget's friends can't believe this declaration.

'Just as you are? Not thinner? Not cleverer? Not with slightly bigger breasts or slightly smaller nose?' asks her friend Jude when Bridget tells her.

'No,' says Bridget.

'Well, fuck me,' says Shazza.

That became the holy grail for my generation: this idea that if you could just find your Darcy, someone who loved you just the way you were, all would be well.

But what if we could just learn to love *ourselves* exactly as we are? Wouldn't that be better than waiting for someone else to tell us we're OK?

And so I looked at the mirror again and at my cheese-on-toast tummy and wine face and smiled. Then I said my very last affirmation:

I love and approve of myself. Just the way I am.

And in my head I expanded: *I love and approve of myself even though my only exercise is walking around the block. I love and approve of myself even though I drink wine and love Netflix. I love and approve of myself even though I am disorganized and crap with money. I love and approve of myself even though I cry at everything . . . including* Bridget Jones *and ads for insurance.*

And, as if on cue, I started crying again because I realized, as I looked in the mirror, that for all the time I'd spent obsessing about my bad bits, I'd rarely given any thoughts to my good bits. And there *were* good bits. Lots of them.

And so I said them out loud:

*I am kind, funny and smiley. I try to be nice to people. I give
to charity. I'm a good listener. I work hard. I make my friends
laugh. And I have such good friends: funny, cool, interesting
friends! And they love and approve of me JUST AS I AM.*

Although they might change their mind if they saw me
talking to myself in the mirror with no clothes on.

I'd once read someone describing success as being able
to look at yourself in the mirror in the morning and be OK
with what you see. And I had got there.

After a long and painful sixteen months, I could look in
the mirror.

But as I dried myself and brushed my teeth, I knew with
absolutely certainty that it was now time to step away from
my real and metaphorical reflection. I couldn't bear to think
about myself for another minute.

In self-help land the news is frowned upon. It's a source of
negativity and misery. It will bring you down. Better to walk
around the block repeating affirmations or read about the
power of positive thinking than engage in the ugly, cruel
world. And for more than a year I'd followed this advice. I'd
gone from someone who read the papers every day to
someone who read motivational posts on Facebook. And in
some ways it was nice. Life felt simpler, cleaner.

But as I neared the end of my challenge, denying the real
world – in all its messiness and tragedy – no longer felt
enlightened. It felt like selfishness. So after I'd showered, I
went to the corner shop, bought the papers and read about
a shipwreck which had killed hundreds of African and Ban-
gladeshi migrants trying to escape war and poverty. Rescuers
described a 'cemetery in the sea', while one of the survivors

told how hundreds perished because they were locked up below deck 'like rats in a cage'. It was hellish. Here was the story of people fighting to just stay alive, children who were dying before they'd even lived. Terrified mothers putting their babies on boats because there was no alternative . . .

My quest to improve myself felt immoral. What on earth did I have to complain about? What was I trying to improve? I was already living a dream life compared to 99.99 per cent of the world.

I was beyond blessed. It was time to appreciate what I had.

Be grateful.

Tony Robbins, Eckhart Tolle and Susan Jeffers all talk about swapping 'expectation for appreciation'. But I hadn't done that. Not at all. I was too busy analysing my self-created problems to see how lucky I was. That was going to change.

'I've come to a decision,' I told Rachel, who was tapping on her laptop while I read the papers.

'OK?' she said. Not looking up.

'I'm done with self-help!'

Now she looked up. 'Really?'

'Yes.'

'Oh, thank God.' She smiled. And for the first time I realized what a nightmare I must have been to live with – between the highs, the lows and the navel gazing. I hadn't been able to have so much as a cup of tea without analysing my feelings for it and making her do the same.

'I've decided to do some volunteer work instead.'

Rachel's face froze: 'You're not going to try and become Mother Teresa now, are you?'

'No! A friend of a friend put a thing up on Facebook. She

is organizing donations for Calais this weekend and is looking for helpers. It's just a day.'

'That sounds good. Can I come with you?'

'Yeah, that would be great.'

While I waited for the kettle to boil, to make another
coffee, I summoned up the courage to ask Rachel the question that had been niggling away at me for months.

The Big Question, really.

All year I'd been waiting for people to comment on how
wise I seemed, how calm and together. I wanted them to
think, 'I'll have what she's having', you know, Meg Ryan-
style. It didn't happen. Not at all.

'Do you think any of this has helped?' I asked Rachel,
keeping my eyes focused on the coffee.

'Do *you* think it's helped?' she asked. She was no better
than the therapist.

'I don't know. In some ways yes, in some ways no. I think
it will take a while to assimilate.'

'Good use of the word assimilate.'

'Thank you.'

'So what are you going to do now?'

'Work, see people, be normal . . . but first I'm going to
tidy up my room.'

Rachel raised her eyebrows.

'Maybe the books *have* helped.'

I sat on my bed and looked at the technicolour volumes on
my bookshelf. All with broken spines and folded pages.
Each my companion through weeks of soul searching, agonizing and, more often than not, crying.

I picked up my well-thumbed copy of *Feel the Fear and Do*

It Anyway which had started my self-help mission, at the age of twenty-four and then again at thirty-six. Both felt like a lifetime ago. The stand-up comedy, the naked modelling, the karaoke – I still couldn't believe I'd done all that. In one month. Susan was right: life really does start the minute you do something, do *anything*.

Next to its battered red spine, the book that introduced me to my tragic money love story. What a month. How had I not known what a disaster I was with money until this book? I'd started the year hoping to somehow – magically – become filthy rich but that hadn't happened. I was still in debt and nervous of the ATM, but at least I was checking my bank balances now. Well, sometimes.

I moved my eyes along to *The Secret* and felt a familiar stab of irritation. That book still did my head in. Was it true? Was it not true? I still didn't know.

I knelt on the floor and looked at my Vision Board, which I'd hidden behind my desk. The pictures of green juice and yoga were now curled up and dusty. I looked at everything I'd wanted in March. The international travel had not yet come my way, neither had the lead singer of a band knocked on my door. I had, however, drunk a lot of green juices and done yoga, with and without clothes . . . So maybe there was something in it?

Thrown behind the Vision Board was the box of angel cards. I pulled out one for old time's sake: 'Believe and Trust.' During my angel month the vagueness of this would have enraged me – but now it felt quite nice. Just a little positive message to help you through the day. What was so wrong with that?

I picked the box off the floor and put it on the shelf, next to my water-damaged copy of *F**k It*. Ah, *F**k It* – just saying it made me let out a sigh of relief. This book was deceptively profound and wise. The younger, sweary brother to *The Power of Now*, which was my favourite of them all.

I flicked through the copy that sat on my bedside table. I turned to its underlined pages most days. With margins full of 'YES!' and exclamation marks, it looked like the bible of a mad woman, but every page contained some bit of wisdom.

As did all the books I'd read. Even the ones I didn't like had something to offer – a sentence of truth. Something to make you see the world differently.

But what to do with them now?

A part of me wanted to throw them away – maybe even burn them – to mark the end of an era but that didn't feel right. We'd been through too much together.

These books and their authors had been my constant companions for over a year. At times it had felt like there were twelve people living in my head commenting on everything I was doing. But, as much as I loved them all, it was getting quite crowded up there.

I called Mum.

'Where are you?' I asked.

'In TK Maxx buying pillowcases. Where are you?'

'At home, having a clear-out. I've decided I'm going to stop the self-help stuff.'

'Oh, good,' she said, letting out a sigh.

There was a silence on the line before she asked me the question that I'd asked Rachel: 'Do you think it helped?'

'Dunno, I'm still not fixed. I'm still broke and single . . .' I said.

She sounded surprised. 'I didn't think you were trying to

fix yourself, Marianne. I thought you were trying to know yourself – and you must know yourself very well by now.'

I took this as a criticism. 'I know you think I've been self-obsessed and self-indulgent,' I said.

'Actually, Marianne, no I don't –' Her voice got all high and tight the way it did when she was lecturing us as kids. 'Well, yes, OK, a bit but I also think what you've done is very brave. You have faced up to things that people spend their whole lives avoiding and that takes courage. I–I–I, I never thought about things or questioned life the way you have. I just accepted what was happening. I never had any ambitions. I wish I had done a bit more thinking like you have been doing. I am very proud of you. I could not be prouder.'

My eyes pricked with tears. It might have been the nicest thing she'd ever said to me. 'Thanks, Mum.'

'You're a good girl,' she said.

This was the highest praise we'd ever get from Mum growing up – all the more powerful for how rarely it was uttered. But I had mixed feelings about her saying it now. Was that part of my problem – always trying to be a good girl? Get everything right? To please everyone? As much as I knew Mum was saying it out of love, I felt it was time to stop trying to be a good girl. Stop *trying*, full stop. To just be whoever I was. For good and bad.

I didn't say this. Instead I said, 'And you're a good mum.'

There was a silence on the line.

'Well, I'm very lucky with the daughters I have. I love you.'

'I love you, too.'

There was another silence.

'Right, I can't stay on chatting. I need to get to the supermarket before it shuts.'

I got off the phone, sat on the bed and had a cry. Again. If this year had done anything to me, it had made me into someone who cried constantly.

So here I was. I'd done it. I'd come to the end of the road. It felt big. Momentous. Emotional. But it was also an anticlimax.

There was no finish line. No prize. No cheque from the Universe for £100,000.

Just me, sitting on the bed, surrounded by self-help books.

I picked up my relatively untouched copy of *You Can Heal Your Life*.

I felt bad that lovely Louise, the grand dame of self-help, was not getting the attention she deserved. But I think she would approve. My lack of desire to do more self-help was, in many ways, a sign that I *had* healed my life.

I had faced my demons one by one and I was still standing. More than that – I was standing tall. I had found peace with myself and my place in the world.

My journey of self-improvement had turned into a journey of self-acceptance and then, miracle of all miracles, self-love.

I hadn't changed myself in any of the ways I'd wanted to at the beginning, but I'd done something better. I hadn't fixed myself – I had *become* myself.

Now it was time to stop thinking about myself, to look out rather than in. To live life rather than analyse it.

I looked out of the window. The London sky was pink and streaky. It would be summer soon. I could hear chatter from the two old women in the garden next door sitting in their rose garden. A dog was barking and a police siren was wailing in the distance. Life was happening in every corner and I wanted to be part of it.

Rachel shouted from downstairs. 'I know you're cutting down but do you want to celebrate with a drink? Shall we go out?'

'Yes!' I yelled back. 'I'll be down in a minute.'

I put my Vision Board under my bed, along with my twelve self-help books.

The phone rang. It was Sheila.

'Hey, how are you?' I asked.

'Fine. Busy. I'm just going to the gym. What about you?'

'I'm heading to the pub for a drink with Rachel. We're celebrating. I've decided to call time on the self-help.'

'So you finally think you're OK now, do you?' she asked.

The thing was, for the first time ever, I really believed I was.

So Does Self-Help, Well, *Help*?

It's exactly three months since I finished my self-help journey and I am in my best friend's cottage in the West of Ireland. Gemma and her baby boy, James, are having a 'cuddly wuddly' on the sofa while I am writing this in the porch, at a desk that looks onto a country road.

This morning half a dozen cows walked right by the house and yesterday four sheep sauntered past like they owned the place. Which they do – more than me, anyway.

The sun is out and the sky is a massive sheet of blue. It seems to get bigger every day and I can't understand how. It blows my mind. Tonight it will go pink and purple with the sunset and I'll say, for the umpteenth time, 'God, it's so beautiful . . .'

Before that, Gemma will make fish for dinner and I'll help to feed James – although he is a big boy now and can do a pretty good job of feeding himself, first by spoon and then, when that seems like too much effort, by hand.

When he's had enough he'll give us presents of his leftovers; delivered from his perfect little food-covered fingers into our grown-up hands. We'll say, 'Ta ta!' and he'll beam pure light and love and joy and his mummy will tell him he's the bestest boy in the whole wide world.

James and I will then go for a post-dinner walk around

the garden and he will pretend to smell the flowers. He'll lean in very close and make a sniffy sound and look at me for approval. Which he'll get. He'll then shout 'Bee!' and point to the buzzy bees that always seem to be in the purple flowers – which are called *Nepeta*, apparently.

We'll keep walking and smelling and bee spotting until it's time for James to have his splashy splashy bath. There he'll play with his rubber ducks and come out looking so shiny and clean and innocent in his fluffy white towel that I could burst with love. If I'm lucky I'll get a kiss. It will be a perfect moment, coming at the end of a summer of many perfect moments.

I am so happy.

Last night, after an afternoon spent swimming in the Atlantic, squealing as the icy-cold waves crashed against us, Gemma and I watched a documentary that featured an interview with the British playwright Dennis Potter who was dying of cancer. Listening to it made me cry. This is what he said about life:

> We tend to forget that life can only be defined in the present tense . . . Below my window, for example . . . the blossom is out in full now . . . and instead of saying 'Oh that's nice blossom' . . . I see it is the whitest, frothiest, blossomest blossom that there ever could be . . . the fact is, if you see the present tense, boy do you see it! And boy can you celebrate it.

That's how I feel right now. I am living life in the present tense. Each moment seems full to bursting in its perfection. Even the banal stuff like hanging out laundry or washing dishes seems weighted with significance. I don't know why. I guess I've just come to the end of a long journey only to realize there is nowhere else I'd rather be. Nobody else I'd rather be. I am here. I am happy.

So does that mean the self-help, well, helped?

In so many ways my year was a disaster.

My debt grew, my productivity plummeted and I am now a stone heavier than when I began. I became irresponsible, selfish and deluded, watching inspirational videos on YouTube instead of doing actual work and spending money I didn't have on the basis that the Universe would provide. Worst of all, I fell out with one of my best friends.

And Sarah was right – I *was* self-obsessed. I cringe at how selfish I was, constantly analysing my every thought and action. I became a self-help junkie, disregarding my friends and family, always thinking the answer was in the next book, the next book . . .

With every book my expectations of life increased. I didn't just want a happy life, I wanted an outstanding one! The higher the bar was set, the more I felt like I was failing. The more I hunted down Perfect Me the more she eluded me. The more desperate I became to be happier, the less happy I became . . .

But I see now that perfection does not exist and happiness comes not from getting what you think you want but from opening your eyes and recognizing that you have everything you could possibly need right now.

In December, when I was cracking up on her sofa, Gemma told me that she hoped I would get to the end of the year and see that I was fine just the way I was, that I didn't need to jump out of planes, chat up strangers or get naked in public to be loved. At the time I thought that was ridiculous. All I could see were my flaws and failings and I thought I needed to fix myself before anyone would love me.

At Hoffman I learned that this was not the case.

Standing up in front of strangers and sharing all the bits of myself that I kept hidden was one of the most terrifying and beautiful moments of my life. Far from being the end of the world, it marked the beginning of a new world, a world where I was accepted for all my flaws, a world where I was loved and belonged just as I was.

During that week we also did an exercise where we had to write out all the horrible things that we say to ourselves on a giant piece of paper and then bash that piece of paper into smithereens using a shoe (it was a weird week) while yelling at the top of our lungs. After twenty minutes of ferocious screaming and bashing, I had the kind of blissful experience I'd had in F**k It and *The Power of Now.*

For a full minute all the crap in my head was gone and I looked around the room and felt pure love for everyone in it, including myself. I realized then that you can't love others when you're busy hating yourself. It's just not possible.

Now, looking back on that moment, I realize something else: trying to find happiness might seem like a selfish endeavour but it really isn't. When you are as unhappy as I was for years, your unhappiness leaches into the air and affects everyone around you. You are not patient, you are snappy. You are not truly kind, you are cut off from others, locked in your own prison of misery. You are also, quite often, a worry to those who love you.

While it is not healthy to think about yourself as much as I had done over the last year, it had allowed me to clear out a lot of junk in my head so that I could finally see beyond my haze of self-loathing to the people around me.

In this way the self-help did help – a *lot.* It, ironically, helped me get past myself. As I listen to Gemma and James sing 'Old Macdonald Had a Farm' in the room next door, I think about Brené Brown's assertion that 'connection is why we are here'.

I think she is right. I have spent my life trying to go it alone, keeping the people who love me at a distance, but no more. As I think back on my year and a bit of self-improvement, the best bits were those moments of connection. It's only with other people that magic happens – a magic that could be defined as love. Or God. Or beauty. Or spirit.

And so for now at least, I am going out in the world with a heart open to love.

Which brings me to men, or rather one man. When I started, some people suggested that if it didn't end in me finding my Prince Charming, it would have been a failure and that made me angry. I did not – and still don't – think that you need a romantic partner to make you complete or OK. I don't think that happiness has to come in the form of marriage and kids. And yet I keep thinking about The Greek. Not because I think that he's the man of my dreams, or because I think that I am the girl of his – but because for whatever reason, out of all the men in London, I walked up to him that day. And for whatever reason, he let me. And even though we only spent a few hours together, a year later we were still talking.

Gemma shouts to me to say she is going to start cooking.

'Thanks,' I call back.

I look out of the window and look at the trees quivering with the summer breeze. I take a deep breath and pick up my phone.

'*How would you feel about a visitor?* ☺' I type and then press send before I can wimp out.

The reply beeps instantly. '*Yes!*' he says, followed by three smiley faces. And this time they blew kisses.

I jump up and down in my seat and squeal. I can't wait to tell Gemma and Sarah but first I just need to write something down . . .

In *The 7 Habits of Highly Effective People* Stephen Covey recommends writing a mission statement that describes the kind of person you want to be. Unlike the funeral exercise, it doesn't involve knowing the kind of person you want to be in the future, just the kind of person you want to be right now.

At the time I couldn't do it, but sitting in Gemma's porch, this comes to me:

Be honest. Be kind. See the funny side. Exercise. Laugh. Lighten up. Have the difficult conversations and do the difficult jobs. Don't run away. Speak your mind quietly, clearly and respectfully. People are not mind-readers. Spit it out. Work hard and enjoy it. Take pride and satisfaction in your abilities, they are greater than you think. Have confidence. Go for the big things – why not? What's the worst that can happen? Failure won't kill you. Say no. Say yes. See the good in people, don't judge. Listen, understand, forgive. Have fun. Be patient. Nothing is forever. Cherish the day and cherish the people in your life – you are so lucky to have them. Be humble: you're no better than anyone else and no worse either. We're all trying our best, we're all the same, really. Love with all your heart and learn from everything. When things are hard, know that it will pass and none of it matters that much anyway. You're just a little dot passing through, so make the most of it. Sing, dance, look at the sky and be grateful. If in doubt, tidy up and make a plan – sometimes it helps to get out of your head and get practical. Most importantly, though, have a cup of tea (or glass of wine) and remember this: You're doing great. You really are.

Acknowledgements

Mum just called me.

'I've been thinking . . .' she said.

'OK,' I said.

'About your book,' she said.

'Yes.'

'Please don't write five pages of thank yous. I'm fed up of all these gushing acknowledgements at the end of books. Anyone would think they'd prevented war the way they go on, instead of writing something that nobody is going to read.'

I decided to skip over the implication that nobody was going to read this book.

'So you don't want me to thank you, then?' I ask.

'No, because then you'd have to thank your sisters and your friends and your aunts and your uncles and where does it end? Before you know it, you're thanking the dog.'

'We don't have a dog,' I say.

'You know what I mean, Marianne.'

'So what should I say?'

'Just say thank you to your friends and family and leave it at that. No names.'

OK. So thank you to my friends and family. No names but I hope you know who you are. Thank you for putting up with me, and in some cases, putting me up. This book would not exist without you.

Thank you too to the wonderful readers who cheered me on as I blogged about this experiment and to the strangers with whom I had the perfect conversations at the perfect time. Thank you to everybody who helped turn my story into a real-life book.

Thank you also to the dog.

But extra-special thanks to my mum.

Author's Note

Writing about yourself is a tricky thing. While I seem to have little problem with spilling my guts to the world (it's surprised me more than anyone) – I am very aware that most people do not feel the same way and to that end I have changed names and identifying details of some of the people in this book.

I had many friends cheering me on (and tolerating me) during my year (and a bit) of self-help and to keep things simple, the friend characters in the book are composites.

I have also changed the order of some events, in the name of (I hope) good story-telling.

That said, every crazy, stupid, naked, embarrassing incident that I describe putting myself through was real and true. I jumped out of the plane. Did stand-up. Chatted up The Greek. Stood up in front of a conference room of business people and asked for a date.

I even thought for a short but agonizing time that I was going to audition for *X Factor*.

As for Mum – I could not have made up, or improved, her effortless one-liners if I tried.